Shopping for Jesus

Published and Forthcoming by New Academia Publishing

Popular culture / Visual Culture / Cinema

To read an excerpt visit: www.newacademia.com

Shopping for Jesus
Faith in Marketing in the USA

edited by
Dominic Janes

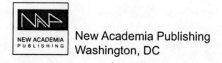

New Academia Publishing
Washington, DC

New Academia Publishing, 2008

Printed in the United States of America

Library of Congress Control Number: 2008921865
ISBN 978-0-9800814-3-5 paperback (alk. paper)

New Academia Publishing, LLC
P.O. Box 27420
Washington, DC 20038-7420
www.newacademia.com - info@newacademia.com

Contents

Marketing Performances

Producers and Consumers

Illustrations

Introduction

Faith in Marketing in the USA

Dominic Janes

Brilliant light, it may be a sunset or a sunrise, flares along a dark horizon and, rising up against it in the foreground, stand the stark silhouettes of three giant crosses. Just below the horizontal beams of the crosses are embossed a series of sixteen numbers. At the top left is the logo of Family Christian Stores and at the bottom right that of Mastercard. The website on which this image is displayed informs us: "The Family Christian Stores Platinum Plus® Mastercard® Credit Card: It's Everything you Need" (FCS, "The Family", 2007. Permission to reproduce an image of the credit card was refused). There are over three hundred Family Christian Stores (FCS) spread across thirty seven states of the Union (fig. 1). The merchandise on offer ranges from Bibles to cards, clothing and ornaments with Christian themes, images or slogans. One of the many things you could use the card to pay for is a book by Ethan Pope, *Cashing it in: Getting Ready for a World without Money*, produced by Moody, publishers whose "mission is to educate and edify the Christian and to evangelize the non-Christian by ethically publishing conservative, evangelical Christian literature" (Pope, 2005 and Moody, 2007). One might assume that this was a work of eschatology; however, the description tells us that what is being

Fig. 1. Family Christian Stores logo.

referred to is a specific sort of financially efficient heaven on earth, a world with currency but without coins:

> With the popularity of credit and debit cards, online bank-
> ing and internet shopping, the idea of a cashless society is
> closer to becoming reality. [This book will] explore the issues
> this raises within a biblical framework and how Christians
> can become wise stewards of their resources (FCS, "Ethan
> Pope," 2007).

Amongst the other items on sale are the "Faith & Friends" dolls which have been, according to their manufacturer, "created to help meet the needs of girls to enjoy and experiment with fashion in a safe and wholesome manner that models femininity and appro-priateness" (Faith & Friends, 2007). The FCS web site expands the way in which this doll, with its diverse accessories, provides for pa-rentally monitored role-playing on the part of the young Christian consumer:

> With Faith & Friends, girls name their doll and write her
> story! Each doll comes with a tiny Bible and blank composi-
> tion book to get girls thinking and writing about their faith
> and encourage wholesome role playing. Your daughter will
> grow developmentally, educationally, and spiritually. And
> you'll have a window into her soul like never before! (FCS,
> "Faith and Friends", 2007).

There is nothing new about Americans who view marketing, capitalism and Christian moral surveillance as entirely compatible aspects of their everyday life. In 1916 Dr Christian Reisner set up a Church Department at the convention of the Associated Adver-tising Clubs of the World. Shortly afterward Norman Richardson of Northwestern University encouraged the future senator, Francis Higbee Case (1896-1962), then a journalist, to draw up submissions from the 1920 convention and to publish these, together with ad-dresses by the Church Department, in the form of a *Handbook of Church Advertising* (1921). The purpose of this book was to reject the notion that the marketing of Christianity was "shameless self-exaltation or of wanton intrusion into the shop and market place. It is rather, the method of the one in the parable of our Lord who went out into the highways and hedges and compelled others to come in" (1921: 186). Moreover, the novelty of such practices was denied. O. J. Goude, of the O. J. Goude Advertising Company was quoted as saying, for instance, in the course of a discussion of trademarks, that "steeples were the first form of outdoor advertising" (1921: 37). Yet even in this triumphal appeal to market evangelism a cautionary note was sounded: "we need to remind ourselves over and over again, and in as many ways as possible, that church advertising is an aid to, not a substitute for, religion" (1921: 177). Why was it apparently so easy to forget the essence of religion amid the heat and light of modern promotion? That, in essence, is the problem that this collection of essays seeks to explore.

The twentieth-century United States had a distinct, if heavily contested tradition of asserting the common causes of the Christian and the businessman (and I do stress the reference to masculinity). We can view this tradition via a series of bombastic literary productions ranging from the classic, *The Man that Nobody Knows* (1925) by the advertising man and future congressman Bruce Barton (1886-1967) - which sold 250,000 copies over 18 months on the back of its vision of Jesus in the image of the author (or the author in the image of Jesus) - right up to such contemporary works as *God is my CEO: Following God's Principles in a Bottom-Line World* (Julian, 2001). The origins of these works have been traced to the muscular Christianity movement of the later nineteenth-century and the desire to assert the consonance of both Church and business with masculinity (Ribuffo, 1981). One feature of such thinking is that spiritual and material success are understood to be linked, however, since, 'in a bottom-line world', financial credit can be assessed much more easily than spiritual merit, the tendency seems to make assumptions about personal piety based on business performance. This leads to suspicions that the business of such literature was, in fact, business. And it is in just this spirit that other management books have been borrowing the language of religious evangelization in order to explicate commercial objectives. This use of religion to provide a provocative source of business inspiration is not just restricted to contemporary American practice as demonstrated, for instance, by

Jesper Kunde, *Corporate Religion: Building a Strong Company through Personality and Corporate Soul* (2000).

Kunde and his ilk tend to present an image of religion as unified realm formed from a generic Christianity in which a hierarchy of Church structures is taken for granted. This is presented in ahistoric terms as a powerful management construct which can inform practices in business (or, some might say, in other non-religious business) endeavors. It is important to be aware of the dangers of anachronism involved in a vision based on such a reductionist image of 'religion'. The challenge, for the contemporary scholar is to establish a a neutral conceptual space between such glib assertions as that identifying St. Paul as the 'first spin doctor' (Institute for Cultural Research, 2000: 9) and the placing of Christianity in a privileged locale entirely separate from commercial processes both in the ancient world and today. Whilst the origins and development of Christianity do hold within them great potential for studying the background to the material under discussion, the present collection of papers cannot seek to find a set of universal answers to such questions as whether Christian denominations can be classified as businesses, or whether businesses should be classified as religious denominations whose purpose is to maintain faith in their corporate brands and to control the nature and reception of its values. Nevertheless, it is important to note that the conceptual boundary between religion and business is blurred and contested in the modern United States. It is the purpose of this collection to engage some of the key areas of this contestation and to explore the cultural landscape of shopping for salvation in our age of the therapeutic ethos (i.e. the idea that contemporary capitalism aims to deliver fulfillment in this life, Lears, 1983). The vital question is whether the engines of material consumption can enable Churches to provide spiritual salvation.

Some say yes. Stark and McCann (1993), for instance, provide a picture of spiritual success ensured by market competition. They argue that attendance at Catholic churches is more frequent in areas in which one finds the presence of the largest number of competing denominations. One of the relatively few recent attempts to study the boundaries of religion and economics to have been carried out by academics from the latter discipline, soundly backs up this viewpoint. The authors of this work, *The Marketplace of Christianity* (Ekelund, Hébert and Tollison, 2006), present their work as an attempt to develop analyses based ultimately on the insights made by Weber in his famous analysis of the Protestant work ethic. They consider the last five hundred years of Christian history as representing the failure of a "dominant company" (the Roman Catholic Church) to contain its competitors in a developing market for religious goods and services. Consumer demand is taken for granted on the basis that existential dread of death is "hard wired"; this cannot be addressed by scientific reason and, therefore, there is an "innate demand for the services of magic, religion, and spiritual experience" (2006: 270). The results have been a triumph: in their concluding remarks the authors celebrate "the competitive revolution in Christianity unleashed by the successful entry of Protestant competitors in the sixteenth century. Just as free and open competition increases the utility to consumers of goods and services, the open and extremely competitive market for Christian and other religious products and product forms creates a variety that maximizes satisfaction for individuals whose demand for such services is unlimited" (2006: 272).

The basis of this view is faith in the free market and the utilitarian notion of the maximizing of the individual and common good. In this analysis the successful denomination is that which outcompetes through offering the maximum spiritual benefit at the most competitive cost. It is important to note that cost refers to time as convertible to money. Those who argue that these processes have been happening, but that they are far from a good thing, tend to pin their arguments on the notion that active commitment is being replaced by spending. In an echo of Reformation disputes over the sale of indulgences, it can be argued that the contemporary American is being encouraged by the use of the familiar business methods of marketing to shop for Jesus-flavored products which provide a temporary therapeutic fix. Michael Budde is amongst the prominent scholars who have warned against such trends arguing, in relation to the Catholic Church, that the "the incorporation of a marketing ethos" undermines "gospel nonconformity and radical discipleship" (1997: 104). His sense is of a threat which is only now becoming critical. He writes: "contrary to the cultured despisers of Christianity, who see nothing new in the Church adopting the best tools with which to bamboozle the gullible, I believe there are *qualitative* differences between the past and the emerging present" (1997: 105).

It is all too easy to universalize when talking about Christianity, but to put such American expressions of peril in perspective, let me give you an example from my own country (the United Kingdom) which is one of world centers of advertising and marketing. On 30th September 2007 the established Church of England held a Back to Church Sunday. As reported in *The Guardian* newspaper clergy received customer-service training from John Lewis' department store, and "the Bishop of Sherwood, the Rt. Rev. Tony Porter, took off in a light aircraft trailing a banner behind him, while the Rt. Rev. John Pritchard, the Bishop of Oxford, will record a podcast reflecting on his appeal to lost churchgoers" (Butt, 2007). The ironic tone of the article suggested that there was no danger that such basic attempts at marketing would have any effect other than to emphasize how out of touch the Anglicans were from contemporary society. The sense of peril in the case of the USA, by contrast, may stem partly from the strength there of both business and religion: the thought being that the two must inevitably influence each other and produce something that is neither quite commercial nor quite spiritual, but a strangely warped hybrid of both. Doubts can be found on such issues on the part of some marketing professionals. For instance Hutton (2001) wonders whether there are dangers in using the "metaphor of the customer" (or not recognizing that it is a metaphor) in the case of non-profit businesses. Moreover, deeper questions arise over whether the market itself is moral, immoral, or amoral (Blank and McGurn, 2004).

This book is not aimed at providing moral suggestions, let alone solutions. Rather, the contributions have been chosen so as to provide case studies across a range of interactions between Christianity, marketing, visual and textual culture. The aim of this is to explore the connections between belief, its presentation, and the processes by which it is sold and consumed. The contributors have all been thinking about the way in which Christianity operates in a market culture and the degree to which one can use the notions of branding, advertising and marketing to understand missionary and revival activities. They come from theology, history, art history, literature and business studies backgrounds. All the contributors want to understand the production and consumption of images of holiness, rather than judging the quality of those images. That is quite another enterprise, one aspect of which, idolatry discourses in Victorian England, I have been researching for the last few years (Janes, forthcoming). Nevertheless, it is important to explain the general approach to the production of images as being derived from the emerging sub-discipline of visual culture.

Key introductions to this field are Walker and Chaplin (1997); Mirzoeff (1999); Mitchell (2002) and 2005); Sturken and Cartwright (2001); Elkins (2003) and Halsall (2006). Images are understood to be culturally mediated productions in which an emphasis is placed on the meaning-making observer, on evolving technologies of representation and transmission, the importance of mass media and popular culture, consumerism and the manufacturing of desire (Sturken and Cartwright, 2001, chapter 6). The effect of this postmodern cultural matrix is understood to be the eroding of the power of institutions in the face of the bewildering patterns of customer attention and choice. Some assert that what nowadays exists is indeed the image rather than the 'actuality' of holiness. However, the studies in this volume are empirically grounded in specific contexts of production and consumption and it is those connections which are the focus of these studies rather than the images themselves. In other words we want to look at the production of images of holiness for what that tells us about business and religion, rather than for what it tells us about the operation of visuality, textuality and the media through which those forms are manifested.

In this regard the current studies are heavily indebted to leading works of American and sacred visual and material culture, notably those of McDannell (1995) and Morgan (1998) and (2005). Two theoretical insights from these works have been particularly influential. Firstly, McDannell's keenness to emphasize processes of consumer agency through bricolage (the personal assemblage of referents to diverse cultural traditions, practices and formations). She notes that "Christian retailing is possible because consumers refuse to separate the sacred from the profane, the extraordinary from the ordinary, the pious from the trivial. For these consumers,

Christianity is intimately bound up in the day-to-day life of the family and its goods" (1995: 261). In other words, we should not assume the authority of religious institutions over the practices of their adherents. Secondly, Morgan helps us to understand that this does not have to be seen in terms of authenticity. For him authenticity is in the way in which things are received. Mass-produced culture can, therefore, be authentic through its manner of reception and use (1998: 134). All of this means that marketing campaigns are to be considering as cultural products which are received and incorporated into believers' lives and practices in an active and engaged manner. This does not mean that people automatically believe what the marketers want, but it does mean that we can study people's beliefs and practices, rather than the mere administering of religious content on the airwaves, movie-screens and the sides of mugs (fig. 2).

What then is marketing? In 1935 the American Marketing Association (AMA) adopted the following definition: marketing is "the performance of business activities that direct the flow of goods and services from producers to consumers." This was revised in 1985, and again in 2004, resulting in the assertion that marketing is: "an organizational function and a set of processes for creating, communicating and delivering value to customers and for managing customer relationships in ways that benefit the organization and its stakeholders" (Keefe, 2004). The equivalent organization in Britain, the Chartered Institute of Marketing (CIM), offers the following definition: "the management process responsible for identifying, anticipating and satisfying customer requirements profitably" (Chartered Institute of Marketing, 2005: 2). What has happened is an evolution over time from the concept of marketing as playing a purely informational role, to one according it a much more important function in relation to the development of products. The CIM describes contemporary marketing as consisting of seven key aspects – the 7Ps - product, price, place (i.e. the shop), promotion, people, process, physical evidence (i.e. plausibility of the process). Understood in these terms, the marketing of religion is intimately involved in shaping the content of religion in response to customer needs and expectations.

The challenge this poses to traditional Christianity should be obvious and, if marketing were to play such a prominent role in a religious denomination, one might expect there to be, at the least, a rigorous code of marketing ethics. The AMA web site gives the following definition:

> marketing ethics - 1... Standards of marketing decision making based on 'what is right' and 'what is wrong', and emanating from our religious heritage and our traditions of social, political, and economic freedom. 2... The use of moral codes, values, and standards to determine whether marketing actions are good or evil, right or wrong. Often standards are based on professional or association codes of ethics.

Yet the AMA web site also features an article which poses the question of whether marketing ethics is an oxymoron! (American Marketing Association, "Is Marketing Ethics an Oxymoron?", 2007; compare Nantel and Weeks, 1996). The discourse and practices of marketing are, it should be clear from this, to be understood as cultural constructs that are evolving alongside contemporary religion in America.

I have stated that the papers provide a set of overlapping studies. This has, however, the disadvantage that it makes selecting the order for the chapters something of a challenge since they are explore related themes. The following summary of the papers, therefore, aims not simply to sum up some of the key points about each one, but to explore the links between them and the rationale for their collection and ordering in this format. The overall structure is to move from contexts of textuality, to those focusing on material and bodily spaces, thence to visual culture and performance, finishing with objects, branding, bricolage and interfaith expression.

The Papers

Rewriting the Scriptures

Holy Scripture is regularly rewritten with each new translation, but in this section of the book I am referring to the more subtle rewriting that occurs when the message of the Bible is reinterpreted and re-presented. The chapters in this section present, respectively, the investigation of satirical and serious rewritings of religion in the USA. **Jennifer Lee's** contribution, "The Commodification of Religion: Fiction that Presents Religion as a Consumer Good and the New Faux Faith" discussed the work of three novelists and one film director who develop more or less (and in a couple of cases much less) affectionate satires on the role of religion in relation to business and its techniques. As Lee comments, "where Harry Crews is cynical, Christopher Moore is good-natured; and where Chuck Palahniuk is sarcastic, Kevin Smith presents a sincere message of faith. These authors have seen America's trend toward a trademarked Jesus, and the opportunity for comment cannot go unmarked". These satirical attitudes may strike a chord with some of the present readers of this collection. However, it is not our intention to present religious practices, however unexpected or problematic, as the legitimate objects of satire or attack. On the other hand the authors of the chapters of this book do not want to take an uncritically reverent attitude to the Churches and persons under discussion. It is important to understand, with Lee, that there is much in the alliance of business and Christianity that provides certain writers with abundant material for satire. We need to think why this should be.

The way in which the messages of Holy Scripture are re-written is of immense importance, above all because many of the potential readers of that script do not necessarily have the resources in terms of time or background knowledge to critique effectively what they are being presented with. This must surely be the case with texts marketed to children, or rather, as **Diane Carver Sekeres** explains it, quoting Simon (2006) in her "Balancing the Mission and the Market: Christian Children's Books for Tweens", to the "four-eyed, four-legged consumer" that is parent with child in tow (or vice versa). Sekeres concludes that Christian fiction for tweens (8-12 year olds) does much to fulfill a religious mission to instill moral values, but that it is sanitized in order to present a limited version of the world in which the readers are growing up. The world of the novels is overwhelmingly white, middle-class and conservative. Here morality derived from the Word has been represented to reflect the lives of those most likely to read it. This has the advantage of making it comprehensible to its audience and so boosting sales, but it does mean that difficult or contentious issues of race, social justice and sexuality are side-lined, if not eliminated altogether.

Evangelism and Purification

The next section explores the location of America in relation to sacred and profane places, spaces and persons. These essays explore some of the ways in which Christian denominations seek to purify contemporary culture, or to ensure their own purity. How do they, in other words, contest or engage with the world? Can marketing, for instance, be used effectively to challenge mainstream attitudes to gender roles and sexuality? Our next contribution suggests that it can. The power of heteronormativity, in many (and indeed, most) Christian denominations, is abundantly evidenced in **Monica Pombo**'s paper, "Capturing the Religious Imagination: Branding and the United Church of Christ's 'God is Still Speaking' Campaign". In 2004 the liberal denomination, the United Church of Christ, launched a TV marketing campaign for their Church which made a virtue of their inclusivity, notably toward homosexuals. Pombo discusses the processes behind the launch of the campaign before examining one of the key TV commercials, *Bouncer*, in detail. In this advertorial bouncers are shown at the door of a church behaving as they might in front of an exclusive nightclub. The result is that a wealthy white couple is let in, but homosexuals are not. The article then moves on to discuss the controversy caused by the campaign and the refusal by certain networks to air the advert because it was "too controversial".

This campaign can be compared with that carried out by the Cathedral of Hope, "the world's largest gay and lesbian church", in Dallas, Texas. The cathedral produced a half-hour infomercial, *Holy Homosexuals*, and failed to get it on six TV channels before WGNTV in Chicago agreed to show it if the title were changed to *The Cathedral of Hope* (Hendershot, 2004: 135). Pombo makes a strong case for such campaigns as marketing watersheds in Christian marketing in the USA, arguing that the United Church of Christ successfully employed professional business methods with which it was previously unfamiliar in order to promote tolerance as a key aspect of the message of Christ. This is an important corrective to notions of the business environment as a bastion of inherent social conservativism, notably because the marketing agency in question worked on this account for unusually low fees. This problematizes oppositional notions of material capitalism versus Christian altruism. It is clear that, although it has been unusual, liberal Christian positions can be effectively advanced through the kinds of unashamed promotional techniques that have traditionally been the forte of the evangelical right.

The question of the sacralization of secular spaces and practices, or, conversely, the secularization of religious impulses is explored in our next paper. **Kathaleen Amende** in "Better than Sex: Working out with Jesus at the Lord's Gym" explores the way in which physical and moral attractiveness are aligned in the marketing imagery of the Lord's Gym chain of health clubs. Amende understands this as a development from the traditions of muscular Christianity. That movement originated in the nineteenth-century and aimed to assert the manliness of Christ and, thus, to ensure that religion did not become sidelined into a focus upon what was then the relatively disempowered feminine sphere of sensibility. What has been referred to as the "cult" of bodybuilding has, of course, developed a strongly secular identity such that even the Young Men's Christian Association effectively hides its origins in its acronym YMCA. Indeed, the Village People hit of 1978 indicates the way in which the cultural meanings of this organization could become divorced from, and perhaps even antithetical to, the aims of its founders. Amende reads the Lord's Gym as an attempt to reconnect physical and moral hygiene through the provision of a space in which bodily fitness is de-queered and the exerciser's body is brought into consonance with that of a heteronormative Christ. However, she argues that this process is far from unproblematic. The modern connotation of muscularity as a key attribute of male sexual attractiveness means that Christ is being set up as an image of desire; explicitly so for women, and implicitly so for men. This leads to the question as to whether Christianity is being used as the cover for the pursuit of material and erotic interests, or whether this organization is helping in the process of Christianizing otherwise profane activities. Does it promote the equality of His people, or does it, in fact, continue traditions of the disciplining and disempowerment of female desire? Is the image of holiness being used to market a specific sexual regime?

Amende's work compliments that of Schippert (2003) which explores the potentially queer dynamics of gymnasia to build an argument that the Lord's Gym is concerned with the production of respectable, heterosexual bodies in which sexuality is focused on eroticizing the marital bond. But this author is also keen to stress that this attempt to construct a heteronormative space for exercise indicates that this has become problematized in mainstream culture. Some of the key evidence of this is the way in which images of Christ in modern America have been actively monitored for inappropriate gender messages such that He must not be too overtly masculine or feminine, since these, respectively, risk raising the thrills of effeminacy or of the adoration of masculinity (Jordan, 2000: 202). It is the latter that we can see shining out from Andy Warhol's *The Last Supper/Be Somebody with a Body* (1985), in which the juxtaposed body builder sports a halo (Heartney, 2004: 38 and Dillenberger, 1998). So how can the Lord's Gym deny the homo-erotic potential of its own imagery? The answer, suggested Mark Jordan, lies in the belief that, "Christianity is vehemently opposed to homosexuality, [and] hence Christian art cannot be homoerotic. Second, faithful Christians cannot be homosexuals, so the main audience for Christian art contains no one who might react to it homoerotically" (Jordan, 2000: 203). The efficaciousness of the Gym is, therefore, based on belief in the purity of those attracted to it. The marketing message, therefore, is not dangerously ambiguous because it will only be heeded by the pure in any case.

This is, of course, a niche marketing strategy aimed more at maintaining the purity of converts than at evangelizing the unconvinced. Terminology can be a minefield, so in the following I am using the terms evangelical and fundamentalist in relation to the way in which they are used as labels in the contemporary United States. As this is not a history-based volume, however, it useful to step back for a moment and take a broader retrospective view of denominational differences. Catholicism fosters strong conceptions of the localization of the sacred as being concentrated in churches generally and in the sacraments in particular (Giles, 1992: 36-8).

The role of relics and shrines, although reduced after Vatican II, represents a strong tradition of the assertion of embodied sacredness. Such embodiment invites comparison with external secular or profane space. By eroding or removing the sacramental authority of the priest, forms of Protestantism vested sacred power in the force of the Holy Spirit as manifested in the blessed persons of the congregation. Evangelical drives seek to ensure the widest expressions of such sacred force through conversions and the act of being born again. There has, however, been a very significant divergence in evangelical thought. One stream, prevalent in the earlier years of the movement refused to actively contest the materialism of the world, despite denouncing many of its ways, because of belief in the need for submission to the power of God's will and, for some groups, because of faith in predestination. Many of those in this tradition looked, and continue to look for the coming the last times and deliverance from the fallen nature of the world. However, it is a variant of these traditions which has become very prominent in the modern United States via a split from fundamentalist elements of Protestantism. This is represented by the view that, even if the last times are imminent, the faithful have the duty to cleanse and sacralize the world rather than to separate from it. The effect of this can be endorsement of the ways of the world when these are accompanied by appropriate expressions of faith. In other words, the doctrine that faith rather than good works ensures salvation ensures a remarkable ability to assimilate all manner of novel social and economic forms to Christianity for which there is no biblical sanction (if only because they did not exist two thousand years ago).

Darren E. Grem, in "Selling a "Disneyland for the Devout": Religious Marketing at Jim Bakker's Heritage USA" gives us a picture of what such an evangelical landscape looks like when examined on the ground. His case study is Heritage USA, Fort Mill, South Carolina, described by Grem as having been "promoted as a Christian amusement park and resort", which opened in 1978 and lasted for eleven years before the financial and moral downfall of its founder led to its closure (it is, however, currently being rebuilt under new ownership). Heritage USA is particularly fascinating in that it attempted to combine the notions of special sacred space which must be defended from external pollution with a full-hearted embrace of the business practices of modern capitalism. In other words, it acknowledged that there was a need for a retreat from the world but not through the denial of it, but through its perfection in microcosm. Grem finds this paradoxical strategy not simply disturbing, but also contributory to the failure of the enterprise. To make fun of Heritage USA for being like a Christian Disneyland is, however, to do a massive disservice to the power, influence and subtlety of the latter (Lyon, 2000). Rather the problem, for Grem, lay in the fact that the park in general and its mall in particular were projected as sacred religious spaces in which the supreme commodity of faith was to be consumed via the purchase of Praise the Lord Frisbees, T-shirts and sun-visors, not to mention Tammy Faye Bakker's own range of maquillage. The vision being sold here was that the capitalist American way of life could deliver heaven on earth: it just needed Christian leadership to reach that state of perfection. But this was no utopia. The presence of tensions between visitors of differing denominations, as well as between management and workers make it clear that this was not a paradise of Christian tranquility.

The theme park is presented in this essay as a failed exercise in wish-fulfillment. However, it is important to note that the reason for its failure did not lie in a misreading of market pressures. For instance, it has been commented of the phenomenally successful *Left Behind* series of novels that the vision of the post Apocalyptic kingdom of God that these provide allows "for Christians to enjoy all the consumer pleasures that secular humanism has allowed citizens of capitalism, but [to] escape responsibility for the [environmental and social] violence on which global capitalism depends" (Dombek, 2007: 152). Heritage Village USA represents the idea of the sacralisation of consumption. The traditionally profane, shopping for instance, is not so any more: "not only is the mall more central within Heritage Village than its church and other facilities, it is also more carefully and elaborately decorated" (McGuinn and Belk, 1989: 231). Guilt has been purged into the joys of spectacle and consumption. As Tammy Faye Bakker commented: "if my utopia could look any way I wanted it to look, I'd like it to look like Disneyland. I love Disneyland, and if I could, I'd have the whole world look like Disneyland" (quoted in McGuinn and Belk, 1989: 232). But it is vital to remember that the diversity of facades and rides in Disneyland are presented as a universe of choice, but they are all variations on a theme, built at the same time from the same materials for the same purposes. The cultural meaning of Heritage USA lay in its attempt to restrict spending choices by shaping consumer desire and, thereby, channel consumer spending into the pockets of the Bakkers. It is important to note that the park was much more successful in this than it was in converting people to the Bakker's brand of evangelicalism. For, fascinatingly enough, Heritage USA had a wide appeal to people who were secure in a wide range of denominations: "despite its firm grounding in evangelical Protestantism, by 1985 Catholics visited Heritage USA as frequently as Baptists". If considered in relation of popular material culture, the spaces of Heritage USA can be read as being consumed through processes of bricolage, whereby people are negotiating their personal paths through what Hendershot refers to as the "complicated osmosis" occurring between the "secular" and the "religious" (2004: 6).

Marketing Performances

Heritage USA can be considered as representing a theater in which interactive performances were being staged. An emphasis on the performative is important, not simply because of liturgical traditions within Christianity, but because of our belief in the notion of the shared construction of meaning by what were once viewed unproblematically as 'producers' and 'consumers' in commercial transactions. What happens when we turn to look at self-conscious acts of promotional performance? Kilde (2002: 216) has criticized modern evangelical auditorium churches for giving the audience what it wants; serving up easily consumable religious product which, as a result, fails to deal with the full power and potential of Christian Truth. Issues such of these are the key concern of Vincent Miller's troubled meditations in *Consuming Religion: Christian Faith and Practice in a Consumer Culture* (2005). He argues that:

> when consumption becomes the dominant cultural practice, belief is systematically misdirected from traditional religious practices into consumption. This makes the moment of choice the fundamental means of self-actualization,

implicitly presuming that the object being chosen, whether a banal commodity, or a profound spiritual tradition, will in itself resolve all the difficulties the consumer faces. Traditional practices of self-transformation are subordinate to consumer choice. This results in a divorce between belief and practice, as people sincerely and mistakenly believe they are acting on the beliefs they are choosing (2005: 225).

Religion, in this theoretical framework, becomes feel-good entertainment that is bought at the collection plate every Sunday. Why bother if all that one gains is a passive audience? Perhaps the answer is that at least they are not watching (and paying) someone else.

An audience drifting beyond denominational boundaries was, as we have seen, a feature of Heritage USA. These features can also be seen in the case of the biggest selling Christian film of recent times:

Clearly Gibson's film would have fallen flat had it not been for the ways it was analyzed, criticized and otherwise promoted by both secular and religious groups through the Internet, television and print news media... there is little doubt that Gibson and his publicity people knew how to work the system (Plate, 2004: xvi).

This helps us to understand the cross-denominational appeal of Mel Gibson's cinematic Biblical epic of 2004 discussed by **Kent L. Brintnall** in "Pursing the Passion's Passions". Gibson is emphatically Catholic; as is his film, in so far as it presents an extraordinarily intense focus on the suffering of the incarnated Christ, combined with an emphasis on the role of the Virgin Mary. Indeed, Roman Catholics flocked to see the movie; however, Brintnall introduces us to its impact on members of the Reformed denominations. He introduces us to the Protestant Branch family who associate their having viewed the film with the seemingly miraculous recovery of their daughter from drowning. The film appears to have functioned for its vast evangelical audience as a marker of Christian solidarity against an "other" which can variously be identified as "secular" culture in general and Hollywood in particular, but which had an ugly spinoff in suggestions of anti-Semitism as an element of the film itself and in some of the support for it. Brintnall calls attention to Gary North's opinion that *The Passion* can be seen as a "decisive turning point in the culture war between a Hollywood elite and a Christian mainstream" (North, 2004: ix-xii, 6-10, 175-89). In this cultural construction the essence of the American people is religious and it is the peddlers of modern and postmodern dreams that are leading the nation astray. The strategy that is suggested here is that by mobilizing their buying power as a mass-audience, Christians can take back control through the mechanism of big (in this case media) business. The capitalist system, in this formulation is the key to the victory of Christ. However, Brintnall explains that the surge of Christian consumption was insufficient to create major change in the output of Hollywood. Instead he finds that *The Passion* can best be understood via the lens of film theories of the "cult film", its form and audience. In other words, the story of Jesus" death is a classical narrative that is adored by a minority in-group but which has no wider purchase on the average viewer. At one level this can be considered as a triumph of marketing. *The Passion* achieved a self-supporting cultural existence, rather than being seen as just yet another version of a well-known story. It is very important to realize that what is being sold here is ultimately the Passion, but most immediately, it is *The Passion* (fig. 2). This raises the suspicion that knowledge of the Passion is used to sell *The Passion* rather than the other way round. Such marketing techniques are not new. Market

Fig. 2. Jesus, a film and a mug are being sold, but in what order of importance? © Bob Siemon Designs 2004, http://www.shareth epassionofthechrist. com/gifts.asp#mugs.

front   back

MUG READS: He was pierced for our transgressions, He was crushed for our iniquities; the punishment that brought us peace was upon Him, and by His wounds we are healed. ISAIAH 53:5

segmentation was being used to formulate strategies for the promotion of Biblical epic film in the 1920s and 30s (Maresco, 2004). What does appear to have changed is the increasing diversity of media, the sophistication of technical effects and processes and, perhaps, an increasing tendency for the commoditized narrative to establish a cultural and commercial life of its own.

Such commercial life-forms exist most easily in environments rich with those who are ready to consume. This means that sales pitches (evangelism) produce the largest returns when addressed to those who are already customers. Marketing to the in-group is explored by **Jennifer Fleeger** in her paper "The Passion and the Profit: Evangelical Christianity and Media Space in Amish Country". The self-consciously pre-modern spaces of "Amish Country" in Lancaster, Pennsylvania are the location for the Millennium Theater, a multi-million-dollar organization which uses the latest high technology to stage reconstructions of biblical stories. The people who are likely to visit the Theatre are already those with some investment in Christian belief. The aim of the Mission is to find ways in which to ensure clients' ongoing and increasing emotional and financial commitment. The form of the Theatre itself helps to train audiences into the experience of attendance at a mega-church and to the sense that attendance and spending represents what is required in exchange for entertainment and salvation.

This does not mean, however, that simple, easily consumed messages must be trivial. After all Jesus Himself preached in the language of the common person. In this collection we take all aspects of popular culture with appropriate respect. For instance, English (2005) has argued strongly that cartoons can be taken seriously by theologians. This argument is based on the notion of the cartoonist as holy fool. Cartoon strips are, in various formats, read by people of all ages, but they have a particular cultural role in the education and entertainment of children. It is clear that youth must present a clear target for evangelization. **Harry Coverston** in "Evangelical Cartoons: the Good News and the Bad" takes us onto a university campus to explore the way in which cartoon strips are employed to draw students into the Christian fold. Coverston explores the pamphleting of the campus of the University of Central Florida in 2006 with a number of cartoon tracts, notably *The Choice* (Chick

Publications, 1999). Jack Chick was inspired to begin a cartoon mission for Christ having seen a group of teenagers and collapsing in tears at the thought that these promising young people were on their way to hell. His company now produces hundreds of tracts which are widely employed as part of evangelization strategies. Coverston analyses these tracts by reference to their use of color, which he sees as a marketing tactic aimed at producing emotive responses, and in terms of their narrative content, which he views as being targeted at primal anxieties for safety as defined by theories of the nature of basic and complex human needs. He links these insights to social survey evidence which suggests that the direct conversion rate from such campaigns is very low and that those who do convert tend to have high levels of mental health and addiction problems. This, of course, can be read in two ways: either these campaigns are successfully reaching the vulnerable, or they are exploiting that very vulnerability. To some extent a decision on which of these is correct must be left to one's own beliefs, however, Coverston does point out what he refers to as "darker questions", notably in relation to the morality of marketing campaigns that seek to target vulnerable groups. There is, of course, nothing remarkable about such a strategy in itself. The fear of inferiority is used frequently to drive desires for consumption in our capitalist system. But this cannot, surely, be morally unproblematic for Christians?

Agency, Producers and Consumers

The commodity-rich world of youth-culture, sport, music and as-sociated "lifestyle" brands is the subject of the next chapter. **Sil-via Giagnoni** explores the way in which the evangelical ministry of Luis Palau has attempted to engage younger people through an extensive program of festivals which feature Christian versions of popular culture staples such as rock music and action sports. Skate parks are one of the main attractions at festivals the appeal of which is modeled on that of the some three hundred skateboard minis-tries that flourish in the USA (as of 2006). The aim is to provide ways in which youth culture can become assimilated into Christian society, rather than standing in rebellious opposition to it. The strat-egy here is to attempt to purify rock and sports of their potential for impiety. By ensuring that lyrics are consonant with the Gospel and that sportswear bears Christian-themed branding, the potentially rival attractions of rebellion and counter culture can be, in theory, harnessed to Christian purposes. It is the purpose of pastors of this emerging trend to go forth with gladness amongst the young un-believers and bring them into the fold, happy in the knowledge that their culture is essentially imperfect, but salvageable. Yet Gia-gnoni discovers some of same problems that Amende saw in her discussion of the Lord's Gym chain of health clubs. She sees skate-boarding focused ministries as attempts to control and discipline aspects of counter-cultural behavior. In her analysis, the effect of the evangelicals is not so much to ensure the success of Christianity as to see that adult social norms are asserted over those of teenage counter-culture. Moreover, Giagnoni also references the downside of sports ministries in so far as they are focused on the harnessing of masculine strength to the Church and, thereby, display gender bias. Beyond all of this, a further problem with the Palau approach is that in openly embracing cultural bricolage, it threatens to open up the essentials of Christian faith to the vagaries of daily consumer choice.

The analysis of bricolage plays a key role in Vincent Miller's at-tempt to find ways forward for religion in America's consumer cul-ture. But though he emphasizes the dangers of passive spectator-ship and the consumption of images as a replacement for social ac-tion (2005: 60), he develops a theory of the positive uses of bricolage (2005: 162). He recognizes that "consumer culture is experienced by most people as liberation. It liberates them from the constraints of closed communities, and tightly scripted class, gender and social roles". It may be that it is in the emergence of blurred ground be-tween denominations and between the religious and secular sphere that we can find significant grounds for optimism,

The challenge of taking the cultural practices of mixing as seri-ously as they deserve is taken on by **Elizabeth Bernstein** in "Escap-ing the "December Dilemma" on Chrismukkah.com". In this paper Bronstein considers the content of the Chrismukkah website which was set up by Ron and Michelle Gompertz. The site is, first and foremost, an online store retailing "our hilarious, best selling Chris-mukkah books, our original design Chrismukkah cards, menorahments, Chrismukkah kipot, holiday music CDs and more"(https://www.chrismukkah.com/content/shop_chrismukkah, accessed 10 October 2007). As Bernstein says "the kitsch sold on the website is grotesque and irreverent and the whole enterprise might appear insensitive, another "superficial fad". After all, Hannukah and Christmas, which Chrismukkah attempts to conflate, have no common ground in terms of Christian and Jewish theology. However, she asserts that this visual and material culture is not simply the result of secular confusion, bad taste and symbolic appropriation; it stems from the specific fact of the sharp rise in the number mixed-faith couples. Accurate figures are in short supply, but in 1990 the Council of Jewish Federations' National Jewish Population Survey concluded that a majority of American Jews take non-Jewish partners (Horowitz, 1999: 303). Accordingly, Bernstein sees in Chrismukkah the reflection of quite specific anxieties on the part of mixed-faith couples in the context of the social threat of exclusion from mainstream celebrations. She (and indeed the website) point out that the American Chrismukkah had its counterpart in the pre-World War Two celebration of Weihnukkah in Germany. In this analysis the humorous aspects of kitsch function to defuse the presence of very real fears about one's place in multi-cultural society.

In Conclusion

Without wishing to do violence to the complexities of the material evidence which is the basis of these essays, I can suggest some of the key themes which emerge. Lee and Sekeres explore aspects of the textual representation of Christian messages and raise the issue of the way in which positive and negative imagery can reshape reader's views and, thus the way in which Christian texts may be adapted to be in conformity with their audience. Pombo and Amende reveal the fact that business methods can be harnessed in support of both liberal and conservative Christian agendas. This suggests that we may wish to reflect on the degree to which ideology is necessarily influenced by the marketing techniques themselves. Grem, Amende and Gignoni's studies highlight attempts to purify the material world rather than simply to reject it, and, moreover, to ensure that purity by Christianizing practices of consumption which are widespread in society at large. In these case studies the tendency to rewrite the Christian script to appeal to the audience finds expression through the embrace of business methods in order to attempt the creation of a better sort of business. The problems with these attempts partly relate to a conflict between the desire to secure new denominational adherents and to retain existing members. Brintnall, Fleeger and Coverston highlight the challenges of both sides of this equation in an environment of competitive marketing and consumer choice. Some of the most effective strategies appear to focus on increasing the loyalty (and donations) of current adherents (loyal consumers). Gignoni and Bernstein, finally, highlight issues of the shifting balance of power between producers and consumers who are busy with the construction of self-identity. The danger, in these circumstances, is that people will be given what they want, rather than what they need. Is the alluring image of holiness generated by marketing morally authentic, or has it, as Zuckerman (2005) argued for *The Passion*, developed into a meta-reality which tells us more about the persuasive power of the media than of Christ?

This line of thought can, of course, be considered in the light of long-standing Jewish and Protestant anxieties about representation, albeit that we now understand that the textual is just as vulnerable as the visual to variant readings. Visiting the Epcot Center, Orlando, Florida, the art historian Annabel Wharton notes that "to fondle the façade of the Georgian structure in [the themed zone of] 'England' [is] to realize that it is constructed of Drivit (stucco on Styrofoam), Werzalite (glued sawdust), or fiberglass, not brick and stone" (2006: 230). Her dismay at the 'unnatural' and the artificial is unmistakable. Such views place a sharp opposition between true and false and between, implicitly, moral and immoral imagery. Wharton bewails the fact that "as the illusionism of both images and the market has accelerated in the West, anxiety about money and representation has, in inverse proportion, diminished" (2006: 238). Has moral and cultural relativism gone too far for it to be meaningful for us to worry about authenticity in art or religion? David Chidester has presented a vision of "authentic fakes" which are "simultaneously simulations and the real thing". He argues that American popular culture is mostly about faking, but this does not mean that it cannot do valuable "religious work". He points out that even "the really real in America, money, hard cold cash, the bedrock of values, is also an arena of trickery, fraud, and deception" (2005:. viii). We can, by thinking in this vein, make the proposition, to take one example, that the Bakkers and Heritage USA were fakes who did a good deal of Christian work. Therefore, the authenticity or otherwise of their associated marketing campaigns simply does not matter. Pete Ward goes beyond this to celebrate the Christian embrace of postmodernity by a "liquid church" of believers who are fully enmeshed in this world but who create Christian fellowship through all media of communication rather than via traditional, static ("solid") forms of worship such as church buildings (Ward, 2002). Perhaps it does not matter too much if truth is destabilized and becomes liquid too, since it might be equally valuable to rediscover the spiritual potential of doubt?

It is easy to assert that this state of affairs is very recent and that is it an aspect of postmodern relativism. However, it is instructive to bear in mind Mrs Bulstrode in George Eliot's *Middlemarch* (1871) who had a "NAIVE [original emphasis] way of conciliating piety and worldliness, the nothingness of this life and the desirability of cut glass, the consciousness at once of filthy rags and the best damask (quoted in Barker, 2007: 36). The attitudes that we see today have been slowly developing for decades, or even centuries. Jhally (1989) argued that materialism in general and advertising in particular was a religion based on commodity fetishism, but Sheffield, in *The Religious Dimensions of Advertising* (2006: 151), has contended persuasively against this: "the new industrial capitalism did not become a new religion; instead, it evoked religious dimensions as a way for the individual to make meaning in a quickly changing society". What has changed is that what was once seen as "naïve" is now regarded as the action of creative personal agency. What is also clear is that Christianity, which was once in pole position as a maker of social meaning, has had increasingly to compete for attention with a myriad of secular and commercial alternatives. Churches, moreover, have to compete against each other as well as against other religions in a world in which the loyalty of adherents is decreasingly assured by tradition. In such an environment there is competition to reduce the barriers (the costs) of conversion and, thus, a tendency to gain and lose large numbers of superficial customers, or to gain people whose true loyalty and understanding is, in fact, focused on the charismatic marketing itself. What is increasingly difficult to sustain in such an environment is a notion of the Church as a counterculture which seeks to lay out an alternative agenda to the processes of worldly consumption (Budde and Brimlow, 2000). If Ekelund, Hébert and Tollison (2006: 270) are right that there is an innate demand for spiritual reassurance, we might wonder at the existential dread which lies ahead in a nation in which Churches each efficiently market their special possession of the Truth. What chance, in the spiritual hyper mart, do people have of remaining secure in their belief that they have picked the right spiritual product?

References

American Marketing Association, "Definition, Marketing Ethics" (Chicago: American Marketing Association, 2007), http://www.marketingpower.com/mg-dictionary-view1869.php, accessed 28 August 2007.

American Marketing Association, "Is Marketing Ethics an Oxymoron?" (Chicago: American Marketing Association, 2007), http://www.marketingpower.com/content24271.php, accessed 28 August 2007.

Badaracco, Claire, "Affinity Marketing and Religion in a Therapeutic Culture", *Public Relations Quarterly* winter (2004), pp. 46-49.

Baldwin, Tom, "America: the New Evangelicals: Where God Meets Big Business – and it's Coming Soon to a Church near you", *The Times* 27 December (2006), pp. 40-1.

Barker, Paul, Review, Cherry, *Household Gods, Times Literary Supplement* 9 February (2007), p. 36.

Belk, Russell W., "Materialism and the Modern U.S. Christmas", *Advertising and Society Review* 1 (2000), http://muse.jhu.edu/journals/asr/v001/1.1belk.html, accessed 18 August 2007.

Blank, Rebecca M. and William McGurn, *Is the Market Moral? A Dialogue in Religion, Economics and Justice* (Washington: Brookings Institution Press, 2004).

Budde, Michael L., *The Two Churches: Catholicism and Capitalism in the World-System* (Durham, N.C.: Duke University Press, 1992).

_____, *The (Magic) Kingdom of God: Christianity and Global Culture Industries* (Boulder: Westview Press, 1997).

_____, and Robert W. Brimlow, *The Church as Counterculture* (Albany: State University of New York Press, 2000).

Butt, Riazat, "Church Mission to Get People Back to the Pews", *The Guardian*, 25 September (2007), p. 21.

Case, Francis H., *Handbook of Church Advertising* (London: Epworth Press, 1921).

Chartered Institute of Marketing, *Marketing and the 7Ps: a Brief Summary of Marketing and How it Works* (London: CIM, 2005), http://www.cim.co.uk/mediastore/FactFiles/Factifile7ps.pdf, accessed 28 August 2007.

Chick Publications, *The Choice* (Ontario, California: Chick Publications, 1999).

Chidester, David, *Authentic Fakes: Religion and American Popular Culture* (Berkeley: University of Chicago Press, 2005).

Cohen, Deborah, *Household Goods: the British and their Possessions* (New Haven: Yale University Press, 2006).

Coleman, Simon and John Elsner, *Pilgrimage: Past and Present: Sacred Travel and Sacred Space in the World's Religions* (London: British Museum Press, 1995).

Dillenberger, Jane, *The Religious Art of Andy Warhol* (New York: Continuum, 1998)

Dombek, Kristin, "Murder in the Theme Park: Evangelical Animals and the End of the World", *The Drama Review* 51 (2007), pp. 138-53.

Dotson, Michael J. and Eva M. Hyatt, "The Impact of Religious Symbols as Cues in Advertising", http://www.sbaer.uca.edu/research/sma/1995/pdf/61.pdf, accessed 18th August 2007.

Ekelund, Robert B., Robert F. Hébert and Robert D. Tollison, *The Marketplace of Christianity* (Cambridge, Mass.: MIT Press, 2006).

Elkins, James, *Visual Studies: a Skeptical Introduction* (New York: Routledge, 2003).

English, G., "Cartoons and Christians: do Cartoons have a Place in Religious Discourse?", *Australian EJournal of Theology* 5 (2005), pp. 1-10, http://dlibrary.acu.edu.au/research/theology/ejournal/aejt_5/english.htm, accessed 18 August 2007.

Faith & Friends, 'Why Fashion Dolls" (Franklin: Mission City Press, 2007), http://www.faithandfriends.com/whyfashiondolls.htm, accessed 11 October 2007.

FCS, "Ethan Pope, Cashing it in" (Grand Rapids: Family Christian Stores, 2007), http://www.familychristian.com/shop/product.asp?prodID=15433, accessed 11 October 2007.

_____, "Faith and Friends, True Blue Doll" (Grand Rapids: Family Christian Stores, 2007), http://www.familychristian.com/shop/product.asp?prodID=18411, accessed 11 October 2007.

_____, "The Family Christian Stores Platinum Plus® MasterCard® Credit Card" (Grand Rapids: Family Christian Stores, 2007), https://wwwa.applyonline-now.com/USCCapp/Ctl/entry?sc=FAAWIE&mc=A00000276Y, accessed 11 October 2007.

Giles, Paul, *American Catholic Arts and Fictions: Culture, Ideology, Aesthetics* (Cambridge: Cambridge University Press, 1992).

Halsall, Francis, "What does Visual Studies Want?", *Art Bulletin* 23 (2006), pp. 6-8.

Heartny, Eleanor, *Postmodern Heretics: the Catholic Imagination in Contemporary Art* (New York: Midmarch Arts Press, 2004).

Hendershot, Heather, *Shaking the World for Jesus: Media and Conservative Evangelical Culture* (Chicago: University of Chicago, 2004).

Hoover, Stewart M., "Visual Religion in Media Culture", in eds. David Morgan and Sally M. Promey, *The Visual Culture of American Religions* (Berkeley: University of California Press, 2001), pp. 146-59.

Horowitz, June Andrews, "Negotiating Couplehood: the Process of Resolving the December Dilemma Among Interfaith Couples", *Family Process* 38 (1999), pp. 303-23.

Hutton, James G., "Narrowing the Concept of Marketing", *Journal of Nonprofit and Public Sector Marketing* 9 (2002), pp. 5-24.

Institute for Cultural Research, *The Marketing of Christianity: the Evolution of Early Christian Doctrine*, Monograph Series 39 (London: Institute for Cultural Research, 2000).

Janes, Dominic, *Sex and Salvation: Idolatry in Victorian England* (forthcoming).

Jhally, Sut, "Advertising as Religion: the Dialectic and Technology of Magic", in eds. Ian Angus and Jhally, *Cultural Politics in Contemporary America* (New York: Routledge, 1989).

Jordan, Mark D., *The Silence of Sodom: Homosexuality in Modern Catholicism* (Chicago: University of Chicago Press, 2000).

Julian, Larry, *God is My CEO: Following God's Principles in a Bottom-Line World* (Avon, Mass.: Adams Media Corp., 2001).

Keefe, Lisa M., "What is the meaning of marketing?" *Marketing News*, 25 September (2004), pp. 17-18.

Kilde, Jeanne Halgren, *When Church Became Theatre: the Transformation of Evangelical Architecture and Worship in Nineteenth-Century America* (Oxford: Oxford University Press, 2002).

Kunde, Jesper, *Corporate Religion: Building a Strong Company through Personality and Corporate Soul*, trans. Helle Nygaard and Nigel P. Mander (London: FT Prentice Hall, 2000).

Kyle, Richard, *Evangelicalism: an Americanised Christianity* (Piscataway: Transaction, 2006).

Lears, T. J. Jackson, "From Salvation to Self-Realisation: Advertising and the Therapeutic Roots of the Consumer Culture, 1880-1930", in eds. Richard Wightman Fox and Lears, *The Culture of Consumption: Critical Essays in American History, 1880-1980* (New York: Pantheon, 1983), pp. 1-38.

Levey, Geoffrey Brahm, "Symbolic Recognition, Multicultural Citizens, and Acknowledgement: Negotiating the Christmas Wars", *Australian Journal of Political Science* 41 (2006), pp. 355-70.

Lynch, Gordon, *Understanding Theology and Popular Culture* (Oxford: Blackwell, 2005).

Lyon, David, *Jesus in Disneyland: Religion in Postmodern Times* (Cambridge: Polity, 2000).

Maresco, Peter A., "Mel Gibson's *The Passion of the Christ*: Market Segmentations, Mass Marketing and Promotion, and the Internet", *Journal of Religion and Popular Culture* 8 (2004), pp. 1-10, http://www.usask.ca/relst/jrpc/art8-melgibson-marketing-print.html, accessed 18 August 2007.

McDannell, Colleen, *Material Christianity: Religion and Popular Culture in America* (New Haven: Yale University Press, 1995).

Miller, Vincent J., *Consuming Religion: Christian Faith and Practice in a Consumer Culture* (New York: Continuum, 2005).

Mirzoeff, Nicholas, *An Introduction to Visual Culture* (London: Routledge, 1999).

Mitchell, W. J. T., "Showing Seeing: a Critique of Visual Culture", *Journal of Visual Culture* 1 (2002), pp. 165-81.

Mitchell, W., J. T., *What do Pictures Want? The Lives and Loves of Images* (Chicago: University of Chicago Press, 2005).

Moody, "Moody Publishers Today" (Chicago: Moody, 2007), http://www.moodypublishers.com/Publishers/default.asp?SectionID=456C4C3264844F37B6E3E50481199218, accessed 11 October 2007.

Moore, Alexander, "Walt Disney World: Bounded Ritual Space and the Playful Pilgrimage Center", *Anthropological Quarterly* 53 (1980), pp. 207-18.

Moore, Rick Clifton, "Spirituality that Sells: Religious Imagery in Magazine Advertising", *Advertising and Society Review* 6 (2005), http://muse.jhu.edu/journals/asr/v006/6.1moore.html, accessed 18 August 2007.

Morgan, David, *The Sacred Gaze: Religious Visual Culture in Theory and Practice* (Berkeley: University of California Press, 2005).

_____, *Visual Piety: a History and Theory of Popular Religious Images* (Berkeley: University of California Press, 1998).

Nantel, Jacques and William A. Weekes, "Marketing Ethics: is there More to it than the Utilitarian Approach?" *European Journal of Marketing* 30 (1996), pp. 9-19.

North, Gary, *The War on Mel Gibson: the Media v. "The Passion"* (Powder Springs: American Vision, 2004).

O'Guinn, Thomas C. and Russell W. Belk, "Heaven on Earth: Consumption at Heritage Village, USA", *Journal of Consumer Research* 16 (1989), pp. 227-38.

Padley, Steve, *Televangelism in America* (New York: Routledge, 1990).

Plate, Brent S., *Religion, Art and Visual Culture: a Cross-Cultural Reader* (New York: Palgrave, 2002).

_____, "Introduction: Re-Viewing as Remembering", in. ed. Plate, *Re-Viewing the Passion: Mel Gibson's Film and its Critics* (New York: Palgrave, 2004), pp. xi-xix.

Pope, Ethan, *Cashing it in: Getting Ready for a World without Money* (Chicago: Moody, 2005).

Ribuffo, Leo P., "Jesus Christ as Business Statesman: Bruce Barton and the Selling of Corporate Capitalism", *American Quarterly* 33 (1981), pp. 206-31.

Rothschild, Michael L., "Marketing Communications in Nonbusiness Situations or Why it's so Hard to Sell Brotherhood like Soap", *Journal of Marketing* 43 (1979), pp. 11-20.

Schippert, Claudia, "Sporting Heroic Bodies in a Christian Nation-at-War", *Journal of Religion and Popular Culture* 5 (2003), http://www.usask.ca/relst/jrpc/art-heroicbodies-print.html, accessed 16 August 2007.

Sheffield, Tricia, *The Religious Dimensions of Advertising* (London: Palgrave, 2006).

Silk, Mark, "Gibson's *Passion*: a Case Study in Media Manipulation", *Journal of Film and Religion* 8 (2004), http://www.unomaha.edu/jrf/2004symposium/silk.htm, accessed 18 August 2007.

Simon, Mary Manz, "Trends in the Children's Marketplace - 2006," unpublished paper presented at the 2006 CBA International Christian Retail Show (Nashville, 2006).

Stark, Rodney and James C. McCann, "Market Forces and Catholic Commitment: Exploring the New Paradigm", *Journal for the Scientific Study of Religion* 32 (1993), pp. 111-24.

Sturken, Marita and Lisa Cartwright, *Practices of Looking: an Introduction to Visual Culture* (Oxford: Oxford University Press, 2001).

Walker, John A. and Sarah Chaplin, *Visual Culture: an Introduction* (Manchester: Manchester University Press, 1997).

Ward, Pete, *Liquid Church* (Peabody: Hendrickson, 2002).

Wharton, Annabel Jane, *Selling Jerusalem: Relics, Replicas, Theme Parks* (Chicago: University of Chicago Press, 2006).

Zuckerman, Bruce, "Where are the Flies? Where is the Smoke? The Real and the Super-Real in Mel Gibson's *The Passion*", *Shofar: an Interdisciplinary Journal of Jewish Studies* 23 (2005), pp. 129-36.

Web Sites

www.chrismukkah.com
www.cim.co.uk
www.familychristian.com
www.marketingpower.com (American Marketing Association)

Rewriting the Scriptures

The Commodification of Religion:
Fiction that Presents Religion as a Consumer Good and the New Faux Faith

Jennifer Lee

Since the end of the Second World War, the globalized world has undergone drastic changes, perhaps the greatest of which is in spending patterns. Consumerism has evolved beyond any rational motivations of "need" or "comfort." Following this development, James Twitchell (2002: 47) writes that, "the average American consumes twice as many goods and services as in 1950; in fact, the poorest fifth of the current population buys more than the average fifth did in 1955". More products are available than ever before, and we spend more money on them, often more than we have to spend. The advent of the credit card has altered the way Americans spend; television has altered the ways that products are sold and the internet has altered the way that America shops. Amid this increased consumption and production, it is hardly surprising if Jesus himself and the religion he inspired become products in this new world of commerce.

A number of variables are responsible for this trend, one of which is the pervasive voice of America's religious groups. Within America, the religious-right movement, which presents one conservative view of Christianity, has grown immense and influential. One such organization, Focus on the Family, receives enough mail to warrant its own zip code (PFAW, 2006b). The religious right has, inadvertently, helped to popularize the use of religion as a sales tactic for both politicians and products. While conservative Christians are not a majority of the voting and consumer demographic, they are the most noticeably active and vocal within the United States, and their cultural influence resonates through many spheres. This influence is not a new or solitary occurrence, as religious groups have always shaped the American Cultural landscape. Movies, in particular, have been affected by America's religious organizations since 1909 when, working for the People's Institute, John Collier participated in a review board that would screen all movies shown in the state of New York (R. Moore, 1994: 223). Similar censors have existed since then, including D. W. Griffiths, creator of the notorious *Birth of a Nation*. By 1930, the Hays Code represented a system of unofficial censorship for America's motion pictures. As with the Comic code of the 1940s, the industry strictly regulated itself to circumvent official, government regulation. This censorship continued until 1950, when European films, such as *The Bicycle Thief* and *The Miracle* drove the American public to challenge the censorship of its day. Such award winning movies as these helped to inspire a revolution in the film industry: "Hollywood was having difficulty turning important pieces of American theatre into credible film because of code restrictions, restrictions that liberal Protestants had once said did not go far enough. For a time the *Christian Century* found itself stymied, literally with nothing to say" (1994: 231). Decades of ad hoc censorship were replaced with a rating system that continues today.

In a review of Kevin Smith's film *Dogma*, critic Roger Ebert comments on this golden age of censorship; he notes that generic ideas of the supernatural are acceptable to Hollywood where specifics might not be, resulting in, what he calls "an emerging anti-religion based on magic, ghosts, reincarnation, mediums and other new age voodoo" (Ebert, 1999: 33). While there is no longer any direct individual or organization that is overtly responsible for approving America's movie content, there are sponsors and patrons who might withdraw financial support should a film attract the negative attention of vocal organizations such as the Catholic Action League of Civil and Religious Rights, which has grown 350,000 members strong over the past thirty-three years (PFAW, 2006a: par. 9). The sectarian views of such religious organizations are not represented throughout American culture. Commercials, infomercials, and television shows often reference prayer and God, but rarely do they mention sect-specific beliefs or controversial convictions. The desire for increased sales precludes any exclusivity of religious conviction, thereby encouraging generic, non-specific notions of faith and God. It is difficult to sit through one hour of American Primetime television without flipping past programming and commercials that raise a vague and generic notion of an all-sect and all-belief-encompassing God to gain mass appeal. Even the National Football League now includes televised prayers on the fifty-yard line (Marquand, 1998).

In addition to this generi-God, the appropriation of Jesus as a marketable good is often segregated from Jesus' teachings. Stephanie Nolen (2002: 243) writes that "a revival is underway, but for a phenomenon with Jesus at its center, it has surprisingly little to do with mainstream religion". She continues to note such Random House bestsellers as *Care of the Soul* and *The New Spirituality* as "sure fire hit[s]". There is an entire industry built around diluted Christianity that caters toward consumers' desires more than it does a life ideology. Numerous products have emerged that directly espouse the notion of God outside of any traditional parameters. Sankara Saranam, a resident of New Mexico, founder of the Pranayama institute, is the author of *God Without Religion*. He explains the necessity for his book by saying that it "offers a way for individuals to discover and define God on their own rather than accepting the interpretation of a religious doctrine" (The Pranayama Institute, 2006: par. 6). This is only one of a number of newly emergent new-age philosophies which have gained popularity in America today, most of which impose their own interpretation of a religion-less God, focusing their teachings more on daily interaction and life improvement than any genuine faith.

Contemporary American media, from *The Simpsons* to *The Onion*, have satirized this increasing trend. Recurrent images are raised of a-spiritual religions based on extrinsic value systems and rewards. Philosophies can be high-profit industries if they promise a high and instant return and low maintenance lifestyle, and many authors target this phenomenon, portraying the consuming masses as too preoccupied with the physical and material to have any "true" spiritual sense. While such satires are found in all media, including TV, movies, graphic novels, internet sites, and literature, this essay will analyze the commodification of Jesus as presented in four contemporary works of fiction that critique mass consumerism as it exists today. Chuck Palahniuk, Harry Crews, Christopher Moore, and Kevin Smith have different approaches to the notion of commodified religion, but all are wary of the extremes to which consumerism has gone.

Chuck Palahniuk has gathered a cult following since the success of his 1996 novel, *Fight Club*. Each of his eight works of fiction use bizarre plot lines with a satiric edge to focus on themes of consumerism within modern-day society. *Survivor* (1999), however, deals largely with religion. Harry Crews is the most prolific of the authors examined here. He is also author of an autobiography, over fifty non-fiction essays, and was even the inspiration for a band in the early 1990s that sung about his novels and performed under his name. Many have studied his tropes of human disfigurement and zoomorphism, but here it is his disapproval of religious profiteering as presented in *The Mulching of America* (1995) that will be examined. Like Palahniuk and Crews, Christopher Moore has developed a large fan base for the nine novels he has written over the past fourteen years. His unique plotlines are developed and fleshed out with a deft combination of humor and intellect. His 1997 novel, *Island of the Sequined Love Nun*, raises questions of religious profiteering and abuse amid a setting of Micronesian cargo cults and black-market organ sales. Of the humorists included here, Kevin Smith is, perhaps, the most lighthearted in tone. Since 1994 when his independent film, *Clerks*, gained a small but dedicated following, Smith has written seven full length feature-films, the newest of which, *Clerks II*, is already the center of minor controversy, as critique Joel Siegel stormed out of the debut screening (Anon., "Critic Flees"). Controversy is not new to Smith, whose *Dogma* (1999) has received national attention for the boycotts and protests it received from Catholic organizations prior to the movie's first screening. Although each work presents a different attitude toward religious faith, all of the authors examined in this paper write against the consumer aspects of religion and the potential for profiteering.

Chuck Palahniuk's *Survivor* presents the harshest criticism examined herein, as his biting and sardonic satire is often negative and with little hope for faith. This work raises the idea of religious officials confusing their wallets with their souls amid a pervasive cultural notion of marketing. In this novel, the last surviving member of a fictitious church colony becomes a popular star, espousing an empty religion at the insistence of his agent. At an auction to determine who will sponsor Tender's fake, artificially designed and produced marriage at the Super Bowl, Tender explains that "the religion will depend on the bidding war, a very hush-hush bidding war going on for me to convert to Catholic or Jewish or Protestant now that the Creedish Church is belly-up" (Palahniuk, 1999: 92). The major religions of America are portrayed as companies seeking profit and customers. Consequently, the agent's ideal possibility for Tender's wedding ceremony is to "avoid the middle man and found our own major religion. Establish our own brand recognition. Sell direct to the customer". Palahniuk describes the process of organizing a religion with consumer terms like "brand recognition," "sell," and "customer." _

Reflecting the commercialism of present society, Jesus is repeatedly portrayed in contemporary satiric literature as a product, another idea or piece of merchandise to buy. He must be designed and redesigned in order to be sold and resold to one generation after the next. Tender, as he undergoes preparation to become a new commercial messiah, experiences this physical transformation as he becomes hopelessly absorbed in the shallow, media-obsessed reality of which the agent is a ringleader. His agent explains that the masses of America want attractive saviors: "these days, people aren't going to fill stadiums to get preached at by somebody who isn't beautiful" (1999: 153). The American masses are presented as mindless consumers, concerned more with surface than substance. To appeal to them, Tender agrees to a complete makeover, one that includes starvation and stairmasters, diet pills, tanning salons, dental caps, hair dye and every imaginable atrocity of contemporary body mis-maintenance. Of course, this works: he sells.

A wave of Tender zealots overtakes the nation and products that endorse or encapsulate his generic and empty "religion" are sold and bought. He is even offered his own "1-976 salvation hotline", a paradoxical proposition for a number of reasons, the most obvious of which is the irony of charging worldly money for otherworldly salvation. Through Tender Branson's inoffensive "religious" products, people are sold aspirations as though they were impossible to find for free. Like America's ever-popular self-help books, Tender's religion provides commitment-free, effortless hope.

As Tender becomes increasingly lost in this superficial reality and the euphoria of an intense workout, he decides that "[e]verything the agent's been telling me makes perfect sense. For instance, if Jesus Christ had died in prison, with no one watching and with no one there to mourn or torture him, would we be saved?" (1999: 152). This is not a real, internal, philosophical quandary; Tender is becoming brainwashed by the marketers and agents around him to believe that public relations matter more than the belief system they tout. More than a product's quality, the advertising campaign attracts customers. The opposite is true of intrinsically valued morals, faiths, and beliefs; their quality to the individual matters more than their perceived quality. This sense of irony heightens the satire throughout many of Palahniuk's key scenes, leading readers to examine the ways in which we blur the lines between intrinsic and extrinsic. Tender's participation in the cycle of mindless production and consumerism fosters his belief in all he is told by the shallow businessmen around him. He begins to replace any "normal" or "healthy" grasp on reality with the conviction that the tasteless, pseudo-religious products he endorses are good and necessary, and that the public is right to long for them desperately. He is lost amid a world of celebrity and faithless belief.

Tender comes to represent a host of "religious" products that span from board games (*Bible Trivia*) to books (*Sex Secrets of the Bible*). Here, Palahniuk reflects on an increasing trend: the popularity of Christian imagery in consumer goods. Writing for the *Toronto Globe*, Stephanie Nolan follows this trend of Christ-based merchandising, noting that Jesus' image is "being silk screened on gowns from Gaultier and Dolce and Gabanna, He has a board game, He is setting the publishing industry on fire. Jesus is the icon of choice on T-shirts and tote bags, sold in trendy shops on Toronto's Queen Street West, and He pops up in the lyrics of some of rap music's biggest acts" (Nolen, 2002: 243). One may wonder what, if at all, an expensive shirt has to do with the teachings of Jesus Christ, and the answer that Palahniuk gives is: nothing. Tender Branson has no spiritual beliefs after the disassembly of the Creedish Church. He has no message to sell. Like many extant companies today, the agent and the Tender Branson Corporation have products that they will market via faux-faith and watered down Christianity. They will spew whatever bland, generic drivel the public is willing to hear and, more importantly, spend money on.

The Tender Branson Corporation mocks the notion of commercial or profitable religion and "effortless salvation." *The Book of Very Common Prayer* is the brainchild of tender's agent, who explains to Tender that it will be "fifty pages, tops. Little tributes to the environment, children, safe stuff. Mothers. Pandas. Topics that step on nobody's toes" (Palahniuck, 1999: 126).   Predictably enough, this book presents no genuine doctrine of faith but instead caters to an audience that wants "prayers" to stop baldness, premature ejaculation, and gridlock. "The Prayer to Stop Smoking" is exemplary of what Palahniuk terms the "Learned Helplessness" that is pervasive in much of American culture:

Our most Holy Father,
Take from me the choice You have given.
Assume control of my will and habits.
Wrest from me power over my own behavior.
May it be Your decision how I act.
May it be by Your hands, my every failing.
Then if I still smoke, may I accept that my smoking is
Your will.
Amen (1999: 125).

Those who recite this prayer have abandoned any personal accountability for their lives, and their idea of God is a parent to whine at and blame for their shortcomings, weaknesses, laziness, and apathy. The speaker of this prayer seeks a scapegoat – not a savior. This hyperbolic example mocks the increase in Learned Helplessness, an idea that Palanhiuk raises to indicate a segment of the population that is not genuinely helpless, but has been taught to feel helpless: people who remain in jobs and relationships that make them miserable under the mistaken notion that there is no alternative. In this "prayer," Palahniuk intertwines his philosophies on Learned Helplessness with the pseudo-religions that have gained popularity in America.

The American population is too diverse in its ideologies to adhere to one specific doctrine, but among the buying population, the bodies of multiple faiths can be boiled down to an inoffensive, ready to sell, commercial ideology of religion. In *Consuming Religion: Christian Faith and Practice in a Consumer Society*, Vincent Jude Miller (2003: 81) describes this phenomenon:

> If the first dynamic of commodification endlessly seeks the exotic and new… this one brings the unobjectionableness of McDonald's french fries, tailored to the need for widespread acceptance. This does not preclude making reference to the transcendent, placing demands on the believer, or calling for subversive action, but it does place serious parameters around these aspects of religion.

The easiest way to turn religion into a "product" is to remove the beliefs from it. *The Book of Very Common Prayer* is a perfect example of a "religious" product in which the religion has been diluted from its original in order to increase mass appeal. Chuck Palahniuk presents exactly this faux religion through Tender, and he exposes its shallow origins: the CEO of Tender Branson Enterprises wishes to profit above all else. While the American spending population may believe that Tender is at the center of Tender Branson Enterprises' ideologies, he is nothing more than a figurehead. These are not beliefs inspired by the Creedish Church Colony or the sudden revelations of a last surviving member. These are mass produced words that are designed solely for their marketability.

Tender's status as a religious icon and product is described as "the same as people wearing clothes printed with Mickey Mouse or Coca Cola, I mean, it's so easy. It's not even a real choice, you can't go wrong. [My friend] Fertility says, praising God is just such a safe thing to do" (Palahniuk, 1999: 123). Through Fertility, Palahniuk equates the commercialized notion of God to the products of mega-conglomerates: Disney and the Coca Cola Corporation. Essentially, that is what Religion becomes when it is altered for retail: another consumer good. Tender's company uses him as the ultimate marketing ploy, because there is little risk and a great likelihood for profit. This reflects an increasing trend in a marketplace where consumers want to experience fast and easy consumption. The Reverend Harry Maier (Nolen, 2002: 244) explains:

> In a highly individual society, religion is very private... People want a personal experience with God. They want an easier, faster, no-fuss, microwavable God... In a capitalistic world, in a world economy, people want an easily translatable God ... They want it tradition free, context free – it's Wal-Mart God, it's generic.

Maier brings Wal-Mart and generiGod to the same level, much as Palahniuk likens commercialized religion to corporate products, as it is the production company that stands to make the biggest profit from such bland "religious" notions. Palahniuk satirizes a global marketplace in which the corporation benefits and the consumer loses sight of the original message.

Tender Branson himself gains nothing other than money and misery and the public spends willingly in exchange for the same temporary hope that a lottery ticket may bring. Customers can wish for a place in heaven without earning it just as they wish for an effort-free million. It is the Tender Branson Corporation, and the agent who designed it, who gain the money and power that Tender lives for. Tender's religion is generic and palatable to a mass market, because, as his agent explains, "we weren't targeting the smartest people in the world, just the most" (Palahniuk, 1999: 135). Tender's speeches to his blindly devoted followers read with the innocuous genericy of an Oscar winner's speech or a television sitcom monologue in which cute little so-and-so explains the value of family or friendship or love.

Christopher Moore's *Island of the Sequined Love Nun* (1997) provides an equally cynical philosophy of commercial or marketable religion and worship. Tucker Case, the novel's protagonist, is employed by Mary Jean Dobbins, a makeup mogul who runs a cosmetics corporation. She incorporates religion into her sales meetings, simply because incorporating religion into sales company policy "just seemed like good business" (1997: 20). Mary Jean's business savvy certainly pays, as she has "a sapphire-and-diamond pin whose value approximated the gross national product of Zaire"

(1997: 14). The irony, of course, lies in Mary Jean's use of the spiritual (the invocation of God in her speeches) to gain the physical (a successful business and mammoth jewels). Moore further describes her religious business tactic by expounding that "sometimes [Tucker Case] would stand in the back of the auditorium and listen to her talk to a thousand women about having God on their sales team, and they would cheer and 'Hallelujah!' and he would feel as if he'd been left out of something -- something beyond the apparent goofiness of it all" (1997: 20). These team members are zealots for makeup and sales that they use God to increase; the scene reads like a revival meeting of which profit, rather than spiritual salvation, is the goal. Without the ability to express himself, Tucker knows that this is neither a true faith nor an ideology, and he cannot share their enthusiasm. In this satire, much as can sometimes be the case in life, organizations and individuals use religion as a faithless business ploy to increase sales by creating a "wholesome" company image through forced enthusiasm.

Behind this pure and wholesome image, a world of sex abounds. Mary Jean Dobbins' motivational speeches inspire arbitrary sex among her saleswomen, which Tucker sees, (along with the travel and an expense account) as one of the many perks of his "perfect" job as her pilot: "inspired by Mary Jean's speeches on self-determination, motivation, and how they too could be a winner, they sought Tucker out to have their one adventurous affair with a jet pilot" (1997: 26). Of course, there is something a little sad in a speech laced with God motivating one-night-stands rather than faith or genuine self certainty.

Tucker begins the novel as a man guided more by his sex drive than his conscience. He only begins to realize this when he injures his groin, loses his pilot's license, and begins to see visions of Vincent, a pilot from World War Two. When his life reaches crisis point, he begins to contemplate God. Tucker asks his friend Jake if he ever thinks of God, to which Jake responds, "yes, I do think about God sometimes. When I'm with a really hot babe, and we're going at it like sweaty monkeys, I think about it then. I think about a big old pissed-off Sistine Chapel fingerpointin' motherfucker. And you know what? It works. You don't come when you're thinking about shit like that" (1997: 27). Moore wants his readers to abandon this image of a cruel and punishing God. Through Vincent, the deceased World War Two pilot, he presents a God who is forgiving, kind, and playful. Nonetheless, readers are meant to receive some shock at this statement (perhaps after a disturbed giggle subsides). Jake is shallow and preoccupied with sex and money, and the only thought that he gives to God is completely inappropriate.

Moore furthers the novel's underlying critique of consumer religion through the cargo cults of the South Pacific. A reporter named Pardee explains to Tucker that the outlawing of Micronesian cargo cults martyred the cargo cults' leaders: "the missionaries railed against the new religions, trying to use reason to kill faith, so some islanders started claiming their pilots were Jesus. Drove the missionaries nuts. Natives putting little propellers on their crucifixes, drawing pictures of Christ in a flight helmet. Bottom line is the cargo cults are still around" (1997: 40). Moore bases this on historic instances of South Pacific cargo cults in order to present characters who literally worship material goods and those who deliver them. The Islander's confusion of goody-toting military pilots with Jesus is comparable to the way that some children (and even adults on a more abstract level) confuse Christianity with the commercial notions of Christmas and Santa Claus. Moore certainly wants us to think in broader, contemporary terms. After meeting a native to the Micronesian crescent who is obsessed with Crips and Bloods (American gang rivals), Tucker tries to make sense of this anachronistic culture. His friend Pardee, an American reporter, explains that: "a few of the islanders have satellite TV. The people who look like them on TV are gangsta rappers. The old rundown buildings they see in the hood look like the buildings here... They buy into the advertising bullshit that Americans have become immune to. It's like the entire Micronesian crescent is one big cargo cult. They buy the worst of American culture" (1997: 52). Just as the developed world often emulates and is influenced by that which it sees on TV, these isolated Micronesians have fallen victim to the worship of chips and colas.

While one small island has been particularly affected by American goods and the pilots who brought them, there are larger implications. At the novel's close, Vincent, the revered pilot who has

died and become a God to the people of Alualu, explains to Tucker
that:

> I had this bet with these guys I play cards with [referring to
> Christ and other deities] that my little cult could go big-time
> if I could get enough citizens. I told 'em, 'two thousand
> years ago you guys were just running cults. Get me to the
> mainland and give me a thousand years and I'll give you
> a run for your money.' All the conditions were right. You
> need some pressure, I got the war. You need a promise, I
> got the promise I'll come back with cargo (1997: 321).

By appropriating the idea of postwar cargo cults, Christopher
Moore is able to imply that we, not simply Americans, but the
world, are already a cargo cult of sorts; we worship products and
the companies that bring them.

These ideas also occur in Harry Crews' *The Mulching of America*
(1995). Rather than a mere business ploy, the business is a religion, and, as in *Island of the Sequined Love Nun*, products are to be
revered. Through Hickum Looney, salesman for the Soaps for Life
Company and a Willie Loman for the 1990s, Crews raises ethical
questions about the role of corporations in America. In the postmodern market, television and magazines play a tremendous role
in what products are bought and elevated. Religion is no different. Vincent Jude Miller writes that "visual media are important
[to commodification]... Televangelism comes quickly to mind:
Televised worship services with high production values – from the
liturgies of the 'Hour of Power' to the high-energy revival preaching of Jimmy Swaggart" (Miller, 2003: 78). Miller's discussion of
televangelism places it on commercial terms of a high-energy, visual field that gains interest and money from its appearance and
offer of hope. Harry Crews shares this notion of televangelism, as
becomes apparent when reading of Hickum's predation on elderly
customers whose mortality and desperation can be used as a marketing gimmick, and he is careful to clarify that the desperation of
the sick and dying is used by many commercial ventures, not just
religion alone. Crews (1995: 24) depicts mass-produced, televised

religion as a product that is designed to cater to the desperation of this decrepit, withering audience:

> Who else but the poor, broken, and troubled...could be sending all that money to all those preachers on television who daily told all the poverty-ridden, death-stricken listeners who could hear their voices that the first thing they had to do was quit taking their medicine and quit eating so much food and quit trying to stay warm in the winter and send every cent they had to the Service of God? Then, magically, the address of the Service of God appeared on the screen.

As with Palahniuk's scrutiny of religion as a consumer good, Crews underscores the idea of commercial profit within what are supposed to be divine, and at the very least, non-profit organizations that function for the good and well-being of their constituencies. Obviously, this is not always the case, and as in *Survivor*, *The Mulching of America* examines the tactic of using God as a safe marketing ploy.

Crews presents an America in which the masses have abandoned the old and traditional religions, and the corporate employer becomes the new governing force of many peoples' actions and beliefs. The Boss Hickum (always capitalized) is God, or, rather, he has become a God to the employees of the Soaps for Life Corporation. He is worshipped and revered by all of his followers. At convention meetings, the Boss' employees become so excited by his speeches that "[s]everal throughout the enormous convention hall would enthusiastically bash their heads together, not because they liked doing it but because they could not help doing it" (1995: 35). This hyperbolic description fits the absurd and violent reality that surrounds the Boss and those who work for him, while parodying notions of Southern revival meetings where parishioners are taken with "the spirit." This fervor is not limited only to such employees; even consumers begin to believe in the Boss and his product. Ida Mae, and elderly woman whom Hickum first meets on his sales route, begins to worship the nonexistent, "divine" power of the Soaps for Life soap (1995: 32).

The Boss is rich and powerful and, for this, he is revered by many. It is his money that keeps his following and gives him the power to do anything he wishes, "he was... a millionaire many times over. And his being a millionaire made them forgive him every fault he may have had in the past, had now, or might have in the future" (1995: 37). His money, his power, and his omniscience within the company critique the American adoration of money. Such recurrent characterizations in contemporary literature reach toward a multifaceted target: what lasting repercussions will we face when intrinsic values are replaced by extrinsic?

The Boss uses his employees' passion and faith in him to force their devotion and zeal for the Soaps for Life Company. At company meetings, the Boss "[c]ould deliver that line about people needing what he had to sell with such fiery passion that people often fainted, especially the afflicted and the very old" (1995: 26). He acts as a warped messiah, delivering his fanaticism among his zealous followers. To further this satiric depiction of America's secular worship of the money and power the Boss embodies, Crews gives the Boss an ironic obsession with Jesus Christ whom he sees as the penultimate marketing gimmick: "the Boss of Soaps for Life loved Christ... Christ himself would go either way on any issue. The Boss loved him for that if for nothing else" (1995: 29). The Boss divorces Christ from any Christin message, choosing to see only what he wants: profit. He is only able to interpret Christianity as he wishes it were: as an advertising device. As with Mary Jean Dobbins from *Island of the Sequined Love Nun*, The Boss uses religion as a part of "good business" (C. Moore, 1997: 29). His definition of good business differs from Mary Jean's. While she uses Christianity to help create a the company image and to encourage her employees' devotion (both to her and God, thereby enhancing company image), the Boss also uses Jesus Christ as a sales scam, and Christ's words as a sales tactic.

The Boss is hardly subtle about his intentions for Christ's appropriation into Company policy and the Company Manual. Through his disfiguring hair lip, the Boss of Soaps for Life shouts at company meetings that:

Nu couldn't pay a man nike Nesus Christ what he was worth. If I had Nesus, I could rule ne world. Wit Nesus, I'd be bigger nan Wal-Mart and IBM both together. I know in my heart nat Nesus Christ could write more orders nan all my other salesmen put together. Nat's one Goddam ning I know about Nesus Christ (Crews, 1995: 29).

As one would expect from such a satirically exaggerated depiction of the contemporary working environment, the Boss of Soaps for Life sees everything, even Christ, on consumer terms. This maniacal little man sees Jesus Christ as a salesman rather than savior.

If Soaps for Life uses religion as the ultimate marketing ploy, then it only follows that Jesus himself would be the most effective figurehead thereof. The Boss is able to love Christ's flexibility, though "nothing else," simply because it can be manipulated to use believers' faith against them, as it can help persuade anyone to buy anything. The Boss seeks power and mega-conglomerate status, and the image and icon of Jesus Christ can draw Americans into spending. Crews places the Boss in the role of the postmodern God, the God of consumerism and commerce and corporate ideology.

Naturally, since Crews portrays the Boss as a postmodern God to his many misguided employees, there must be a new postmodern doctrine: consequently, the Boss' rules are law and his Manual is a Bible. Hickum repeatedly quotes directly from this Company Manual when pitching his sale to Ida Mae, firm in the conviction that "[s]he needed hope. She needed love, and Hickum Looney had it all, or at least he had everything she needed right there in the Company Manual… Hickum believed that to be the truth. He had no alternative" (1995: 24). Hickum is so blind in his worship of the Boss that he believes all that the doctrine says, always and without question. Just as Tender Branson experiences Learned Helplessness in Palahniuk's *Survivor*, Hickum Looney believes himself to be choiceless in the major decisions of his life. His position in the Company forces Hickum to believe in its word and law. The salesmen of Soaps for Life Corporation are forced to memorize this handbook so that they can recite selections from it as they canvass neighborhoods selling soap. They follow the Boss, his word, and his organization. The end result of this is that when the company redesigns its image, Hickum is let go. In a strange and satiric twist, Hickum, and others like him who do not coincide with the new

Soaps for Life persona, are killed, run through a mulcher, and used to fertilize the headquarters' garden. This metaphor adequately expresses what it can feel like to be abandoned by a company to which one has devoted his or her life.

As with all the works of fiction presented herein, Kevin Smith's film, *Dogma* (1999) questions the commercial aspects of Christianity. Film Critic Roger Ebert (1999: 33) summarized the movie excellently by writing that *"Dogma* grows out of an irreverent modern Catholic sensibility, a byproduct of parochial schools, where the underlying faith is taken seriously but the visible church is fair game for kidding". This is exactly what so many Americans love about this movie, and it is exactly what so many religious organizations protested upon its release into movie theatres, often without watching the film (Mottram, 1999: 6). Film Critic Joel Holleman's review is less favorable than Ebert's, opening with a litany of those features most guaranteed to cause outrage among those least likely to watch it:

> Why would this movie cause such a stir? Could it be that . . .
>
> *One of the characters, Bethany, a descendant of Jesus, works in an abortion clinic.
> *Or that another character, Rufus, claims to be the 13th apostle, who was left out of the Bible because he is black.
> *Or because God often loses track of what's going on in the universe because he (or she) is in Jersey playing skee-ball.
> *Or because a celestial muse, now working as a stripper, compares the Catholic Mass to bad sex.
> *Or a newly designed crucifix, to coincide with a "Catholicism, Wow!" promotion, as a smiling Jesus giving a "thumbs-up" sign (Holleman, 1999: p. f1

These potentially scandalous features are intended as humorous satire with an overt underlying message: faith is separate from the details of organized religions. At Bethany's (Linda Fiorentino) introduction, the viewer learns that, while she participates in Catholicism, her faith is faltering. Her coworker, Liz (Janeane Garofalo), explains "faith is like a glass of water. When you're young, the glass is small, and it's easy to fill up. But the older you get, the bigger the glass gets, and the same amount of liquid doesn't fill it anymore. Periodically, the glass has to be refilled" (Smith, 1999). This question of faith continues throughout the film. Rufus (Chris Rock) poses an answer to Bethany's crisis of faith when he explains to her that God "still digs humanity, but it bothers Him to see the shit that gets carried out in His name – wars, bigotry, but especially the factioning of all the religions. He said humanity took a good idea and, like always, built a belief structure on it... It's better to have ideas. You can change an idea. Changing a belief is trickier". Serendipity, a retired Muse/stripper, echoes this remark: "When are you people going to learn? It's not about who's right or wrong. No denomination's nailed it yet, and they never will because they're all too self-righteous to realize that it doesn't matter what you have faith in, just that you have faith". By the movie's close, Bethany's faith has been restored as evinced by her response to Rufus' question, "Are you saying you believe?" "No," Bethany replies, "but I've got a good idea".

This parallels Kevin Smith's own struggle with faith. As he explained to Steve Murray of *The Atlanta Journal and Constitution* (1999: 13):

> Once you become a certain age, it gets harder and harder to hold on to [sic] your faith, because the world throws so much at you. Also, you start to learn a lot more. And with education comes the danger of replacing God with science or knowledge or something like that... I was one of those people that really wanted to stay with it, because it was so much a part of who I was when I was younger. But there are times in life when it is hard to reconcile your faith with the world around you.

And while The Catholic League protested this film, Smith made it because he "wanted to do something to celebrate the faith".

While the underlying message of faith is paramount, more than this underlies the movie. The commercial aspects of religion saturate much of the film's content. Cardinal Glick (George Carlin) is a primary vehicle for the examination of the commercial machinations within America's religious institutions. His first scene opens the movie with the idea of the redesigning of Christ in order to "sell" the Catholic Church. Glick explains that, trying to spread a more positive image of the Catholic Church, the crucifix has been redesigned: "the holy mother Church has decided to retire this highly recognizable, yet wholly depressing image of our lord crucified. [Christ] was a booster. And it's with that take on our lord in mind that we come to a new, more inspiring sigil... The Buddy Christ" (Smith, 1999). This figure outraged certain viewers and critics, one of whom described it as "winking, pointing and giving the thumbs-up, like Bill Clinton on some future comeback trail" (Bradshaw, 1999: 14). Others were able to see the social commentary inherent in such a figure. Peter Howell of the *Toronto Star* adroitly explains: "older Catholics will recognize it as a sharp jab against the liberal reforms of Vatican II during the Swinging Sixties, reforms which, ironically, Smith's harshest critics would deem worthy of satire" (Howell, 1999: 12). Smith intends his viewers to see this satire of sixties reform, as the scene of Buddy Christ's unveiling satirizes the re-envisioning of Christ. With his friendly, goofy smile, sly wink, and giant thumbs-up, Christ is presented as a mascot to be designed for the consumer, presenting the image of a commercialized religious organization. Cardinal Glick's view that the traditional Crucifix is "wholly depressing" presents him as a man who has undergone his religious training only to lose sight of the faith it espouses. The image of Jesus' crucifixion is "depressing" for an obvious reason; he was martyred.

Glick preoccupies himself with the popularity and commercial potential of Christianity, rather than the belief system. Never in this scene does he raise any tenets of Christianity. Here, the "Buddy Christ," is divorced from any genuine message of faith that Jesus inspires. "Buddy Christ" and this renovation of the Catholic Church are segregated from the doctrine of faith that Christianity is supposed to hold. By this, Kevin Smith forces viewers to acknowledge and question the way in which one or many individuals within the Church could potentially weigh the commercial prospects of religion over its spiritual values. Smith reinforces this notion of religion as a corporate product, as Cardinal Glick disclaims that Buddy Christ is "not the sanctioned term we're using for the symbol – just something we've been kicking around the office" (Smith). Here, the Church is represented as an office, and Jesus is portrayed as a marketing gimmick. As Glick says, this is not a "sanctioned" move, which further divorces the act from most conventional notions faith.

Glick later explains in a private meeting that "mass attendance is at an all-time low… fill them pews people. That's the key. Grab the little ones as well. Hook em while they're young," and when Roofus, the thirteenth apostle, compares Glick's attitude to the smoking industry, Glick only laments, "Christ, if only we had their numbers". To Glick, "believers" are a demographic, as present in any industry, by which the Church can profit monetarily. Here, Glick ignores Christianity's messages that worldly wealth is irrelevant compared to spiritual wealth and heaven. He turns Christianity into a business. Here we see an individual whose view is unethical and inappropriate; this is comparable to a doctor considering what treatments would be most beneficial to his wallet rather than to a patient's conditions. Neither is impossible, and the consequences of each would be dire. This scene, however, parodies the extent to which consumerism has spread. Marketing and PR were relatively unknown to average citizens until recent decades in which they have become a "science" of their own. Through this scene, Kevin Smith shows how expansive these fields have become and the ways in which they've penetrated all realms of interaction.

Consumerism itself wears a bull's-eye, as Smith not only mocks the material facets of the Catholic Church, but all American materialism. The two evicted angels, Loki (Matt Damon) and Barnaby (Ben Affleck), punish the Mooby Corporation (a Walt Disney spoof) for its presentation of false idols, explaining to Mooby Corp's public heads that "you and your board are idolaters. You are responsible for raising an icon [i.e. Mooby, the Golden Calf, which looks quite like Mickey Mouse], which draws worship from the Lord. You have broken the first commandment" (Smith, 1999). As with the Tender Branson Corporation of Chuck Palahniuk's *Survivor*, this is a mega-conglomerate that started small and quickly grew to include television shows, records, films, primetime specials, videos, magazines, and theme parks. This Disney parody poses a new God for American audiences, and it implies that some Americans give more time, thought, and effort to the products they buy than the God they worship. As in Crews' *The Mulching of America*, many have replaced God, but here it is not the Boss and the job, but the product itself that is a new icon of worship.

American policy currently favors the de-regulation of commerce, increasing corporate tax-cuts, while lowering the fines and penalties that once helped force most major corporations to maintain a façade of morality. This is a new era of commerce, and Jesus' role in it is often plastic and mass-produced. As his presence becomes more pronounced within American Media, so does a critique of the ways in which his presence is felt. Each author examined herein adopts a different, underlying tone for his satire. Where Harry Crews is cynical, Christopher Moore is good-natured; and where Chuck Palahniuk is sarcastic, Kevin Smith presents a sincere message of faith. These authors have seen America's trend toward a trademarked Jesus, and the opportunity for comment cannot go unnoticed. The globalized marketplace, and particularly America, has reached a new juncture in its depictions and appropriation of Jesus. By diluting Christianity so that it no longer appears sect-specific within the mass media, profiteering corporations can sell Jesus to all without causing such offense that it would limit sales. Kevin Smith, Chuck Palahniuk, Christopher Moore, and Harry Crews have described and criticized the mass-production of generic, faux religions which are devoid of any sincere message of faith or of an ethical code. Ultimately, none criticizes the belief system of Christianity. Instead, their criticism is of religious profiteering by organizations or individuals who alter Jesus' image, or a Christian message, to increase their sales.

References

Anon., "Critic Flees 'Smut' Screening," *The New York Post*, 19 July (2006), p. 10.

Bradshaw, Peter, "Hail Mary, Hi Buddy; Kevin Smith's Satire *Dogma* is Smug but Surreal," *The Guardian* 24 December (1999), p. 14.

Crews, Harry, *The Mulching of America* (New York: Simon and Schuster, 1995).

Ebert, Roger, "Sing, oh Sinners! *Dogma* Provides Food for Thought in Catholics," *Chicago Sun-Times* 12 November (1999), p. 33

Holleman, Joe, "The Movie Disney Dumped may Ride Wave of Controversy: *Dogma* Opens Friday, and Catholics Plan Protests," *St. Louis Post-Dispatch* 7 November (1999), p. F1.

Howell, Peter, "Yes, *Dogma* is Insulting, but only to Blasphemy," *The Toronto Star*, edition 1, 12 November (1999).

Marquand, Robert, "More NFL Players Embrace Higher Game," *Christian Science Monitor* 14 January (1998), p. 34.

Miller, Vincent Jude, *Consuming Religion: Christian Faith and Practice in a Consumer Society* (New York: Continuum, 2003).

Moore, Christopher, *Island of the Sequined Love Nun* (New York: Avon Books, 1997).

Moore, R. Laurence, *Selling God: American Religion in the Marketplace of Culture* (Oxford: Oxford University Press, 1994).

Mottram, James, "Defender of the Faith," *The Scotsman* 19 December (1999), p. 6.

Murray, Steve. "Man behind Spoof of Religion Claims Film is Defense of Faith," *The Atlanta Journal and Constitution* 19 November (1999), p. 13.

Nolen, Stephanie, "Religion and Jesus Are Popular Now," in ed. Megan O'Neill, *Popular Culture: Perspectives for Readers and Writers* (Boston: Heinle and Heinle, 2002), pp. 243-5.

Palahniuk, Chuck, *Survivor* (New York: Anchor Books, 1999).

PFAW, "Right Wing Organizations: Catholic League for Religious and Civil Rights," (Washington, D.C.: People for the American Way, 2006a), <http://www.pfaw.org/pfaw/general/default.aspx?oid=23325>, accessed 26 September 2007.

_____, "Right Wing Organizations: Focus on the Family," (Washington, D.C.: People for the American Way, 2006b), http://www.pfaw.org/pfaw/general/default.aspx?oid=4257#, accessed 29 August 2006.

The Pranayama Institute, "An Interview with Sankara Saranam, Author of God without Religion," (Albuquerque: The Pranayama Institute, 2006), http://www.godwithoutreligion.com/interview.shtml, accessed 21 July 2006.

Smith, Kevin, *Dogma*, dir. Kevin Smith (1999).

Twitchell, James, "Two Cheers for Materialism," in ed. Michael Kelle, *Reading Popular Culture* (Dubuque: Kendall Hunt, 2002), pp. 47-56.

Website

www.pfaw.org

Balancing the Mission and the Market:
Christian Children's Books for Tweens

Diane Carver Sekeres

Christian publishers who print fiction books for children in the United States take the narrow path to fulfilling their mission of providing literature that is highly moral, exciting to read and eminently marketable. The path is hedged by conservative, traditional beliefs about morality and Christian doctrine, all of which infuse publishers' mission statements and the content of the books. The path is also hedged by the marketplace, whose influence shows up most clearly in book-jackets, advertising, internet tie-ins, and venues of sale. However, the competing goals of the Christian mission of publishers and their capitalist business practices result in an undeniable tension. This also influences book content, limiting plot and characterization in response to and support of the consumer base. This chapter explores the competing goals of mission and marketplace as revealed through the content of books that are offered for sale for the tween age group, 8-12 year olds.

The largest publishers of fiction for this age group include Protestant, often evangelical companies such as BethanyHouse, Zonderkidz, Tyndale, Tommy Nelson, and Moody Publishers, though many companies publish anywhere from one to dozens of books per year for the tween market. Roman Catholic publishers in the United States market a few books written for Catholic young adults, but they publish little for tweens beyond hagiography. The Church of Jesus Christ of Latter Day Saints (Mormons) also publish books for the tween group, though few in number.

Sales of Christian fiction have enjoyed phenomenal growth over the last fifteen to twenty years. There are many reasons: a resurgence of interest in spirituality amongst the general public, improved quality of the literature, and significantly, broadening of marketing venues beyond the Christian bookstore all have contributed to growth in this genre. Sales of books targeting the tween age group, which have been carved out of children's and young adult fiction to create a new category, have contributed to this growth.

The tween group is marked out psychologically in respect to their developing sense of personal identity, a personal faith, social consciousness, and awareness of the wider world. Secular publishers have led the way for Christian publishers to target this group with book series, related products, virtual sites that attract tweens, and retail schemes to draw them to bookstores with their parents, usually moms, in tow. As consumers, they are still restricted for the most part to parental buying power, although Simon (2006) reports that "credit cards with training wheels," that is, pre-paid cards for children's use on Internet sites, are a virtual reality for this age group. The following sections begin with a discussion of the history and missions of Christian publishers of tween books; then, a description of the market for Christian books frames how publishers' establish a trusting relationship with customers. Throughout, I will give examples from tween books to show how the books can be interpreted in the light of mission statements and related to the consumer.

Publishers

The publishers who print most of the children's books have entered the children's market at different times and from different backgrounds. Tyndale began in 1962 as the publisher of *The Living Bible*. They publish the long-running *Adventures in Odyssey* audio tapes from Focus on the Family in 1987. They publish the explosive, evangelical series, *Left Behind* (e.g. LaHaye and Jenkins, 2007), which has sold over 65 million copies, and C.S. Lewis' (1950-1956) *Narnia* books and audio adaptations. The company is still run by the family that started it, and they seek to "minister to the spiritual needs of people primarily through literature consistent with biblical principles" (www.tyndale.com).

Zondervan, established in 1931, is known as the publisher of the New International Version of the Bible, and has printed 30 million copies of *The Purpose Driven Life* (Warren, 2002), a book that comprehensively, though simply, outlines a way of living a Christian life. Zondervan is the only one of the five I discuss that is a division of a conglomerate, HarperCollins, which purchased the publishing house in 1988 and also owns an evangelical publisher in the UK, Marshall Pickering. Zondervan has a Spanish-language web site to support their line of Spanish language Bibles and books, and has been innovative in its interactive web sites for tweens as Zonderkidz. Their mission is focused on "meeting the needs of people with resources that glorify Jesus Christ and promote biblical principles" (www.zonderkidz.com).

Moody Publishing exists to fund, in part, Moody Bible Institute, an evangelical college. D. L. Moody, the evangelist, began the publishing company in 1894 to produce inexpensive Christian books: "the Moody Bible Institute exists to equip and motivate people to advance the cause of Christ through ministries that educate, edify and evangelize" (www.moodypublishers.com). Moody's children's books are few, but unlike others, include African-American series. BethanyHouse has been a leader in publishing Christian fiction for fifty years. Its tween books are almost exclusively published as part of a series. BethanyHouse's mission statement, "to help Christians apply biblical truth in all areas of life" (www.bethanyhouse.com) lacks the evangelical tone of Tyndale, Zonderkidz, and Moody. Tommy Nelson is the newest children's division of a major publisher, established in 1996. Their mission is "to nurture the faith of every child" (www.tommynelson.com). They publish a few series such as Bibleman, and the DVD versions of Focus on the Family's *Adventures in Odyssey*. The parent company began in Scotland in 1798, and opened a division in New York in 1854. Besides many adult fiction bestsellers, Thomas Nelson is known for the American Standard, Revised Standard, and New King James Versions of the Bible.

Most publishers' web sites, with the notable exceptions of Moody Publishing and Bob Jones University Press, do not define what a Christian is, what the spiritual needs of people are, or what constitutes biblical principles—all common phrases in mission statements. There is historical information about the companies on some sites, and an explanation of goals, but these, too, use terms which are general and undefined. One advantage of such ambiguity is that readers can interpret the missions and goals of the companies to fit their own ideas of the Christian life. The books themselves perhaps give the clearest description of how the mission statements are realized. However, many publishers belong to the Evangelical Christian Publishers Association (ECPA), which is an international organization that promotes cooperation among the publishers and does seek to define Christian doctrinal beliefs in a statement of faith. Membership in ECPA is open to companies that

> maintain an ongoing program of publishing evangelical Christian literature. The term 'evangelical Christian literature' is meant to include any book...that promotes, encourages, confirms, defends, or establishes the individual in his or her Christian belief...and is not in conflict with the Association's statement of faith (www.ecpa.org).

ECPA includes the following in its seven-point statement of faith: the Bible is inspired, infallible, and authoritative; there is one God, in three persons; Jesus' death provided for the atonement of sins; the Holy Spirit indwells Christians; and believers are united spiritually in Jesus Christ. The publishers' mission statements reasonably can be said to operate as a guide to working out the statement of faith through the medium of literature. In fact, based on textual analysis of a wide selection of tween books (Sekeres, 2003), these points *are* borne out to a greater or lesser degree in the dialogue and events of the stories, yet only the first three are made explicit in the ideological foundation of many books.

The publishers' mission statements are not just in reference to how they hope that their books will affect people's faith; they also include statements of business practices. The rest of Bethany-House's mission statement is representative of those of other ECPA members:

> we are diligently committed to offering the best in editing, design and marketing to make each book as inspiring,

challenging, enjoyable and attractive as it can be (www.
bethanyhouse.com).

There are fewer disputes, perhaps, about what it means to be
diligently committed to providing good books than about what it
means to be a Christian, which makes it easier to be specific about
the marketing function. The mission statements themselves hold
the tension between Christian mission and business practice in balance. By addressing both, however, they are making a claim that is
difficult to realize.

The Marketplace

In a recent survey of the book-buying habits of adults and teenagers, Barna Research Group (2003) reported that overall, 70% of
American adults purchased at least one book in 2002 with an average of five books per person. One third of all adults reported buying at least one Christian book (besides the Bible) that year, representing about half of all adult book buyers. A Christian book is a
title published by a Christian publisher and/or counted in industry
statistics in that category. Thirty percent of teenagers reported buying a Christian book (not including the Bible), and half had read
one. In fact, millions of people who are not Christians purchase and
read Christian books. Barna (2003) wrote, "[these sales figures give]
rise to realistic hope of being able to increase the penetration levels
for Christian books among those audiences".

Christian publishers have turned hope into reality. Even Jour-
neyForth, children's imprint of the extremely conservative publishers Bob Jones University Press, has two lines of books. The more
general line of books is comprised of works they:

> consider classic fiction which have a Christian worldview…
> but they would not be found offensive in a public library or
> in a public school. They're just good solid literature. Those
> books we feel could have a market in places like WalMart,
> or spinners in grocery stores (Lohr, 2003).

The larger customer base has also been influenced by changes in
the publishing industry. Taxel (2002) describes what has occurred in

the last two decades in publishing and the effects those have had on children's literature generally: independent houses have been gradually bought by corporations, their editorial departments merged, and the processes involved in obtaining manuscripts, printing and selling books streamlined. The result has been a proliferation of readily marketable book product. However, the Christian publishing industry has been a step behind the secular publishing industry in market exploitation. The boom in inspirational sales is young, and so are the divisions that service the children's literature market. They have had to work hard to improve the quality of the books they offer in order to be competitive, beginning with the writing, but also considering format and design. Yet, because of increased sales, Christian publishers have been bought up by secular publishing houses, or the media conglomerates have opened divisions for religious publication.

In a move to capitalize on the synergy created when products are cross-marketed, Christian publishers have begun to create brands, similarly to the general publishing industry. The characters and/or titles of series become brands, with the books just one product of the brand. Licenses are sold for the brand name to be used on clothing or toys or lunchboxes (Simon, 2006 and Sperling, 2001). Brands are based primarily on series books. For example, in 2003, HarperEntertainment announced that they would publish a "surfer-themed *Luna Bay: A Roxy Girl Series*, a venture co-partnered by HarperEntertainment and Roxy, a unit of Quicksilver Inc. that produces sportswear for girls" (Lodge, 2003). Roxy also produces a reality TV series about surfing competitions for girls. The paperback series is independent of the TV show, although HarperEntertainment cross-promotes the book series and the show. The process of producing the book product included a search for an author who was experienced in surfing to provide authenticity and who could provide a new title every month. Christian series are also often conceived within the marketing team and authors sought who have the expertise and stamina to write the books. For example, Beverly Lewis wrote nine books in the *Girls Only (Go!)* series, also about girls in sport competitions, between 1998 and 2002. During those years she published in six other series and wrote several stand-alone novels.

Figures are unreliable for sales of Christian children's books in all outlets; however, a new system for gathering data on sales of Christian books, STATS: Sales Tracking Analysis Trends Summary, was launched in 2003, an indication in itself of increased profitability of inspirational books. Annual retail sales in 2003 just for Christian bookstores were nearly $94 million for youth and children's titles (STATS, 2003). This figure includes both literature and Bibles, and over 40% were trade paperbacks. Demographics of purchasers show that most people who purchase products from Christian bookstores are middle-aged, white women, a telling point when publishers consider editorial decisions on book content or themes. The largest increase of sales, though, is through big-box retailers such as WalMart, libraries, and the internet. However, the sales are not reaching a different type of customer so much as new customers with the same demographics who simply did not shop in Christian bookstores.

Christian publishers have also worked at expanding their market by copying the successes of secular publishing in new genres. In some cases, they have targeted particular populations. Christian legal thrillers, futuristic tales and adventure stories, for example, are reaching male readers. A number of publishers have been cautiously moving toward expanding their multicultural offerings as well. Thomas Nelson has worked with Big Ideas to create Spanish translations of their books. Still, as Heuser (2001) said, any multicultural book is a "tithe" book: they do not have the distributors or consumer base to profit by multicultural titles. Publishers have begun imprints, and new publishing houses have emerged to publish in ethnic markets. Moody Press has an African American imprint, and Walk Worthy Press is an example of a new publisher that has been successful in the African-American Christian market. The tween market, however, has few books with major characters of color. Sales of Christian books have increased because of the marketing strategies noted here and the new venues in which the books are sold. Though the mission statements noted above are broad and inclusive, the bulk of the customer base still represents a narrow slice of conservative, Protestant Christians, which in turn influences the contents of the books they buy to represent only those Christians in their pages.

Building Trust with the Consumer

Publishers work hard to balance biblical authority and market pre-rogatives. They want their consumers, who are primarily white, middle-class mothers, to know that they can "trust" books published by their companies to be wholesome and inspiring. In terms of content, scenes don't allude to sex, profanity, or drug abuse, for example. The books mostly show families with two, heterosexual parents who work well together with the parents lovingly in charge and the children looking to them for wisdom, security, and correction. An unexpected element, which contradicts the sense of a wholesome book and provides excitement in many plots, is violence. Authors such as Frank Peretti, Jerry Jenkins and Tim LaHaye or Chris Fabry, are writing books that place their characters at the mercy of crooks that kill and steal without conscience.

For example, in the eighteenth book in the series, *Left Behind: The Kids, Judgment of Ice: Darkening Skies* the story opens with a main character being shot at, a security guard killed, and a guard captain ordering, "find the rabbi and those others! I want them dead before they get out of the stadium!" (Jenkins and LaHaye, 2001: 1). In *The Cooper Kids Adventure Series* (Peretti, 1997), the children and their widowed father are alternately attacked by smugglers, dishonest archaeologists, idols, and often a peripheral character is killed. However, the trustworthiness of content remains despite dangerous, even horrific events because the child characters are protected by their trust in God and by what they have learned from their parents. Also important is the fact that their being in danger is not usually a result of their disobedience, but of machinations on the part of the evil characters.

Publishers' products are also trustworthy in the sense that they are predictable. They build on customers' comfort with series that have familiar content, attractive cover designs, and are sold in venues where they shop. Conversely, publishers depend on those who buy their books to help them plan new books. They solicit feedback from bookstore owners and parents about what they like, closely track sales of titles, seek ideas that "fit" the market from agents, and research kids' interests. Popular themes for series include riding, training, or working with horses (Pistole, 2002), important Christians in history (e.g., *Trailblazer Books* by a variety of authors), or children who constitute a gang that has adventures (Wilson and Dengler, 2001). Trust also results from unconscious resonance with the ideological foundation of a book.

As with any genre, readers (who are also consumers) rightly trust that the features that create the category, Christian literature, will be present in the books they read, even though they may define 'Christian' differently from one another. Hollindale's (1992) discussion of the ideological foundations of literature helps describe what instantiates a Christian genre as distinct from secular science fiction, historical fiction, or realistic fiction. The cultural context of life in the United States is historically grown from and bounded by biblical law and morality. As a whole, from the beginning of European migration to North America until the 1860s, children's literature imported to or published in the United States was predominantly written for Protestant religious and moral instruction (Hunt, 1995). In many secular books today, Judeo-Christian morality still grounds the characters' actions and beliefs about how society works. This societal level of ideology is a uniform influence across children's literature in the USA. However, a crucial difference in today's Christian literature for children is the further assumption that God, not society, is the author of religion and moral law and the Bible, not federal or state statutes, is the guide for living. A life of faith is the ultimate goal, however that is defined.

For example, in *The Year of Abi Crim*, which is a stand-alone book rather than one of a series, there is a scene in which the children are practicing for an orchestral performance. The conductor says to them: "think of the sacrificial love the Savior had for us to leave heaven on our pitiful accounts. Play with that feeling in mind" (Hambrick, 2000: 23). Prior to this reference to Christian belief that Jesus, the son of God, died in atonement for our sins, the reader has encountered the family saying grace and knows that the school is a Christian school. The next morning, Abi's mother asks her: "have you thought about what God might want you to learn through your audition experience yesterday?" (2000: 34). This example shows the expectation that the adults have for the children to look to God or Jesus for inspiration and education.

In another book, *The Case of the Dinosaur in the Desert*, five children win a contest for which the prize is to go on a dinosaur dig. The paleontologist in charge does not want them there. One of the children asks his father by phone what to do. His father discusses part of Matthew 5 and Romans 12 with his son and advises him to pray. The children then talk about the situation and decide a as group to "kill her with kindness" (Romans 12: 20, in Wilson and Dengler, 2001: 65) so as to overcome evil with good. The children expect that their parents can help them, and they expect that the guidelines they read in the Bible will be useful and effective.

Some of the difference between Christian and secular books lies in overt markers of Christianity, such as prayer or reading scripture as in the case above or a conversion scene. However, many publishers have found that a good story sells better when there are fewer didactic elements. Hollindale (1992) identifies a third kind of ideology that suffuses books: the author's beliefs that are implicit in her/his work. This also engages the reader with a comfortable sense of rightness about a book when both reader and author accept a conservative worldview. In *Detective Zack: Secret of Noah's Flood* (Thomas, 2002), a family goes on a summer trip to gather 'evidence' for the truth of the biblical story of Noah's ark. The book begins with a description of Zack's encounter with a friend who laughs at his belief in biblical stories. Zack says to him, "'what are you talking about? Don't you believe the stories in the Bible are real?' I thought he was just kidding. But he was being serious" (2002: 9). The conversation continues, and Zack's friend remarks that the earth is a million years old, and it must be true because his science book says so. The overt belief that would be apparent to someone of like mind is that evolutionary ideas are expressed in school textbooks and are in discord with biblical stories.

Christian writers conceive of the children's books they write as an instantiation of a gift God has given them. In the words of Sharon Hambrick, a writer of two popular series and several other books, "my writing is defined (you could use the word *limited*) by the fact that I am a Believer. I can't step out of that and write something that would dishonor the Lord." This dimension creates trustworthiness in the literature that is recognizable and reassuring to the Christian reader as in the example above. Beyond the literature's content, predictability and ideology, the way that the books are marketed is also an effort to earn consumers' trust.

Publishers' marketing plans target buyers' trust through several means. First, the more familiar the customers are with the authors and themes, the more likely they are to buy; therefore publishers promote brand name awareness of authors, series titles, and an individual book as one product of that brand. Publishers also encourage known authors of adult books to try their hands at books for the tween crowd. For example, the series, *Left Behind: the Kids*, (e.g., Jenkins and LaHaye, 2001) have sold over 11 million copies and bring into the children's market the dangerous, apocalyptic world that is explored in the adult series. The end times are presented as a series of horrific events that must be endured by those who were not believers when the rapture occurred.

Second, publishers gain parents' trust because other products representing brand names provide alternatives to secular toys and games which may have objectionable content. The book characters or the brand theme include videos, plush toys, jewelry, and stationery that are designed for tweens. Far less diversity of products are available in the Christian market than in the secular market in terms of branding. Christian publishing is both smaller in scale and more conservative than the secular industry, though it mimics successful, secular marketing strategies. Offering branded products is a strategy only recently applied to Christian series. Compare, for example, the over 500 products that are sold under the Harry Potter brand (Taxel, 2002), with the four or five products that are branded in a Christian series. The updated versions of an 1870s book series, *Mildred Keith* (Finley, 2001 - first published 1876), offers a doll, who is the main character in period costume, a website, companion books, and a girls' club (www.alifeoffaith.com).

Third, publishers emphasize safety, especially with internet tie-ins. For computer savvy readers, virtual sites such as Faithgirlz. com at Zonderkiz, or Cool2Read.com at Tyndale, offer discussion boards, biblical devotions, and also shopping in a safe environment. The virtual sites can teach children about consumerism within a Christian community of buyers, which appeals to parents and their children. Since 9/11, a consistent theme in marketing books and other products has been children's safety. Parents trust the oversight the companies provide for their children's forays into the virtual world. Fourth, the covers on books, specifically designed to be interesting but not provocative, are calculated to appeal to both the children and the parents. When parent and tween shop together, Simon (2006) calls them the "four-eyed, four-legged consumer," a new conceptualization of the buying power of articulate children and discriminating parents. Community outreach, in the form of book clubs for tweens at bookstores, for example, also attracts customers. These, then, are a few of the ways in which publishers build trust with their customers and build up their consumer base: wholesome book content, product reliability and predictability, and increasingly, a monitored approach to consumerism. Broadening the customer base to include a greater diversity of Christian consumer would require publishing books by more diverse authors and books that were about more diverse peoples.

Fulfilling the Mission

Publishers' mission statements are reflected in the content of the books through the different ways that the Christian characters approach their relationships with God and live their lives. The books acknowledge that there is no single way to live out one's faith and as such many Christian readers can resonate with the views of a life of faith reflected in the books. The books do assume that those who read them have a shared understanding of how people come to have faith, why people pray, read scripture, and actively seek to model their lives on biblical teaching. There is little overt teaching about these issues, but they infuse the stories. The wide variance in the extent to which characters rely on God provides a continuum of Christian life.

Earlier, I proposed that the publishers' mission statements are a guide to working out the points in the ECPA's statement of faith through the books. However, only the first three are obvious in the books for tweens: the infallibility and inspiration of the Bible, the nature of God, and the role Jesus plays in a Christian's life. Those that deal with the spiritual unity of Christians, or the role of the Holy Spirit in a Christian's life, are not concepts that arise in the books. None of the books challenge the depiction of God as male, so I will refer to God as "he" for the purposes of this discussion.

The Bible's authority is portrayed through characters' reliance on scripture to come to terms with events in their lives, as Abi does in *The Year of Abi Crim* (Hambrick, 2000). She confronts racist attitudes in her friends through her father's help and through remembering verses to give her courage. The children in *The Case of the Dinosaur in the Desert* (Wilson and Dengler, 2001) also depend upon the Bible to learn how to live rightly, when they use the scripture to guide their decision about how to treat the surly scientist. Biblical and more broadly, Christian authority is portrayed ethnocentrically, even arrogantly in some books with a mission storyline. *The Mystery of the Sunken Steamboat* (Wiggin, 1995), for example, is primarily about how pride gets in the way of one's relationship with God. A visiting missionary, who is asking for money to send supplies to African children, talks about the Masi children who need Jesus. In *The Kerrigan Kids* (Morris, 2001), a family also goes to Africa to spend a few weeks, and the native people are portrayed throughout as unsophisticated and immature in contrast to the Christian children from the United States.

The books are sometimes ambivalent about who God is. In some, God is simply a divine presence, without definition. In others, God is presented in more than one person. However, God the father is predominant; the person of Jesus is rarely addressed or discussed in characters' prayers and conversations and the Holy Spirit even less so. That there is only one God is emphasized by characters' expressions of dependence on him for food and safety. In *The Wooden Ox* (Hardy, 2002) a family is captured by guerillas in Mozambique during the civil war in the 1980s, and the story's theme is about how God meets us in our moments of pain and anger and graciously answers our prayers. *Charlotte's Rose*, a book set in the 1850s, describes a Welsh, Mormon community as they travel to the Unites States then walk pushing handcarts with their household goods across the Great Plains to Utah. Throughout, Charlotte has both irreverent and serious discussions with God about the difficulties they face and the things she wishes to have happen. As the group climbs to the top of the last mountain and can see their goal in site, one character recalls that the missionaries far away in Liverpool told her

God only wanted a broken and contrite heart. She says, "after much sorrow and even more sin, I offer you a contrite heart…but it is not broken…I give you instead a stout and loyal heart. It is yours, God, to do with what you wish" (Canon, 2002: 238).

Some books treat God as though He were a wise man who is occasionally consulted about the day-to-day problems of life, but who is not included in the resolution of those issues. Characters pray to check in with him, but not urgently as those in the books discussed above in which characters directly ask for God's immediate help. The characters may read scripture or talk about God, but they do so as an intellectual exercise and not as an interactive search for answers. In yet other books, God is not present in the story at all; Christianity provides a moral template on which the stories are written. Characters pray only in a perfunctory way, such as saying a grace before a meal. Neither scripture nor conversations about God are resources they use for life choices. There is awareness that God is real, but he is not important to the events of the story. For example, in *A Time to Keep Silent*, Clair is unhappy with her father's decision to leave his church in the city to go to a remote location and plant a church. She befriends a young girl, Dorrie, who comes from an abusive family, and in the climax of the story, when Dorrie's drunken father catches them he slaps Dorrie. Clair thinks:

> I had never seen an adult hit someone. Suddenly I understood that there had always been rules in my life and that because things like that were against those rules they had never happened to me. But outside of my life, in the lives of some other people, there were no rules and anything could happen. (Whelan, 1979: 108)

The presence of Jesus in books is more likely when all the markers of Christianity are present. For example, in *The Year of Abi Crim*, there is the reference to Jesus' role in salvation mentioned above, and in a grace before dinner, Abi says, "Dad thanked God for the day, the food, the family, and mostly, Dad said, for the great Redeemer, the Lord Jesus Christ" (Hambrick, 2000: 7). In *The Palomino*, Jenny works at a barn for the summer and rescues a starving horse who turns out to be a beautiful Palomino when her coat is cleaned. Jenny thinks, "Jesus redeemed me with His blood, and Mom and I redeemed Sunny with a hundred dollars. Sunny and I would both be dead if someone hadn't saved us. Thank You, Jesus for giving your life to save me, and thank you, Mom for helping me save Sunny (Pistole, 2002: 89). Prayer, devotions, scripture reading and conversations about God are present throughout both books. The variety of ways that characters rely on God in their lives provides a realistic spectrum of faith in action. Where the books are unbalanced, and where they challenge the universal nature of the publishers' mission statements, is in the cast of characters and the settings.

Taken together, the books show children in circumstances of life that only a middle-class, white Christian would experience, and then only if that person lived a very sheltered life. Many of the books are set within the sphere of the family, private Christian school, and church, with no interactions depicted outside that sphere. Most of the main characters have the same demographics as the real people who buy the books. The books do not invite Christians that live outside of this narrow range of experiences to "apply biblical truth to their lives," (mission statement, www.bethanyhouse.com) nor do they help children who do recognize themselves in the books to learn to live in the world in all its diversity. Even the range of diversity within the Christian world is not served by the books, as the mission statements imply they are.

Characters attend church, but the particular denominations are not identified, and there is no discussion of the forms and functions of religion beyond personal salvation and living a moral life, and usually implicitly, building a relationship with God. While the books do include multicultural characters, their ethnicities and class are often window-dressing, a nod to a sensibility of the real world's diversity among Christians. Diversity of race or ethnicity is expressed through one or two comments about their color or age, but differences among characters are not substantial and have no effect on the events of the stories. Gender barriers are not often challenged; books are overwhelmingly about families of two heterosexual parents and their children. The parental roles are conservatively portrayed: fathers working and having ultimate authority in the family and mothers at home, caring for the family.

In a more pernicious vein, if there is a villain in the story, that person, usually male, is often lower class, uneducated, or in some other manner marked out as stereotypically undesirable. The implication is the villain is not a Christian, or one who does not practice a moral lifestyle.

Some books do engage issues of race and class through the events of the stories. Most of these are historical fiction books that deal with immigration, war, or the westward movement of the population before the United States took in all the land to the Pacific Ocean. For example, in a complex story titled *The Discovery* (Rue, 2001), Will Hutchinson moves to New Mexico during World War II so his mother can take a job teaching. His father is missing in action. Shortly after they move there, Will finds out that his real father was his mother's first husband, who repudiated his Christianity and who died in jail. Will rejects his mother's faith and seeks God through a Native shaman he meets. He eventually learns to live with and value the Mexican and Native peoples in the town as well as his own Christian heritage.

Few multicultural books reflect the contemporary world; publishers are reluctant to risk publishing books that picture a more diverse world because of the uncertainty of profitable returns. Publishers also are risk-aversive when it comes to acquiring books written by people with diverse backgrounds. Truly, secular children's books suffer from the same lack of diversity, but secular publishers are not making the claim that they print books that will help all Christians live faithfully. There is a reciprocal relationship between publishers who are driven by a profit motive and the customers who indicate their interests and preferences through the book titles they select which works to keep the books from representing a diverse worldview.

The books are also limited in the biblical concepts that they explore. Conversion, forgiveness, humility, charity, or reliance on God are examples of the uncontroversial topics that the books discuss. Few people would argue that these are not important ideas for children to understand and apply. The moral choices characters make are primarily limited to their private lives: should I lie, should I steal? The storyline is often constructed around such how personal choices play out in the character's life. Only secondarily, if at all, do the stories explore how such choices can have an impact in the broader community. Social justice is not a topic that is often explored. One reason for this is that the books discussed here are written for the tween market; young adult books do explore more controversial topics. Another reason is that publishers are trying to reach the broadest market with their books, and so the book topics and range of characters are controlled to appeal to the most people possible. Effectively, such a common denominator creates a narrow range of content. Even when the topic is how to live in community, it is usually only the Christian community that creates the frame for the story's events. It is the rare book that explores how to engage in community with those who think differently about faith.

To look at the books from another perspective, they are recognizable as a genre by what is not in them. There are no abandoned children, divorced parents, same-sex parents, or drug problems; no one is starving or homeless. Violence is usually kept to fistfights or thefts or threats of bodily harm, though adventure book series or apocalyptic series do include violent, but not graphic, crime. Death of a parent or sibling or friend is sometimes a plot device. Abusive parents are alluded to in the lives of a few antagonists as a reason for their immoral behavior.

Despite the narrowness of characters' demographics and the settings in which they live, the books' strength is in the portrayal of people living their lives through a conscious application of Christian principle. As mentioned in the beginning of the paper, the books make present that the reason for choosing a moral life is more than a cultural acceptance of right and wrong; it is an acknowledgement of divine authority. Characters consistently choose to abstain from or turn away from evil behavior. Child characters always know when they are choosing to do something that is not right to do. Their families give them guidelines and consequences for their actions and cheer them on when they chose rightly. There is really no question that they *would not* choose rightly. The possible universes for these child characters and their families do not include failure in the long run, because they choose to follow the precepts of Scripture, explicitly stated or implied by the ideological foundation of the books. The books clearly and strongly travel the 'narrow way' in terms of morality.

Conclusion

The goals of the marketplace, to sell books at a profit, are perhaps incompatible with the goals of Christianity, as what may be sacrificed in either instance in order to achieve the goals is quite different. The marketplace is never focused on service to others; making a profit means minimizing costs and maximizing revenue, which only allows for decisions that primarily concern financial feasibility. Christianity is focused on creating a relationship with God, the result of that relationship being an expression of love that is service to God and other people, with the ultimate aim, in a temporal sense, of people living together peacefully and without oppression. Publishers do successfully achieve their Christian missions in some tangible ways: certainly more people are reading books that celebrate a personal relationship with God, and the profits of the publishing companies often go to other ministries such as international missions or colleges.

Tween books explore topics that do help Christians apply biblical truth to their lives. However, the challenges characters face are those that most often help them develop a personal morality that strengthens their faith. The importance of a faith that is expressed in missions to alleviate suffering in the world, for example, or reach out in other ways is not an important component of books for tweens. In my opinion, tweens are at an age where they are defining who and how they will be in the world. Helping them see beyond themselves to the greater work of Christendom through fictional representations of characters who are also learning to make an impact in the world would be a greater fulfillment of the Christian mission.

In terms of race and class, a steady diet of tween books would give a false impression of the diversity of Christians; or of the denominational life of people and the ways that they worship and include 'biblical principles' in their lives; or poor impressions of those who live in difficult circumstances. If books perpetuate a view of Christian life that is compatible only with the views of the buyers, this lack of diversity is something that proponents of multiculturalism have identified long since as a prescription for the perpetuation of injustice (Harris, 1993; Sims-Bishop, 1997; Taxel, 1994), which is antithetical to biblical themes of justice. If the purpose of publishing is to provide Christians stories about applying biblical truth to their lives, then it is vital that the Christian worldview in the stories be based on a complex understanding of those truths. Since there are books such as *The Year of Abi Crim* or *The Wooden Ox* that do raise issues of social justice in substantive ways, albeit from a white perspective, this is evidence that the market will accept this depth of story. Those books that include a multicultural facet can be held to a higher standard.

It is important to the characters in these books to recognize God's authority—to turn to him for provision, for protection from evil, and for help in distress. Characters express through their dialogue and actions that God is both loving and forgiving and he is waiting to be in lifelong relationship with them. They respond to him in thankfulness for his gifts and in praise of his goodness. I submit that the books' appeal would be strengthened through exploration of more complex biblical concepts. Characters can interact with people who do not have such a conservative worldview in ways that do not violate biblical truths nor impose them on others, yet allow for the love of God to be expressed in that interaction. Such books will continue to uphold the standards of high morality and exciting reading and continue to be eminently marketable. The morality of such books not only will be traditional, but also will be a morality that views others in the fullness of their humanity.

References

Barna, *Half of All Americans Read Christian Books and One-Third Buy Them*, http://www.barna.org, accessed 27 January 2003.

Cannon, Ann Edwards, *Charlotte's Rose* (New York: Wendy Lamb Books, 2002).

ECPA, *Sales Tracking Analysis Trends Summary* (Phoenix: Evangelical Christian Publishers Association, 2003).

Finley, Martha, *Millie's Unsettled Season* (Franklin: Mission City Press, 2001).

Hambrick, Sharon, *The Year of Abi Crim* (Greenville: BJU Press, 2000).

Hardy, Leanne, *The Wooden Ox* (Grand Rapids: Kregel Publications, 2002).

Harris, Violet J., "African-American Children's Literature: the First One Hundred Years," in eds., T. Perry and J. Fraser, *Freedom's Plow: Teaching in the Multicultural Classroom* (New York: Routledge, 1993), pp. 167-81.

74 Diane Carver Sekeres

Heuser, Susan, Interview with editor of Tommy Nelson, Inc., 17th October 2001.

Hollindale, Peter, "Ideology and the Children's Book," in ed. Peter Hunt, *Literature for Children: Contemporary Criticism* (London: Rutledge, 1992), pp. 18-40.

Hunt, Peter, *Children's Literature: an Illustrated History* (Oxford: Oxford University Press, 1995).

LaHaye, Tim, and Jerry Jenkins, *Kingdom Come: the Final Victory*. Vol. 13, *Left Behind*. (Wheaton: Tyndale House, 2007).

Lodge, Sally, "What's Novel in Kids' Series?", *Publishers Weekly*, http://publishersweekly.

reviewsnews.com/index.asp?layout=articlePrintandarticleID=CA284756, accessed 17th March 2003.

Lohr, Nancy, Interview with editor of Journey Forth, 7th April, 2003.

Morris, Gilbert, *The Adventures of the Kerrigan Kids: Travels in Africa: Painted Warriors and Wild Lions* (Chicago: Moody Press, 2001).

Peretti, Frank, *Flying Blind* (Nashville: Tommy Nelson, 1997).

Pistole, Katy, *The Palomino*, The Sonrise Farm Series (Nampa: Pacific Press, 2002).

Rue, Nancy, *The Discovery*, Focus on the Family: Christian Heritage Series: the Sante Fe Years. (Minneapolis: BethanHouse, 2001).

Sekeres, Diane Carver, "The Profit Motive and the Prophet's Message: Multiculturalism in Christian Children's Literature," PhD dissertation, University of Georgia (2003).

Simon, Mary Manz, "Trends in the Children's Marketplace - 2006," unpublished paper presented at the 2006 CBA International Christian Retail Show, Nashville (2006).

Sims-Bishop, Rudine, "Selecting Literature for a Multicultural Curriculum," in ed. Violet J. Harris, *Using Multiethnic Literature in the K-8 Classroom* (Norwood: Christopher-Gordon, 1997).

Sperling, Natasha, interview with editor of Bethany House, 3rd December 2001.

Taxel, Joel, "Children's Literature at the Turn of the Century: Toward a Political Economy of the Publishing Industry," *Research in the Teaching of English* 37.2 (2002), pp. 146-98.

_____, "The Politics of Children's Literature: Reflections on Multiculturalism and Christopher Columbus," in ed. V. J. Harris, *Teaching Multicultural Literature in Grades K-8* (Norwood: Christopher-Gordon, 1994), pp. 3-36.

Thomas, Jerry D., *Secret of Noah's Flood*, Detective Zack (Colorado Springs: Faith Kids, 2002).

Warren, Rick, *The Purpose Driven Life: What on Earth Am I Here For?* (Grand Rapids: Zondervan, 2002).

Whelan, Gloria, *A Time to Keep Silent* (Grand Rapids: Eerdmans, 1993).

Wiggin, Eric, *The Mystery of the Sunken Steamboat, Hannah's Island* (Lynnwood: Emerald Books, 1995).

Wilson, Pauline Hutchens, and Sandy Dengler, *The Case of the Dinosaur in the Desert*, The New Sugar Creek Gang (Chicago: Moody Press, 2001).

Websites

www.alifeoffaith.com
www.bethanyhouse.com
www.cool2read.com
www.ecpa.org
www.faithgirlz.com
www.moodypublishers.com
www.tyndale.com
www.zonderkidz.com

Evangelism and Purification

Capturing the Religious Imagination:
Branding and the United Church of Christ's "God is Still Speaking" Campaign

Monica Pombo

"Who we see and who we do not see; who is privileged within the regime of specularity; which aspects of the historical past actually have circulating visual representations and which do not; whose fantasies of what are fed by which visual images?" (Rogoff, 1998: 15).

"Ideologies usually remains hidden and self-effacing until controversy reveals them" (Breen and Concoran, 1982: 133).

"That they may all be one" (John 17:21) [words within the United Christ of Christ logo].

Advertising has been studied as a form which perpetuates, reflects and creates culture (Barthes, 1972; Jhally, 1990 and Fiske, 1987). While culture was once defined by some as a static realm in which strict codes and traditional values are reproduced (Kluckhohn, 1951), theorists such as Clifford (1986) see culture as a contested terrain where codes and representations are constantly challenged. Clifford writes that the "focus on text making and rhetoric serves to highlight the constructed, artificial nature of cultural accounts" (1986: 2). An advertising campaign is a cultural text. It helps to visually define a product or company and the culture that surrounds them. Sayre (1994: 98) writes, "by its nature, image advertising is value-expressive." As a medium, advertising sells products and ideas. It helps to create a brand and with it brand loyalty. Brands encapsulate the identity and values associated with an institution or product through visual culture. Mirzoeff (1998: 6) writes, "visual culture examines why modern and postmodern culture places a premium on rendering experience in visual form".

Visual culture helps to shape culture. Visual symbols and signs of Christianity define what and who constitute Christianity. Barthes explains this process as "cultural discourse that seemingly moves from mythical invention to natural fact" (quoted in Fuery and Fuery, 2003: 93). In a process which helps to shape and to create ideology. Hall (1995: 18) defines ideology as... those images, concepts and premises which provide the frameworks through which we represent, interpret, understand and 'make sense' of some aspect of social existence." Hall adds that ideology is a "collective process and practice" (1995: 19). Therefore, it is through a system of representation and knowledge that certain belief systems are perpetuated within culture. According to Barthes ideologies and their values are interlocked in symbolic signs. Poststructuralism as a theory helps to explain how cultural process turns signs into ideology and how counter ideology can then be produced; in this case, how Christianity's signs can be reinvented.

In the past, churches have used media to represent and promote their identity. Clarke (2005) and Armstrong, Kallmark and Williamson (2005) look at the representation of religion on television. Collins and Rothmyer (1981), McCleary and Saxton (1983), and Lynch (1990) analyze the promotion and marketing of religion. Studies that look at the impact of consumer culture and 'mass branding' of Christianity are starting to emerge. Hunt (2004: 1) describes Alpha courses which got started in England at Holy Trinity, Brompton. Hunt describes Alpha as a "crash course in Christianity for beginners" and he looks at the mass marketing of religion through what he calls the 'spiritual marketplace' where one's identity often helps shape a sense of belonging within churches.

There are numerous studies that cover the debate over the issue of homosexuality and the church. Olyan and Nussbaum (1998) evaluates how mainline protestants, Jewish, Catholics, and African American churches are debating the issue of sexual orientation within the context of the church. The authors explain that conservative religious groups in the U.S. see the world as a fight of good against evil which is to be understood via a literal interpretation of the bible and a focus on the Old Testament. Liberal Christians tend to favor criticism and interpretation of the bible with a focus on the New Testament. Studies also focus on conservative Christian groups. Heman (1997) writes about the Christian Right in the U.S. and the role of conservative Christians in shaping moral values and policies toward gays and lesbians. Linneman (2003) focuses on the Christian Conservatives movement and the gays and lesbians civil rights movement as they relate to public opinion and the political climate in America. While many studies focus on Christian conservatives, not as much has been written about progressive churches in America and how they are using media to communicate their messages and perspectives on gays and lesbians. In this chapter, I will analyze the United Church of Christ's *God is Still Speaking* campaign and its inclusive representation of homosexuality in the commercial *Bouncer*. I will look at the campaign and the production process which created *Bouncer* as visual text, noting how the campaign and the commercials at its heart break away from the traditional visual symbols of Christianity.

The Campaign

During advent 2004, Gotham, an advertising agency in New York City, released the United Church of Christ (UCC) national television advertising campaign with a commercial entitled *Bouncer*. The commercial was part of a larger identity campaign: *God is Still Speaking*. The final cost of the campaign was $1,200,000, including the costs of production and distribution of the television commercials. It was a new venture for Gotham, an advertising agency known for its make up ads and its worldwide "Maybelline" account. The campaign comprised three spots: *Ejector Pew* (which also appeared in Spanish), *Bouncer*, and *Steeples*. The campaign had several goals. First, it became part of an effort by the leadership of the United Church of Christ to help formulate the church's identity to the public, second to help the church become more visible, third to help increase membership and stewardship and finally to create a recognizable brand for the church.   The original concept was developed by Ron Buford who, at the time, worked at the national offices of the United Church of Christ in Cleveland, Ohio.   Past Church efforts had focused on communication issues related to the public interest. The UCC, through its Office of Communication, has a history of activism and of lobbying the Federal Communication Commission.   In 1959, Everett Parker, head of the Office of Communication, won a "federal court ruling that the airwaves are public, not private property" after a fight against television stations in the south that were not covering the civil rights movement (www. stillspeaking.com/about/firsts.htm). With a long history of advocacy and lobbying at the Federal Communication Commission (FCC), the United Church of Christ explored new territory with the new campaign.   While the campaign depicted persons of color, persons with disabilities, the poor, and gays and lesbians being refused by a Church, the campaign caused nationwide controversy when two of the major United States networks, NBC and CBS, refused to air *Bouncer* calling it too controversial.   Despite the setbacks caused by the networks decision, the advertising campaign proved to have the right ingredients to have an impact on American culture: controversy, a provocative and surprising message and powerful corporations blocking religious freedom of speech.

What follows is a description of the *God is Still Speaking,* campaign with the focus on the commercial entitled *Bouncer.* The 30-second spot was chosen due to the fact that it was the first spot release by Gotham under the guidance of the United Church of Christ Offices of the Stillspeaking Initiative, a separate office established for marketing, advertising, and evangelism with the cooperation of Proclamation, Identity and Communication. It was the commercial that provoked the greatest impact and greatest controversy in the U.S. The challenging spot raised many issues around ideology and visual representation of Christianity in contemporary American life. The spot also raised questions around how the United Church of Christ, through the structure of consumer culture and advertising, translated its sense of identity and theology into a brand that could be reproduced by its local churches. By working with Gotham, the United Church of Christ went through a process of decision making on a new visual style and a brand for the Church.

This study intends, therefore, to address the process of creating a Church's brand, through a textual analysis of the *Bouncer* commercial and interviews with key individuals involved in the creation of the campaign. This study shows how the *God is Still Speaking* campaign moved away from traditional iconic ways of visualizing Christianity.

The United Church of Christ campaign also broke away from hegemonic values associated with traditional modes of Christianity. Under the current historical moment of a right-wing Christian conservative government in the United States (Wallis, 2005; Suarez, 2006), the United Church of Christ had to think about what visual representations it should create to show the audience the Church's progressive voice. Finally, this chapter will also address the role of network television in maintaining its gatekeeping power which helped to define and maintain a representation of Christianity that is allied with a right-wing Christian conservative movement in America. Conservative Christians maintain that God is a strong male authority and the world is divided between good and evil. It is also a God who sees homosexuality as a great threat to the moral fabric of American life.

This chapter will also include textual analysis and political economy of communication. Textual analysis entails a close reading of media texts and it involves three stages: description, meaning and judgment (Buckingham, 2003). Calabrese (2004: 2) explains the political economy of communication as "the institutional structure, organization, and production processes of the media industry". Political economy is also preoccupied with issues of representation and who gets to delineate who and what is represented in the media (Garnham, 1995). Political economy looks at the production process of "cultural industries" (Stokes, 2003 and Hesmondhalgh, 2005) and it helps to reveal the producers' thinking during the creation of images and media texts. Whereas one can see religion as a commodity, political economy focuses on the process of production, distribution and consumption of religion both in its products (such as mugs, T-shirts, pens) and values (belief systems and identities) which are sold within consumer culture. In this paper, I will focus on the production and distribution of the *God is Still Speaking* Campaign. Interviews were conducted with key individuals involved in the creation and distribution of the spots. Interviews provided an insight into the UCC identity campaign as it was constructed through a collective creative process. Key individuals within the campaign were: from the national offices of the United Church of Christ: Ron Buford, Rev. Robert Chase, and Marilyn Dubasak; from Gotham in New York City: Ted Pulton, and Michael Jordan.[1] Ron Buford originally came up with the campaign idea. Robert Chase managed the concept and worked closely with Gotham to produce the commercials. Marilyn Dubasak currently directs the *Stillspeaking* initiative. Ted Pulton is chief marketing officer at Gotham and Michael Jordan is the creative director who has been responsible for the UCC account for the past three years.

Background: the United Church of Christ

The United Church of Christ is a relatively small denomination with 1.4 million members and 6,000 churches across the United States. The UCC was formed June 15, 1957 by uniting the Evangelical and Reformed Church and the Congregational Christian Churches. In its foundation the church had a strong belief in "freedom of religious expression" (United Church Board, 1986: 6). The Church functions under a non- hierarchical system where local churches do not have to abide by resolutions approved at its General Synod. While individual churches have a great degree of independence, the fight for social justice unifies the Church. Working at the national offices of the United Church of Christ between 1993 and 1997, I had several opportunities to record theologians and authors speaking about oppression and its common roots. In the Office of Communication, I worked on several documentaries related to social justice such as environmental racism and welfare reform. I was sent to South Carolina to videotape recovery efforts after a series of African-American churches were burned by white supremacists in the 1990s. The church also asked for my assistance in the videotaping the media literacy video/guidebook entitled *Kids Talk TV Inside Out*. Ministers, theologians and the prominent authors Jim Wallis and Barbara Ehrenreich spoke of a Jesus who fought the powerful and who preached social justice for silenced and disenfranchised groups in society.[2]   Rev. John H. Thomas, General Minister and President, United Church of Christ writes:

> We are a "united and uniting" Church seeking renewal through the vision of Christ's prayer "that they may all be one that the world might believe." We are a "just peace" Church committed to overcoming violence and oppression. We are a "multi-racial, multi-cultural Church" yearning for the day when our congregations more fully reflect the vision of Pentecost. We are an "open and affirming" Church where no one's baptismal identity can be denied because of his or her sexual identity. We are an "accessible" Church cherishing the gifts of all regardless of physical or mental abilities. More recently we have been thinking about what it means to call ourselves "the Church of the still speaking God," a Church that believes God has yet more light and truth to break forth from the Word (http://www.stillspeaking.com/about, accessed March 15, 2007).

The Church, in fact, has a long history of fighting for issues that were unpopular in their time. The denomination's history involves many firsts: from being a leader in the antislavery movement of the 1700s, to the first mainline denomination to ordain an African American minister (1785), to the first to ordain a woman minister (1853). Under its general synod the church approved the ordination of gays in 1972, and in 2005 it passed a resolution for marriage equality for gays and lesbians (http://www.stillspeaking. com/about/firsts.htm). Due to its non-hierarchical nature, however, churches can decide whether to welcome gays and lesbians by becoming what is called "open and affirming", a process which involves open dialogue and education about gays and lesbians and the Church.

Homosexuality and the Context of Religion in the United States

The visibility of Christianity in the United States is closely associated with right-wing Christian conservatives. Conservative Christian groups such as the Christian Coalition have gained political power through their ability to fundraise and influence the American political landscape. Politicians backed by the Christian Coalition have shaped legislation based on traditional moral values. The issue of homosexuality has proven central in the unification of conservative churches. Homosexuality becomes a polarizing issue, one that goes against traditional values as defined by conservative American Christian morality. Cobb (2006: 4) writes that:

> as a policy issue, the publicity around homosexual condem-
> nations proves to be crucial, enabling the so called religious
> right to gain, lucratively, stronghold on conservative con-
> stituents of the market-driven United States ... When 'ho-
> mosexuals' are a religious issue, the reproductive family
> is cast as in decline and in need of 'traditional values.' A
> resurgence of strong, religious emotion inevitably follows.
> Homosexuality, in the early 1990s, became a major topic of
> policy making – a topic that still helps win elections.

A representation of homosexuality shaped by conservative Christian groups dominates U.S. mainstream media, further developing a discourse that creates a negative view of homosexuality within religious institutions. Conservative Christians groups are given front page cover in mainstream media in the U.S. and their beliefs have helped shape the landscape of religion in America in the beginning of the twenty first century. Moderate and liberal churches are often not represented within mainstream media. The majority of Americans have not been exposed to the United Church of Christ and its progressive stands. It took a controversial commercial, which represents gays and lesbians in a positive and welcome way, to get the media to listen.

Branding: Creating the God is Still Speaking Campaign

After a successful career in "corporate product development" at AT&T, the largest U.S. telephone company (Wilson, 2005: 33), Ron Buford came to work for the United Church of Christ national offices, in the office of Proclamation, Identity and Communication (PIC). As he has stated in his sermons, Mr. Buford is an African-American man who grew up in the Church of God, a conservative denomination based in Anderson, Indiana. He remembers his parents speaking of Rev. Dr. Martin Luther King who was then leading marches and speaking against injustice. He is an American living in a country which today is still divided by racism. While his original position at the United Church of Christ encompassed selling advertising for United Church News, it is as the media spokesperson for the Church and through working on the Church's identity that his prophetic voice emerged. He became the life force behind the *God is still Speaking* campaign as creator, spokesperson, and brand manager. Buford brought to the national offices a new outlook in how to deal with the difficult task of defining the Church's identity and shaping agreement among UCC members (at national, conference and local levels.) At first, the stakeholders of the Church were very hesitant to have someone define them. There was also hesitation around the idea of using the tools of consumer culture to market Christianity (Wilson, 2005: 35).

Buford worked against great odds, however, creating a clear vision and fighting for it. The campaign first came to Buford in a dream while he was on vacation in California in January 2002. Earlier that day he had bought a postcard with Gracie Allen's quote, "Never place a period where God has placed a comma." In the middle of the night the slogan "God is Still Speaking" came to him (interview with Ron Buford). From something that started as a dream, the campaign evolved into a national campaign involving the UCC national offices, board members, conference ministers, local churches, a multi-billion-dollar Madison Avenue advertising agency and two of the major U.S. networks. By June of 2003, Gotham agreed to produce the commercials at cost. By December 1, 2003 the project became so large that Buford left the PIC offices and became the interim manager of The *Stillspeaking* initiative. The *Bouncer* commercial aired in December 2004 and March 2005.

The campaign goals involved increased engagement in the church through "identity, giving, evangelism and action" (Buford, 2005a: 8). The hope was to increase membership of UCC churches, to increase stewardship, to create a consistent and clear identity through branding, and to create a connection between the brand and the UCC itself. To achieve these goals, Buford engaged all levels of the Church in the project. In order to invite churches to join in this effort and to create cohesiveness where there is a great degree of diversity, churches had to join the *Stillspeaking* campaign. In order to join, churches had to follow a three-step process: to opt into the program (which allows their church to be listed as a *Stillspeaking* church on the Stillspeaking.com website), go through training (in order to better understand the purpose of the campaign), develop a website (the national offices of the Church helped 1,000 churches create their websites during this process). To become a *Stillspeaking* church, a church would have to commit to the church's brand and its message. Members were encouraged to come to a one day *Stillspeaking* training, to form a hospitality committee in their churches and to join a "Reformation Day worship" a week before the commercial was to air on television (Buford, 2004c). In addition, the national offices provided *Stillspeaking* churches with evangelism resources such as *God is Still Speaking – Outreach, Welcome and Hospitality* manual. In addition, a Media Tool kit with two CDs and a DVD entitled *Ron in a Box* was produced. The CDs contained posters, banners, print ads, radio ads, guidelines for airing local radio advertising, graphics, logos and color/font guidelines so as to maintain the UCC brand.[3] Finally, it included a 38-minute DVD in which Buford explained the campaign to trainers and to local churches. The resource was easily purchased through United Church Resources to help trainers in their local church. In a chapter of the *Ron in a Box* DVD entitled *Creating an Identity Brand*, Buford explains the need to create a Church brand. He says:

> sincere advertising is a ministry of transformation in new and compelling ways. In a world of consumerism we need to build a brand. Jesus was a brand. The name Jesus became synonymous with healing and holiness, with the new, with liberation and so much more. How did the brand of Jesus become so popular? The same happens today, consistence and brand. Is there a symbol or phrase that causes our children to say United Church of Christ? We want people to say through the course of the campaign: the United Church

of Christ. God is still speaking.   Once they encounter the brand they are much more likely to accept our message. They will associate their experience with your signs and symbols (Buford, 2004d)

So, part of the efforts of The *Stillspeaking* initiative was to explain to UCC members and staff the necessity and benefit of allying the Church with marketing.

The Church brand involves three basic elements: the color red which was chosen due to its modern and vibrant appeal; the comma which is a symbol of pause, interpretation and reflection; the signature phrases which are: "God is still speaking", "Never place a period where God placed a comma" and "No matter who you are or where you are in your life's journey. You are welcome here." Marilyn Dubasak explains:

the comma is critical. The comma is a symbol we can use in the public arena to engage people who might otherwise not give the idea of Church a chance. The comma creates a pause. It is a moment for engagement. If someone is wearing a comma pin and they are at a grocery store and somebody says: 'what is the comma?' You can say: 'it is the symbol of my church and we think God is still speaking.' It gives them a way to engage people, a way to get people to do evangelism. In a lot of places evangelism has a negative connotation and it is also a way to break through to people who would never even have looked at the Church. They feel like they already know what it is about. So we don't use a cross which is immediately associated as a Christian symbol, or a fish. So, we don't do that because people look at that, and they say, I already know what is about. I don't like it. I am not interested in that. It is not for me. The comma does not bring up all of that. The brand has a feel. It is a little bit edgy, little bit hip. The ads are provocative. They are meant to grab attention. To say: "oh my gosh, what is happening here? What is going on there?" (interview, Marilyn Dubasak).

The main audience for the commercials was not current members of the United Church of Christ. The targeted audience involved persons who never went to church, individuals who felt alienated by the Church, individuals looking for a new denomination and those who were young and had never attended church. David Schoem, Minister and Team Leader for Evangelism at UCC, explains that 80 percent of twenty-year-olds in the United States have never been to church (Buford, 2006). While some were angry with the church for creating the *Bouncer* commercial, many saw it as a courageous and bold move in a very hostile political and Christian climate in the United States.

Gotham: Visual Culture and the Branding of the United Church of Christ

Gotham clients include AT and T Wireless, Bank of America, Lufthansa, Lindt Chocolates, American Online, among others. Besides the United Church of Christ, Gotham has also worked with the Chicago Theological Seminary (www.gothaminc.com). The agency manages global brands through its parent company McCann Erickson which, in terms of billings, is currently the second largest advertising agency in the world (www.adbrands.net). Ted Pulton explains that the resources of McCann Erickson "allow us to distribute work around the world. Their office structure optimizes and meets the demand of 86 countries" (interview). Gotham decided to work with the UCC even though they would have to work with a small budget by Madison Avenue advertising agency standards. The agency became intrigued by the church's message. In an initial meeting with Ron Buford and PIC director Bob Chase, Gotham asked, "if you have 6,000 churches and 1.2 million members, how come we never heard from you?" (interview with Bob Chase). Gotham became intrigued by UCC's message of welcoming.

Michael Jordan, creative director responsible for the UCC account, explains that clients either come to Gotham with a product or business and they want the agency to find a market solution or the client has a market solution and wants the agency to find a way to communicate that to the public (interview Michael Jordan).

UCC had a market solution with the *God is Still Speaking* campaign. UCC wanted Gotham to create an advertising campaign that would bring the campaign to life. From their initial meeting in 2003, it took a year for the Church to raise the money needed to shoot and to buy air time on the networks. Gotham was very engaged in this process doing, for instance, something that they had never done before: Ted Pulton and Michael Jordan went to the UCC General Synod in Minneapolis. At the General Synod, they met UCC leaders to show them the storyboards for the campaign and to convince them to raise the money needed to produce and air the commercials (interview Michael Jordan).

Jordan also explains that there is no right structure to create an advertising campaign. At Gotham the structure includes: research, analyses, insight, strategy and execution. Gotham researched the 'faith market' to be able to see how other Churches had used commercials to visualize their identity:

> we look at the competitiveness. We look at what messages are out there so we saw everything from different faith based institutions to the Church of Latter Day Saints to the United Methodist Church. Churches that had campaigns and had funding substantial amount of dollars... what we saw was what we call the expected feel-good message... In order for those messages to penetrate and make a difference in terms of outcome... We had to do something that was far more striking so as to break through (interview with Ted Pulton).

Research for the commercials involved focus groups, as Ted Pulton explains:

> because of our size and structure, there was a lot of secondary research. We looked at the face of the market, what trends were going on, a lot of consumer data that looks at people's attitudes and lifestyles and disenfranchisement. What is going on in their lives? What they like and what they don't like. What they connect with and what they don't connect. So we formulated a lot of hypotheses, developed

some ideas that we could use to probe in focus groups. Our first hypothesis was that there was a huge disconnect

That proved true during focus groups. There were ten to twelve focus groups conducted around the country on the West Coast and in Chicago, Cleveland, Pennsylvania and Florida. Focus groups involved eight to ten individuals. Individuals invited to the focus groups were either faith-based people who believed in a higher authority but said they were not religious or were not practicing and people who had been churchgoers but left their Church for some reason. The agency was looking for an insight into consumers and what makes them change their behavior, in this case, to have consumers find out about the United Church of Christ and to join. To get to an insight about a product, there must be research about the competition, the unique characteristics of your brand, and "the deeply seated kind of emotions and to how people relate to things in their lives" (interview with Ted Pulton). From this preliminary research Gotham created "ad-like objects": these are visuals and key word statements that encompass the key elements of the campaign. "Ad like objects" work as a compass, by using them during focus groups, the agency is able to see whether thoughts and feelings behind the commercial concept are working. Gotham used half a dozen concepts during focus groups. "One of them showed the white bread family which is Mr. and Mrs. Mainstream America polished and looking great and proper. That was the image of what the church goers was and by in large what most people would say acceptable". Individuals were given a pad to write their thoughts and this was followed by a discussion. The discussion gave Gotham the insight they were looking for, "what came out was that people felt a sense of rejection. What really stood out was the notion that those people don't want us there. They don't want people like me sitting next to them. It was unbelievable." So, individuals felt rejected by Churches whether because of doctrine or because they felt unwelcome.

From research Gotham produced a creative brief: "the brief identifies the target market and the persuasive outcomes to be achieved... The brief presents the problem to be solved by advertising, and, ideally, it should contain enough background or 'clues' to find the solution" (Koslow, Sasser and Riordan 2006: 83).   At Gotham, a creative brief emerges from a 'brand platform.' Brand platform includes three aspects: brand equity, brand personality and brand positioning. The following e-mail from Ted Pulton explains the components of a brand platform and the UCC creative brief:

> **Brand Equity Audit** – A disciplined process by which we identify the brand's core rational and emotional values. By establishing a desired audit, we construct a strategic blueprint for achieving the desired shift in brand perceptions that are relevant across all key constituencies.

> **Brand Personality** – A statement that captures the intangibles and spirit of a brand. It provides the framework for all creative development and defines a consistent "brand voice" which is distinctive, ownable and instantly recognizable no matter where it appears.

> **Brand Positioning** - We believe that a brand must have some unique value to somebody in order for it to stand out in its competitive environment. This is a concept statement that defines the unique value and qualities of a brand versus its competition in a proprietary and distinctive way.

> THEN, we have our creative brief. I have extracted these elements below:

> **UCC Desired Equity Audit**
> RATIONAL
> Diverse Christian Community
> Progressive Center of Faith/ Spirituality
> Independent Minded
> Insightful, Relevant
> Flexible, Responsive
> Uniting Force

> EMOTIONAL
> Expressive, Individualistic

In Touch
Unexpected
Welcoming, Supportive
Pragmatic
Freeing
My Unique Connection

Brand Positioning
The United Church of Christ is a unique, inclusive religious community that encourages members to explore their spirituality in ways that are meaningful and relevant to them

UCC Desired Brand Personality
My roots go back 2,000 years, but I am very much now and today. I am not strict with tradition or dripping in rituals. Instead, I embrace modern intelligent thinking: Acceptance. Inclusiveness. Justice. I can even be light-hearted. My open-armed approach is appealing to people of all races and life-styles. Which might explain why my Congregations are diverse and individualistic. Another funny thing happens when you're less judgmental. You allow people to search, discover and flourish. My friends come to me to seek their own answers, look inside themselves and explore their spiritual selves. In the end, my personality is reflective of Christ's. Open. Embracing. Nurturing. And always modern.

UCC CREATIVE BRIEF
1. What are we trying to sell?
The United Church of Christ, a place of diversity and inclusiveness for those who seek new, relevant insights and God's help for living today.

2. What should we know about who we're selling it to?

• **Open-minded prospects** who are on their own spiritual journey, seeking new insights and an understanding of God in today's world. They tend to be parents with children under 11 years of age or empty-nesters.

- **Current UCC members** who are diverse in composition, and who we must convince to maintain active participation in and support of the Church and its membership.

3. What is the #1 thing we want to say about it?
No matter who, no matter what, no matter where you are on life's journey, you are invited and welcome.

4. Why will that help membership go up?
UCC is a community of inclusiveness and flexibility.

5. How can we support that?
UCC affirms the ideal that Christians need not always agree in order to live in communion and is one of the most diverse Christian churches in the United States (Ted Pulton, e-mail, 23rd February 2007, quoted with permission, Ted Pulton, Chief Marketing Officer, Gotham).

After the creative brief was completed several creative teams tried to solve the creative problem presented by the Church and one team had the idea of Bouncer who through a red velvet rope guarded the entrance to a church. After Gotham sold the idea and storyboard to the Church, the production process began. Michael Jordan's job was to execute the message of the campaign. He had to translate the vision of the campaign through the production process. He hired Bob Purman, a director from Wisconsin who had previously worked with Gotham on America Online advertising. Since the *Bouncer* advert was shot in January, they had to move the production crew to a warm climate and Gotham choose Florida. To cut costs Ron Buford had originally found a church building in Miami to be the unwelcoming church in the commercial; however, the church did not fit the style required. They needed a church building that was generic and could be found anywhere in the USA. The production process in Florida took about a week of which two days were taking up shooting the *Bouncer* and *Steeples* commercials. To cut costs, cast involved both actors hired by a casting company and members of local UCC congregations. Back in New York City, Gotham hired a company called *Bug* to edit the commercials. During the editing process the editor (so to be able to time the piece and also to see how the pictures were matching the audio track) recorded a voice track for the piece. Interestingly enough this New York City Jewish editor with his sincere and unthreatening voice was engaged to do the voice-over for *Bouncer*. Gotham hired a company to produce the music and gave them the narrative structure which the music had to follow. Jordan mentioned during our interview that the intent was to give the viewer a modern parable, like the good Samaritan. Gotham was trying to create a "metaphorical story of good and bad examples. We were trying to keep with the spirit of the Bible" (interview with Michael Jordan)

Gotham ran the commercial in several test markets around the country. The commercial ran in Cleveland, Tampa, St. Petersburg, Okalahoma City, Springfield, Massachusetts and Harrisburg, Pennsylvania. Advertising time was bought from local network affiliates. The cost of running *Bouncer* during this test marketing ran at $800,000 (interview with Ron Buford). Despite having no problems while showing the commercial at local independent affiliates of the national networks, but two of those networks, NBC and CBS, refused to air the *Bouncer* and suggesting a cable-only run. Bob Chase found that unacceptable since he wanted the commercial to be viewed by the largest possible audience, which would require the networks and free television. While cable television still provides a large audience, it only includes those who can afford to pay for cable (interview with Bob Chase), The networks were willing to air *Steeples*, however, both UCC and Gotham wanted to open the campaign with the edgier piece, *Bouncer* (interviews with Bob Chase and Ted Pulton). *Bouncer* was considered too controversial and it never aired at the national networks, even though, in order to fight the networks' decision the UCC's Office of Communication started an online campaign to pressure the networks to include mainstream and liberal religious voices on the airwaves. (www.accessibleairwaves.org). Ted Pulton explains:

we thought that it was provocative but in no way we expected to cause the furor that it did, particularly with respect to the networks not airing it. We were stunned. We went back to try to do some more negotiations with the networks standard and practice [policy] and they were very firm, that the reaction from the viewers would be such that would be unpalatable. They would not be able to cope with it. There is always a standard and practices policy but there is always a grey line... One of the networks was afraid of a political backlash more than a specific rule within the standard and practices... [during the 2004 election many states in the U.S. had ballots against gay marriage and these ballots let to increase in voting by conservatives across the USA]. Here is something that says we are welcoming... it is a message of inclusion. Why would that message not fly in the market place of ideas?"

The message created a fissure, a rupture in the mainstream discourse of how Christianity should be represented to mainstream America. A message of acceptance, suddenly, became a tool for change, a shifting in the terrain of Christianity and its visual representation.

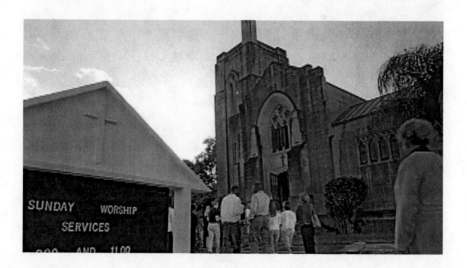

Figs. 3-15. United Church of Christ, *Bouncer*, 2004, http://www.still-speaking.com/media.

Jesus didn't turn people away.

God is still speaking,

UNITED CHURCH
OF CHRIST

UCC.ORG

Bouncer: Visual and Textual Analysis

The commercial opens with an establishing shot; a low-angle, pan. Audio of church bells ringing. The sun is setting and we are outside an old traditional church building. To the left of the frame there is a church sign with a cross on top announcing the Sunday worship times. Middle of the frame we see worshipers walking toward the church. Voices are talking softy in the background. Second shot is a low-angle medium shot. In the foreground, there are two bouncers. One is white and the other one is African-American, both are wearing black and have a cold, tough expression in their faces. The African American bouncer is wearing dark sunglasses. In front of them, a red rope (that works as a gate) is closed. The bouncers are guarding the entrance to the church and the rope is opened by the African-American bouncer only if the white bouncer approves a guest. Low camera angle emphasis the bouncers' wall-like posture and their arms' bulging muscles. In their background is the church's main entrance, the cross and an ornate window. At the church's gate, some observe as individuals try to enter the church. An African-American male wearing dark sunglass stands in the background observing. The white bouncer with a stone face stops two gay white males from entering the church. Gay characters are frail and skinny and have shaved heads. The white bouncer in a strong, mechanical tone tells them: "No! Step aside please." A somber piano tune plays in the background. Eye-level shot, a white couple steps in front of the bouncer, she has blonde long hair and is dressed up in a formal Sunday church dress. He is white, has short blonde hair and is wearing a suit. The heterosexual man smiles as the couple pass the bouncers. Eye-level shot of the heterosexual couple who is invited inside the church. The couple walks toward the entrance and the man turns around for a brief moment to look toward the bouncers and the ones left behind. High-angle camera (angle that makes the character look small) of a white male in wheelchair; he is also turned away. The white male bouncer stretches his arm and his hand signal the man in a wheelchair to go away. The bouncer says: "No, no way..." The next shot shows a high-angle shot of an African-American girl. She looks unemotional. The white bouncer says: "Not you. No." Eye-level, close shot, of bouncer's hand closing the gate. Loud sound of metal as the gate closes.

Fade in upbeat music, which continuous until the end of the commercial. Black background and white text: "Jesus did not turn people away. Neither do we." Fade in long-shot individuals who are standing next to each other in a group shot, like a family portrait. Children, a man and a child in wheelchairs are in the front row, a man is holding a baby. We see an elderly couple, teens, African-American and gay and lesbian couples in the picture. We do not know this family but they are warm and welcoming and they are happy to be with each other. Background is of a building with many large windows and an open door to the right of the frame. Voice over, warm male voice, saying kindly: "the United Church [emphasis and brief pause] of Christ. No matter who you are or where you are in your life's journey. You are welcome here." Series of medium-shots, eye- level shots of Asian girl and white girl, a Hispanic teen male, an African-American male and female in their twenties, a white lesbian couple in their twenties holding each other with a confident smile in their faces, an elderly white couple, all individuals have a warm smile in their faces. Medium-shot of the group fades out and the United Church of Christ logo with red background fades in like a sunrise.

Messaris (1997) explains the importance of visual information to convey meaning in advertising. This following section will explain the meaning behind the images chosen for *Bouncer*. The commercial is broken down by three different phases following a basic narrative structure. "Stable situation 1, situation disrupts (question, enigma, desire, goal) and stable situation 2, resolution" (O'Shaughnessy and Stadler 2005: 23). Stable situation 1: The first half shows bouncers who are working as gatekeepers of the church's gate, or perhaps a metaphor for the gates of heaven. The church-building chosen for the commercial is imposing in its traditional American church architecture but its walls are also old and dirty. It is interesting that in real life the building is not a church but a mausoleum. The tone and feel of the first half of the commercial is somber in the song chosen but also in people's expression, color of clothing and the quality of the bouncer's voice. The bouncer turns people away with no explanation. He knows, and the audience knows, why he is saying "No!" There is a cold, distant determination grounded in tradition which stands behind the bouncer, and also is seen in the church building behind him. The text (character generator) in the middle of the commercial works as a pause (comma), a moment of reflection. Situation disrupts: the words, "Jesus didn't turn people away." "Neither do we," embodies the theological beliefs of the United Church of Christ. Situation 2: the resolution of the commercial opens with uplifting music and smiles on every character's face. There is a warm focus to the pictures. The first shot is like a family portrait showing diversity and unity. The voice-over carries the visuals with warmth and determination in its message of welcome. The logo at the end fades in like a sunset or new beginning for Christianity in a postmodern world.

The commercial takes the audience on an emotional ride from rejection to warm welcome. At a time when Christian conservatives have so successfully colonized American faith and when so many feel alienated by its monolithic way of thinking, the commercial is both provocative and courageous. The UCC's message and the *God is Still Speaking* campaign hit hard at the center of how U.S. mainstream religion has visualized itself. The Church moved away from traditional visuals associated with Christianity to a new system of signs: no longer crosses but commas. It was no longer a statement of dogma but of questions and interpretations. For once, visual culture and Christianity had a representation which was welcoming to gays and lesbians. Conservative Christian institutions which have gained through homophobia and a policy of exclusion were angry about the commercial. The United Church of Christ was labeled "liberal", meaning that its views should be discounted. In the current U.S. political climate "liberal" has meant "radical," "out of touch," and "not to be listened to." There was also some angry criticism directed toward the commercial, as seen in an editorial entitled: "the God Who's Still There: Why Few Mistake Liberal Religion for Christianity." In this editorial Hutchens (2006: 4) writes: "a United Church of Christ kind of God, who hasn't the strength of character to kick anybody out of anywhere, much less out of his churches".

The *Bouncer*, in a superficial reading shows the audience that the United Church of Christ is welcoming to gays and lesbians in its congregations. Visuals in *Bouncer* include gays and lesbians, within the UCC identity. The commercial also works as a parable. Gays and lesbians in the commercial are a metaphor for all who feel unwelcome at church. The closet is in many ways a part of many people's lives, whether gay or straight, white or black. The closet becomes a metaphor for loud silences of unspoken oppressions. Sedgwick (1993: 48) writes that some scholars "refer to the sixties as the decade when blacks came out of the closet." The closet becomes a metaphor for all that we hide from ourselves and each other, the elements of our lives that keep us apart or are not welcomed by others. In a theological reflection written by the Proclamation, Identity and Communication Ministry (United Church of Christ, 2004: 3) the United Church of Christ explains that the *Bouncer* commercial is:

> a metaphor, a modern-day parable. The bouncers on the screen are symbolic of the alienation separating many people from the church. Imagine if Jesus told the commercial's story without the aid of television cameras, actors, music background, voice over narration, and electronic editing. It might sound like this: once there was a Samaritan woman who, seeking spiritual enlightenment, undertook a journey to visit the temple in Jerusalem. Upon arriving at the main gate, she was barred entrance by a scribe and a Pharisee, who said, "we do not allow your kind, a woman and a Samaritan, to set foot within the holy place. Only the righteous and just may enter to receive God's blessing. Be gone." And the woman left, never to return. If I do not turn away the oppressed and the outcast, why should you? God is Still speaking. If you have ears to hear, then listen.

Conclusions

The campaign had a positive impact on the United Church of Christ. In a report on the strategic visioning of the *Stillspeaking* campaign Buford writes that, "the *Stillspeaking* Initiative has provided a language and a brand that lifts up a clear and broadly affirmed strategic vision for the United Church of Christ" (Buford, 2005b: 2). The commercial was successful in reaching the audience. Stations that aired the commercial were, among others, *CNN, CNN Headline News,* and *The History Channel.* I first heard of *Bouncer* when someone from my local church, High Country United Church of Christ, mentioned the advert: "have you seen the UCC ads and the controversy with the networks?" There was a great degree of word of mouth related to the commercial (Elliot, *New York Times,* March 27, 2006). It is estimated that 40 % of the market-place saw the commercial 2 or 3 times even without the national networks (Interview with Ron Buford). The commercial's life still goes on at www.ucc.org where they can be viewed.

By February 2005, the number of visits in the UCC.org website rose from 3,000 a month to 476,670. International visits rose to 24,000 per month. Sales of *Stillspeaking* merchandise reached $431,525 (State of *Stillspeaking,* February 18, 2005: 2). In an 18- month campaign period, the UCC website had 7.1 million visitors and 661,000 visitors tried to find a church near their home. (Gunn, 2006) By September 2005, 42% of UCC congregations had voluntarily joined The *Stillspeaking* Initiative, representing 59% of the church's membership (Buford, 2006: 1). The *Bouncer* commercial won the Association of National Advertisers 2005 Multicultural Excellence Award. Most e-mails were saying "thank you for your courage."

I have argued in this chapter that the United Church of Christ's *God is Still Speaking* Campaign tried to create a brand for the Church that matched its identity. The UCC placed itself in the religious marketplace as a progressive Church. The brand for the Church moved away from traditional signs of Christianity in an attempt to reach its target audience. Despite the refusal by two major national networks to air the *Bouncer* commercial, the little known UCC was able to become visible to the mainstream culture. Through the production and distribution of UCC's brand and through its cohesive and provocative advertising campaign hegemonic representations of gays and lesbians and religion were now being prominently challenged from within the Christian community. Christianity plays a key component in defining homosexuality within American culture (Cobb 2006 and Jakobsen and Pellegrini 2003). The UCC has proved that the definition can be changed through visual expression and branding in the market place of ideas. It is through religious discourse that some of the most violent language against gays and lesbians is articulated within American mainstream culture. Cobb (2006: 7) writes that "religious language has always been part of the strongest, united descriptions of American communities." The United Church of Christ campaign has helped to destabilize conservative Christian discourse. It created a brand that spoke of a God who is alive and still speaking in His acceptance of all. The UCC also broke a symbolic tradition of how gays and lesbians are represented in the media and of how Christianity itself had been represented. Barthes (1982: 213) writes:

> The symbolic consciousness sees the sign in the profound, one might say its geological dimension, since for the symbolic consciousness it is the tiered arrangement of signifier and signified which constitutes the symbol; there is a consciousness of a kind of vertical relation between the Cross and Christianity: Christianity is *under* the Cross, as a profound mass of beliefs, values, practices, more or less disciplined on the level of its form.

Through visual culture and branding, the United Church of Christ was able to create new symbols for what it means to be a Christian. The new symbols and visuals presented through the *God is Still Speaking* campaign helped lift some of the symbolic burdens mentioned by Barthes. The church, grounded in scripture, moved to create new language and symbols that would associate the UCC with a place in which spirituality is alive and where all are invited to be part of God's family. While many denominations are striving to be welcoming of gays and lesbians in the U.S. (Siker, 2007), the United Church of Christ, with its history, was one with the courage to stand up for its convictions. Through the marketplace of ideas, focus groups and branding, the voice of a progressive God was heard in mainstreet America.

Notes

[1]Interviews were carried out as follows: Ron Buford, March 13, 2007; Rev. Robert Chase, January 31, 2007; Marilyn Dubasak, March 14, 2007; Ted Pulton, February 2, 2007 and Michael Jordan, March 26, 2007.

[2] Jim Wallis is president and executive director of *Sojourners* magazine and author of several books including *God's Politics: Why The Right Gets It Wrong and the Left Doesn't Get It; Faith Works: How Faith-based Organizations are Changing Lives, Neighborhoods and America; The Soul of Politics: Beyond "Religious Right" and "Secular Left"* and *Who Speaks for God?: a New Politics of Compassion, Community and Civility,* among other books. Barbara Ehrenreich also has written several books including *Nickel and Dime, Bait and Switch: the (Futile) Pursuit of the American Dream* and *Blood Rites.*

[3] Brand specifications were very clear: PMS colors at PMS 186 C; CMYK Color Breakdowns at Red: C=5, M=100, Y=100, K=5 and Black: C=0, M=0, Y=0, K=0; font for comma should be bodoni, with adobe impact for headlines and franklin gothic for body copy (Buford, 2004a).

References

Armstrong, Richard N., James R. Hallmark and Keith L. Williamson, "Televangelism as Institutional Apologia: the Religious Talk Show as Strategized Text," *Journal of Media and Religion* 4.2 (2005), pp. 67-83.

Barthes, Roland, *Mythologies* (New York: Noonday Press, 1972).

Bass, J., and R. Cherwitz, "Imperial Mission and Manifest Destiny: a Case Study of Political Myth in Rhetorical Discourse," *The Southern Speech Communication Journal* 43 (1978), pp. 213-32.

Bourdieu, Pierre, "Structures, Habitus, Power: Basis for a Theory of Symbolic Power," in eds. Nicholas B. Dirks, Geoff Eley and Sherry B. Ortner, *Culture/Power/History: A Reader in Contemporary Social Theory* (Princeton: Princeton University Press, 1994), pp. 155-99.

Breen, Myles and Farrel Concoran, "Myth in the Television Discourse," *Communication Monographs* 49.2 (1982), pp. 127-36.

Buckingham, David, *Media Education* (Malden: Blackwell, 2003).

Buford, Ron, *God is Still Speaking, Identity Kit – Graphics Toolkit Version 3.0/Ron-in-a-Box Version 2.01,* disk 2 (Cleveland: United Church of Christ, 2004a).

_____, "Creating an Identity Brand," in Buford (2004a) [2004b]

_____, "Letter to Churches", in Buford (2004a) [2004c].

_____, "The Power of Invitation and Welcome", PowerOfInvitationAndWelcome.pdf, in in Buford (2004a) [2004d].

--------, "State of *Stillspeaking*," unpublished internal document, 18 February (Cleveland: United Church of Christ, 2005a).

_____, "Strategic Visioning for the Stillspeaking Initiative," unpublished internal document, 22nd April (Cleveland: United Church of Christ, 2005b).

_____, "Executive summary", unpublished internal document, March (Cleveland: United Church of Christ, 2006).

Calabrese, Andrew, "Toward a Political Economy of Culture," in eds. Andrew Calabrese and Colin Sparks, *Toward a Political Economy of Culture: Capitalism and Communication in the Twenty-First Century* (New York: Rowman and Littlefield Publishers, 2004), pp. 1-12.

Clarke, Scott H., "Created in Whose Image? Religious Characters on Network

Television," *Journal of Media and Religion* 4.3 (2005), pp. 137-53.

Clifford, James, "Introduction: Partial Truths," in eds. James Clifford and George E. Marcus, *Writing Culture: The Poetics and Politics of Ethnography* (Berkeley: University of California Press, 1986), pp. 1-26.

Cobb, Michael, *God Hates Fags: The Rhetorics of Religious Violence* (New York: New York University Press, 2006).

Collins, Catherine Ann, and Sue Rothmyer, "Promotion of the Church: The Church and PSA's," *Religious Communication Today* 4 (1981), pp. 32-36.

Croteau, David, and William Hoynes, *Media Society: Industries, Images and Audiences.* (Thousand Oaks: Pine Forge Press, 2003).

Doty, Alexander. *Making Things Perfectly Queer: Interpreting Mass Culture* (Minneapolis: University of Minnesota Press, 1993).

Elliott, Stuart, "Turning to Mammon to Spread the Gospel," *The New York Times,* 27th March (2006), p. c10.

Fiske, John, *Television Culture* (London: Methuen, 1987).

Foucault, Michel, *History of Sexuality* (New York: Pantheon Books, 1978).

Fuery, Patrick, and Kelli Fuery *Visual Cultures and Critical Theory* (London: Arnold, 2003).

Garnham, Nicholas, "Political Economy and Cultural Studies: Reconciliation or Divorce?" *Critical Studies in Mass Communication* (1995), pp. 62-71.

Gunn, Dorothy, "*Stillspeaking* Ad Buy Resurrected for Easter," *United Church News,* http://www.ucc.org/ucnews, accessed 3rd February 2006.

Hall, Stuart, "The White of Their Eyes: Racism Ideology and Media," in eds. Gail Dines and Jean M. Humez, *Gender, Race and Class in Media: A Text Reader* (Thousand Oaks: Sage, 1995), pp. 18-22.

_____, ed. *Representation: Cultural Representations and Signifying Practices* (Thousand Oaks: Sage, 2002).

Herman, Didi, *The Antigay Agenda: Orthodox Vision and the Christian Right* (Chicago: Chicago University Press, 1997).

Hesmondhalgh, David, "The Production of Media Entertainment," in eds. James Curran and Michael Gurevitch, *Mass Media and Society* (Oxford: Oxford University Press, 2005), pp. 153-71.

Himmelstein, Hal, "Kodak's 'America': images from the American Eden," in ed. Horace Newcomb, *Television: The Critical View* (Oxford: Oxford University Press, 1994), pp. 224-48.

Hunt, Stephen, *The Alpha Enterprise: Evangelism in a Post-Christian Era* (Burlington: Ashgate, 2004).

Hutchens, S. M., "Editorial: the God Who's Still There: Why Few Mistake Liberal Religion for Christianity," *Touchstone: A Journal of Mere Christianity* (2006), pp. 3-4.

Irvine, Janice M., "A Place in the Rainbow: Theorizing Lesbian and Gay Culture," in Seidman (1996), pp. 212-39.

Jagose, Annamarie, *Queer Theory: An Introduction* (New York: New York University Press, 1996).

Jakobsen, Janet R., and Ann Pellegrini, *Love the Sin: Sexual Regulation and the Limits of Religious Tolerance* (New York: New York University Press, 2003).

Jamieson, Kathleen Hall, and Karlyn Kohrs Campbell, *The Interplay of Influence: News, Advertising, Politics, and the Internet* (Belmount: Wadsworth, 2006).

Jhally, Sut, *The Codes of Advertising* (New York: Routledge, 1990).

Kluckhohn, Carl, "The Study of Culture," in eds. D. Lerner and H. D. Laswell, *The Policy Sciences* (Stanford: Stanford University Press, 1951), pp. 12-35.

Koslow, Scott, Sheila L. Sasser and Edward A. Riordan, "Do Marketers Get the Advertising they Need or the Advertising they Deserve: Agency Views of How Clients Influence Creativity," *Journal of Advertising* 35.3 (2006), pp. 81-101.

Linneman, Thomas J., *Weathering Change: Gays and Lesbians, Christians Conservatives and Everyday Hostilities* (New York: New York University Press, 2003).

Lynch, James, "Marketing and the Religious Right: an Application of the Parallel Political Marketplace Conceptualization," *Journal of Public Policy and Marketing* 9.1 (1990), pp. 154-166.

McCleary, Robert F., and Judith E. Saxton, "The Effectiveness of a Media Evangelism Campaign: Factors for Consideration," *Religious Communication Today* 6 (1983), pp. 34-39.

Messaris, Paul, *Visual Persuasion: The Role of Images in Advertising* (Thousand Oaks: Sage, 1997).

Mirzoeff, Nicholas, ed. *The Visual Culture Reader* (New York: Routledge, 1998).

_____, "What Is Visual Culture?" in ed. Mirzoeff (1998), pp. 3-13.

Namaste, Ki, "The Politics of inside/Out: Queer Theory, Poststructuralism and a Sociological Approach to Sexuality," in Seidman (1996), pp. 194-211..

Norris, Michelle, "Lesbian Methodist Minister Defrocked," *Lesbian News* January (2005)
      p. 17.

Olyan, Saul M., and Martha C. Nussbaum, *Sexual Orientation and Human Rights in American Religious Discourse* (Oxford: Oxford University Press, 1998).

O'Shaughnessy, Michael and Jane Stadler, Media and Society: an Introduction (Oxford: Oxford University Press, 2005).

Rogoff, Irit, "Studying Visual Culture," in Mirzoeff (1998), pp. 14-26.

Sayre, Shay, "Images of Freedom and Equality: a Values Analysis of Hungarian Political Commercials," *Journal of Advertising* 23.1 (1994), pp. 97-109.

Scissors, Jack Z. "Another Look at the Question: Does Advertising Affect Values?" *Journal of Advertising* 7.3 (1978), pp. 26-30.

Sedgwick, Eve Kosofsky, "Epistemology of the Closet," in eds. Henry Abelove, Michele Aina Barale and David M. Halperin, *The Lesbian and Gay Studies Reader* (New York: Routledge, 1993), pp. 45-61.

Seidman, Steven, ed. *Queer Theory/Sociology* (Oxford: Blackwell, 1996).

Siker, Jeffrey S., ed. *Homosexuality and Religion: An Encyclopedia* (Westport: Greenwood, 2007).

Stokes, Jane, *How to do Media and Cultural Studies* (Thousand Oaks: Sage, 2003).

Sturken, Marita, and Lisa Cartwright, *Practices of Looking: An Introduction to Visual Culture* (Oxford: Oxford University Press, 2002).

Suarez, Ray, *The Holy Vote: The Politics of Faith in America* (New York: Harper Collins, 2006).

United Church Board for Homeland Ministries, *History and Program - United Church of Christ*, 5th ed. (New York: United Church Press, 1986).

United Church of Christ [Proclamation, Identity and Communication Ministry], *God is Still Speaking: 30 Second TV Commercial: Theological Reflections* (Cleveland: United Church of Christ, 2004).

Wallis, Jim, *God's Politics: Why the Right Gets It Wrong and the Left Doesn't Get It* (San Francisco: Harper, 2005).

Wilson, David, "The U.S. Church that Sold Itself Without Selling its Soul", *United Church (of Canada) Observer* June (2005), pp. 32-5.

Web Sites

www.accessibleairwaves.org
www.adbrands.net
www.gothaminc.com
www.stillspeaking.com
www.ucc.org/god-is-still-speaking

Fig. 16. Lord's Gym, 2007, photography by Amende, used with permission of Cole Bailey, director, the Lord's Gym, Panama Beach, Florida.

Better than Sex:
Working out with Jesus at the Lord's Gym

Kathaleen Amende

In early 2001 I was driving along Interstate 10, through some small towns in eastern Texas where there are more signs for churches than there are for restaurants. It was thus a huge surprise to see, in the middle of this Bible-belt territory, a large billboard advertising what appeared to be a local, male strip-club. As I drove towards the billboard, I could see the well built, long haired hunk who watched out over the road with sultry eyes. His chest was bare and his arms open in flirtatious embrace. It was only when I was practically upon the sign that I saw the banner underneath – a banner advertising an upcoming Easter mass. Yes, my well-built male stripper was in fact Jesus. The crown of thorns, placed lightly on his head like a tiara, was only visible upon up-close scrutiny. Almost immediately, I regretted not stopping to take a picture with my digital camera. At first, I must admit, I found myself wondering who would believe that a church would resort to using a masculinized, sexualized Christ image to draw worshippers (particularly, it would seem at first glance, female worshippers) and even now, years after the sign has been removed, I find myself curious to know if it worked. For it seems that, much to my earlier surprise, that advertising church was not the only institution relying on sex to sell its religious services.

In his critical work *Closet Devotions*, Richard Rambuss (1998) discusses a number of advertising images that combine sexual and religious connotations including one for a "cross" used as furniture for sadomasochistic purposes and flyers given out at a San Francisco gay pride event telling people to "jack off for Jesus." Although his text deals specifically with considerations of sex and religion in medieval devotional literature and art, many of these images he provides as modern day examples of using sex to draw attention to religion and vice versa dovetail interestingly with those used not only by shock groups but by religious groups and organizations themselves. Certainly few (if any) churches are going to suggest one "jack off for Jesus," but there are plenty of organizations such as Christian teen magazines, newsletters, and online "advice sites" that are not afraid to use the same tactics to draw consumers to their products. Oftentimes these same books, magazines, etc. have suggested that one turn to Jesus and imagine Him when sexually aroused with the stated purpose of quelling sexual desire. There is a definite sense, however, that Jesus is the proper conduit for channeling the same sexual energy that might also lead to masturbation. Rambuss, in fact, argues that:

> through an osmosis of eroticism fueling religious affect and religiosity heightening erotic desire, devotion to Christ becomes sexualized, becomes ... a state of the body and its passions, no less than it is an exertion of the soul ... This is to say that religion and sex have done, and still continue to do, each other's affective work (1998: 101).

If religious passion and sexual passion are so affectively similar, then it really is no wonder that religious literature and advertisements will appeal to sexual and physical desires as well. Furthermore, as will become obvious, one of the ways that churches sometimes appeal to people is by trying to place Jesus and the Church itself as the proper receptacle of sexual and romantic desire. Jesus is often painted as not only an appropriate lover, but one who should have full reign over the bodies and hearts of women (and possibly men as well). Finally, even when churches are not explicitly advertising with or referring to sex or bodily images, people are still using church and religion to find such gratification based, in part, on the way they encounter such things. In fact, even if Jesus is not presented as a sexualized being, He still often inspires erotic thoughts – a concept that perhaps the creators of the Jesus billboard had in mind.

MEEK. MILD. AS IF.
Discover the real Jesus. Church. April 4.

Fig. 17. *Meek. Mild. As If!*, 1999, used by permission of Francis Goodwin, Chairman, Churches Advertising Network.

It seems that when it comes to selling religion, as in regular advertising and sales methods – power and sex sell. Not long ago, I came across another Christian billboard, very similar to the one above with a picture of a masculine Jesus, modeled on Che Guevara, under whom the words "Meek Mild As If" stand out in bold, black letters (fig. 17). Next to the image of Jesus were the words "Church: It isn't as churchy as you think." While no one would be surprised to open a popular magazine such as *Vogue*, *Maxim*, or even *GQ* and see a well or skimpily dressed model advertising jewelry, clothing, spirits or foods, it might be more surprising to see such billboards, or to open a church bulletin, Baptist newsletter or youth-oriented magazine and find similar advertisements. The meaning behind such advertising techniques is obvious and well studied: if you use this product, wear this watch, dress in this brand, etc., you will be sexy. Ellen Rosenberg, in her essay "Serving Jesus in the South" (1989), however, shows how a Christian publication, a magazine published by the Women's Missionary Union (a division of the Southern Baptist Convention) aimed mostly at southern women, has urged women to "spread the word as she would if she were involved in a human love affair, telling the world about this person who made her life so special" (1989: 133), and Heather Hendershot (2004) writes of articles in the youth magazines *Brio* and *Breakaway* (published by the Evangelical organization Focus on the Family) that urge teenagers to make their bodies beautiful and strong, not only to glorify God, but because "'members of the opposite sex are keeping an eye on you'" (2004: 105). These magazines provide linguistic analogues to the almost erotic billboard and even if they do not explicitly maintain that readers will increase their sex appeal and/or find sexual gratification and pleasure, the intent and implications are as obvious as the swimsuit model suggesting housewives use BrandX vacuum cleaner to leave time for the "special things" in life. Although the BrandX vacuum cleaner is made up, there is, of course, a long history of using sexual imagery and text to sell products. For a more in-depth pictorial essay of the history of sex in advertising, see Gallup and Robinson (2007).

That sex sells is no surprise to anyone and one of the most obvious uses of sex appeal as advertising is in advertisements for gymnasiums and health and fitness clubs. After all, the stated purpose of such places is to make its clients more healthy *and* more physically appealing not only to themselves but to others as well. One of the most popular of such places is Gold's Gym, an international chain of health clubs centered in the United States but with branches in cities as varied as Sydney, London and Tokyo and in 27 countries including Haiti, Jamaica, India and Hungary. A quick visit to the Gold's Gym website will reveal an ad slogan that Gold's Gym has "40 years of making bodies better, thinner, stronger, faster, harder, tougher, sexier, improved, successful" (www.goldsgym.com). Pictures fill the site with images of young, hard, sexy bodies that hint at what could be a consumer's for only a low cost per month with a one year contract. Gold's Gym, however, is not the only gym offering sexier and healthier bodies for low, low prices. These days, the market has boomed, and the Christian community has claimed its section of this growing market. Many of the so-called "megachurches" in the United States now boast their own gymnasiums that offer the same services as the larger fitness centers. The Hartford Institute for Religion Research defines a "megachurch" as "a very large Protestant congregation usually having 2000 or more persons who attend weekly services" and a constantly active community, usually focused around a charismatic ministry (Thumma, 2007). Preston-wood Baptist Church, Plano, Texas is one of the more famous of these Mega-Churches because of its coverage on ABC News (for instance, see http://abcnews.go.com/GMA/print?id=617341). However, such churches are growing in such numbers that even in my own small city of Montgomery, Alabama there is the Frazier Baptist Church which has its own gymnasium, daycare centers, shopping outlets and so forth.

Beyond these mega-churches, with their built-in consumer base, are other commercial gymnasiums such as the expanding chain "Lord's Gym" who compete with the larger clubs. The Lord's Gym website, however, unlike its competitor's site, does not offer a number of hard bodies lifting weights. Instead, people with a variety of body types are working at various lifting exercises with a promise of fitness "for the whole family." However, the first image to show up on the site *is* a very muscular, toned Jesus bench-pressing a huge cross with "The Sin of the World" written across it (fig. 16). Immediately I find myself remembering the Jesus on the interstate billboard. Here is a Jesus who resembles physically, not just spiritually, someone consumers should want to emulate. This is a Jesus who will not take any nonsense from anyone. It is hard to imagine this Jesus as the often-depicted "effeminate", sacrificing young carpenter who cries tears of blood and meekly submits to His fate. In fact, in some versions of the Lord's Gym logo (as in the one above), Jesus is *sweating* blood as opposed to crying it. And although the site advertises "an atmosphere of Christian fellowship" and "spiritual, mental and physical growth in one setting," it would be hard not to make the comparison between Lord's Gym and Gold's Gym, and to see that both places are using images and promises of leaner, healthier, and sexier bodies to draw customers. In his book *God's Gym*, Stephen Moore (1996) draws a similar comparison when he creates an extended analogy comparing Jesus in the temple to a bodybuilder in his home gym. The "interior Court" filled with "gold" where only "priests" may go to pray is converted to the gym's bodybuilding court filled with iron where only men who are physically fit and ritually garbed may gather to work out. Further, the "wholeness" and "purity" of religious holiness becomes the purity and perfection of body that the bodybuilders seek.

It also is not difficult to find examples of sexually alluring religious materials – or at least materials that seem meant to draw
consumers in through a sexually appealing cover. A simple walk
into the local large bookstore (or even the smaller Christian oriented bookstores) will reveal books with titles such as *Bad Girls of the
Bible, Sex and the Bible, 60 Things God Said About Sex*, and even *Real
Sex: The Naked Truth About Chastity*. These books and many others
jump off of the shelves with covers that depict half-clad or sexily
dressed women from ancient times, or men and women holding
hands or engaged in romantic moments. Whatever the contents of
the books, the covers certainly visually privilege romance, love and
sex, with the aim of drawing consumers (usually women) through
a prurient interest into picking up the text itself. Another interesting example, however, is the controversial "Jesus Loves Porn Stars"
Bible produced by the anti-pornography ministries of XXXChurch.

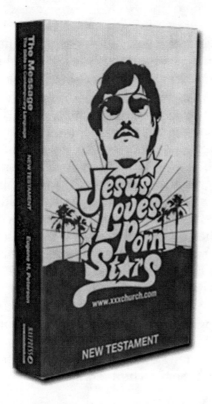

Fig. 18. Cover, Eugene
H. Peterson, *The Mes-
sage: the Bible in Con-
temporary Language:
Jesus Loves Porn Stars,
www.xxxchurch.com,
New Testament* (Colo-
rado Springs: NavPress,
2006).

com (fig. 18: Peterson, 2006). This church, based in Grand Rapids, Michigan and largely made up of internet parishioners has finally found a publisher willing to publish their Bibles with bright pink and yellow covers that read "Jesus Loves Porn Stars," to give out at adult expositions and what they refer to as "porn shows" (http://www.xxxchurch.com). While this particular Bible is perhaps not aimed at a mainstream crowd, it is hard to deny the spark of interest that undoubtedly crops up at its title; nor is it hard to imagine why the church chose to use it. Like other religious advertisers, they intend to pull in consumers by appealing to the individual's prurience and then to make them aware of alternative paths to fulfilling their desires.

One book that stood out, for me, from many of the others was Dee Brestin and Kathy Troccoli's *Falling in Love With Jesus: Abandoning Yourself to the Greatest Romance of Your Life* (2002). In this text, the authors urge women to "understand the amazing parallel that Scripture makes between falling in love on earth and falling in love with Jesus" (2002: 4). Further, the book's advertising blurb reads:

> Dee Brestin and Kathy Troccoli introduce readers to the ultimate love relationship of all time: a relationship with Jesus Christ. Using humor, contemporary love songs, real-life stories, and solid Biblical teaching, Dee and Kathy help women discover a life-changing intimacy with Jesus. No matter your age or marital status, you are His bride, the object of His affection. The secret to an abundant life lies not in ten steps, but in developing a deep love relationship with Jesus, abandoning yourself to the greatest romance of your life! (http://www.amazon.com/gp/product/0849943345).

Once more we are reminded not only of the WMU newsletter, but of the Interstate Jesus with his appealingly handsome features and strong, inviting arms. Especially in the Southern United States where evangelical religions have taken such hold, privileging a personal and close relationship between a woman and Jesus may draw even more worshippers, particularly women who are lacking or craving those relationships in their secular life. Johanna Miller Lewis (1997: 75), moreover, argues that southern evangelicalism's "emphasis on an individual relationship with a loving God... may have appealed to dependent and vulnerable women". Brestin and Troccoli's text may appeal to an even more widespread group of Christian women. Although, interestingly enough, at least one reviewer at the Amazon.com page for the book found the book to be *too* sexually suggestive, arguing that "I personally feel that this book suggests Christ as our Bride-Groom an in UN-PURE way... It's very wrong to suggest we see our Bride-Groom Christ with the same romantic, intimate, etc, eyes as we would our husbands" (http://www.amazon.com/gp/product/084993345). This review, however, was the only one of many that had anything negative to say about the book. The other reviewers felt the book was personal and inspiring and that it would help guide their relationships with Christ. The authors find that they model their relationships with men on their relationships with Jesus, and almost by default, their relationships with Jesus on their relationships with men.

What the authors do not seem to recognize, however, is when women are trained, as they often are even in modern society, to sacrifice themselves for men or to make their bodies pleasing in order to find a mate, this can make such modeling both more complicated. Of course, men are increasingly under the same pressure today, but traditionally this has been the kind of pressure most often asserted over women by both men and other women. In action, it is simple. Women will treat their husbands or lovers as they would treat Jesus – through sacrifice and worship. But in motivation and emotional investment, such a relationship becomes incredibly complicated, particularly when, on the flip side, these same women begin to expect or find quasi or even fully erotic release in prayer, church services, and personal relationships with God. Such an example will be provided shortly.

If theories of sacrifice and submission of the heart, mind and body prevail in Christian's women's literature, the opposite seems to exist in books aimed at men. For example, in *Temptations Men Face*, a book aimed at teaching Christian men how to lead a Christian life and have Christian relationships, the author, Tom Eisenman, promises to tell men "in straightforward language" how they might "fight" and "win the struggle against sin and its power" (1991: 17). The cover of this book depicts a busy city street in the midst of skyscrapers. Its visual focus on a world of business differs from the ever-present focus on emotion and love depicted on women's literature, and men are taught that theirs is an *active* struggle, one they are compelled to fight, and that sin is a "powerful" adversary that they must overcome with "almost no help at all from society" (17). They are taught they must, like a masculine soldier under their general (Jesus), stand and face the onslaught of enemies in order to *actively* create healthy relationships not only to women, but to the world around them. This focus on activity as opposed to submission parallels the secular tendency to ascribe activity to men and passivity to women. Other books such as *No More Christian Nice Guy: When Being Nice—Instead of Good—Hurts Men, Women and Children* by Paul Coughlin and *A Husband After God's Own Heart* also teach men that being a good Christian in a relationship means being the masculine care-taker who *guides* the family, *leads* it, and actively strives to *control* situations instead of submitting to them (emphasis my own). The way they avoid temptations (including sexual ones) is to fight for control, and if they are, as they are in many teen Christian magazines aimed at males, also taught to turn to Jesus, it is through activity rather than through submission. This literature, however, as different as it may seem from that aimed at women, ultimately has the same message – the body and the mind must be controlled. If control for women must come through submission, then for men it must come through action. But in either case, there is an absolute insistence upon it. One is reminded here of Michel Foucault's description in *Discipline and Punish* (1995), of the history of the penal system wherein control and punishment of the body eventually leads to control of the mind. Ultimately, much of this Christian literature serves the same purpose not by punishing the physical body, but by enticing it through promises of gratification in one form or another.

In fact, when we move away from such books to Christian magazines and newsletters, particularly those published in the United States, we find that even without explicit advertising, alternatives to secular searches for sex and romance are nonetheless being advertised, that Jesus is being "sold" as an alternative to sex. While the ministries of "Christian Women for Jesus" at christianwomen. net, suggest that if a woman wants to find a husband she, "attend

church as often as those doors open. Get busy. [She] will hopefully be noticed and approached by a Godly man who admires [her]
walk and obvious love of God" (http://www.christianwomen.net/
marriage.html), most of these magazines and websites, instead of
encouraging man-hunting at church, attempt to provide "alternatives" to extra-marital sexual and romantic entanglements. In general, these alternatives involve missionary work, turning to Jesus, or
devoting oneself to chastity and purity. Flipping through teen-oriented magazines such as *Divo, Breakaway,* and *Brio,* or through any
of the myriad of websites that come up with a quick Google search
for "Christian teen magazines," will show that sex is on the mind of
Christian teenagers no less than it is on the mind of non-Christian
teenagers. In fact, because of the focus on chastity, self-identified
Christian teenagers may think *more* about sex. They want to know
if it is okay to "pet," if it is going too far to kiss, how to find a true
love, when it is right to marry, how to avoid the temptations of pornography and masturbation, and what to do to keep one's mind off
of sex when one is aroused. These magazines all offer very similar
answers: if one is aroused, he or she should think of Jesus. Or,
as Heather Hendershot points out, "magazines, videos, and advice
books urge sexually aroused teens to stymie sexual feeling by picturing the faces of all their relatives, as well as Jesus" (2004: 95). As
she further points out, even if the intention is "simply to make kids
feel guilty, there is also a creepy Oedipal dimension to picturing
your mother's or father's face whenever you are sexually aroused".
This argument can be taken even further, however, when we look at
what happens when teenagers do imagine Jesus instead of their in-
fatuation, or when, as was recommended by the WMU letter above,
women imagine Jesus "as they would a human love affair."

Rosemary Daniell, a Southern writer, living in Savannah, Georgia was a Christian teenager in the 1950s and 60s who not only
heard this advice but internalized it. The author of many poems
and a number of autobiographical writings including *Fatal Flowers:
On Sin, Sex and Suicide in the Deep South* (1980), Daniell grew up
shuffled between Methodist and Baptist churches, depending on
where and with whom she was living. For Daniell, there was never
any question but that Jesus was the ideal man. As a child and
a young adult in the sixties and seventies, Daniell learnt, like the

younger generation who read modern Christian teen magazines, that she must give up all sexual thoughts in favor of chastity and religious virtue. However, because she (and indeed anyone) cannot simply negate her sexuality, she begins unconsciously to merge the image of Christ with that of a mortal erotic partner. The eventual result of this merging was the union of sexual and spiritual love. Daniell ultimately eroticized Christ and exalted her mortal partners simultaneously, sometimes using the Christ figure as a sort of Girardian mediator of sexual eros, and occasionally using sexual expression as a mechanism for coping with the strictures and rulings of religion. She eventually began to sublimate her own sexual feelings by turning them into a desire for Christ and salvation. When, in *Fatal Flowers*, she and her young boyfriend argue, for example, Daniell decides to "dedicate [her] life to Jesus and try to save the lost" (109). By turning her desire for her boyfriend into a desire for Jesus, Daniell subconsciously merged the two male figures at an early age. This merging shows itself when Daniell reveals her childhood fantasies, including one she often had while walking through the dump that had become her private hideaway: "I was suffused with images of Jesus that mixed with a vague sense of arms around me, of flesh rising warmly toward mine" (96). Like most children, the young Daniell is given to fantasizing when alone, but her fantasies are ones of a *physical* melding with Jesus. According to Daniell, the idea of sexual desire was "tied into [her] mind, at the time, with the image of Jesus because He was such a large part of the role of goodness." With her unconscious (or, one might even say, conscious) eroticization of Christ, she retained a central fantasized male body and found, in her religion, both spiritual *and* sexual expression, rather than one instead of the other.

In an article seemingly aimed at a young Daniell, Lisa Anne Wiggett (2005) wrote in *Brio* Magazine (a magazine aimed at females), that "you *can* have what you're looking for; you'll find it in the arms of Jesus" and that "When the time is right, you'll be able to recognize a godly guy because he'll treat you like Jesus does – like the priceless treasure you are". She encouraged girls to think of chastity and pre-marital abstention not as "time you have to endure," but "a time that God has you all to himself". It hardly seems surprising that, given these admonitions and advice, girls would find themselves turning, as Daniell did, to ideas of purification and redemption through a perfect relationship with Jesus. Furthermore, if teenagers and pubescent girls, as hormonally driven as they already are, are singularly focused on Jesus as a romantic partner, it seems even less surprising that they would also eventually focus their libidinal passion and desires upon Jesus. In the evangelical churches of the last decade or two, more and more teenagers are being encouraged to turn themselves over to Jesus and in large celebratory events, to declare their chastity and purity. In the 1990s, the "re-virgination" movement began, a movement dedicated to the idea of a second virginity for girls (and boys) who have had pre-marital sex. The idea is that by giving up sexual activity and committing oneself to chastity before marriage, a person can claim to be a virgin once more. Huge events such as the "True Love Waits" revivals and other "Chastity Celebrations" are often full of music, dancing and mixed-gender mingling that would seem almost to belie the reason for the celebration. In fact, Heather Hendershot, in examining Christian Rock Music Concerts, some of which are designed to celebrate chastity, points out that "reviewers of [Christian rock music] concerts consistently note a writhing ecstasy among aroused concertgoers that clearly defies any dualistic conception of body and spirit where music is concerned" (2004: 39). The Church, in its desire to steer teens away from sexual and physical behavior, often seems to be, she argues, sanctioning "the very behavioral traits... that supposedly compel unchaste behavior" (2004: 92-93). Hendershot here is making a point about more than just the Purity Balls where fathers offer their daughters "purity rings" instead of engagement rings, and more than just concerts where "writhing in ecstasy" occurs. She is also making an argument about the very traits that magazines and newsletters encourage in boys and girls. Her focus on *Brio* and *Breakaway* highlight the ways in which girls are trained to be romantic and 'soft', passive to the world around them, while boys are trained to be 'hard' and aggressive (2004: 92-93). These traits, she argues, will lead to sexual behavior (boys will be aggressive and girls will submit to that aggression), but the church encourages them nonetheless. I argue that the Church, in encouraging these traits, is also attempting to control them, refocusing them on "proper" conduits including chastity and purification for the sake of Jesus and, for boys, offering them gymnasiums, weight classes, skating parties and other physically oriented social outlets where they may *actively* pursue interests that will lead them away from temptations and towards desirable forms of spiritual and physical control.

What becomes interesting, beyond the ways that religious bodies consciously attempt (often, as we have seen, unsuccessfully) to manipulate sexual desire into spiritual desire, is the way that they can themselves unconsciously mingle the sexual and the spiritual, creating, within the very church buildings themselves, sexualized spaces. In looking at traditional Protestant services in the United States, Critic Margaret Wolfe explains that:

> Religious services... provided social outlets for young and old alike, and temptation often lurked nearby. Lusty youths particularly valued churchgoing for the assistance it lent to courting. Evening services had the additional advantage of providing them with cover of darkness as they played the gallants escorting fair members of the opposite sex to the safety of their homes. (1997: 115)

Church services, such as revivals, have also presented youth with not only an opportunity for clandestine sexual activity but also for "proper" passionate outpourings. Typically revivals involve singing, dancing, jumping up and down and crying out on the part of the revivalists. Physical activity is not only allowed, but even encouraged and, in some instances, can result in speaking in tongues or dancing with wild abandon. In some smaller, rarer sects the handling of snakes is part of a wild, physical celebration of life and Jesus, and the pastors expect and encourage spiritual ecstasy as part of the service. These are the times when passion, celebration and even physical exertion and expression are properly channeled. Of course, as Lee Smith points out, more often than not the physical expression doesn't end with the service. Talking about a boyfriend she once had in West Virginia, she writes: "I would go to the revival with him and be saved – constantly. So religion and sex – you know, excitement, passion – were all together. I couldn't differentiate between sexual passion and religious passion. This was what we all did on dates, was go to the revival. It was a turn-on" (Smith, 2001: 46). Like the teenagers at Christian Music festivals and chastity celebrations, these kids have found a way to manipulate the sacred in favor of the secular, and have ended up inadvertently combining them into one.

The music and words of the services within the churches help to enhance these sexualized spaces. While, for Catholic children, the near-naked Jesus on the cross may be the first unclothed male form they encounter and may thus subconsciously be subsumed into early erotic fantasies, the same could not be said of Protestant churches, many of which are empty of all icons and images. When talking of southern Baptist churches, sociologist Miles Richardson (1995: 14) explains that:

> Having stripped the meeting place of all statues and crucifixes, having renounced all sacraments and having introduced ordinances whose message is 'purely symbolic and free of magic,' and having secularized their meetings and having reduced the hand to a metaphor, the Baptists opt for the word.

The Baptist religion, like many of its evangelical counterparts, is concerned not with iconography but rather with words; thus, it seems paramount to look at the words being said and sung in these churches. It is, however, also valuable to remember that words and images are inextricably linked. Jacques Lacan, among others, reminds that humans do not think in words but rather in images and these images can have a powerful influence on the way people think and formulate reality. Religion theorist Susan Tamke develops this idea, explaining:

> our perception of reality is formed by the images in our minds. The images we carry with us locate us in time and space, they make the unknown concrete, they express symbolically our affective experiences ... Insofar as human beings are rational creatures, their behavior is directed by the complex of images carried within the mind (1978: 155).

The images that children within a Protestant context are likely to internalize are ones of sensuality, blood, pain, ecstasy, and sacrifice. The hymns sung in these churches are filled with imagery of Christ as a lover, savior, and martyr. In "Just as I Am," Charlotte Elliot's hymn for example, Christ is the redeemer whose "blood can cleanse" and "relieve" (Methodist Book Concern, 1935: 6-7). Similarly, in Francis Xavier's "My God, I Love Thee!" Jesus is the lover who suffers for His beloved – and in particular is penetrated and bleeding for his lover: "But, O my Jesus, Thou didst me // Upon the cross embrace; // For me didst bear the nails and spear, // And manifold disgrace" (1935: 5-8). And in Paul Gerhardt's "Jesus, Thy Boundless Love," singers beg Jesus to "knit my thankful heart to Thee // and reign without a rival there" (1935: 3-4). Here the singer begs Jesus to come to his or her heart and then refuses all others, allowing no one to come before Jesus and implying that He is the only or supreme lover that the singer should or will ever know. Indeed, Jesus is often considered the *only* proper outlet for emotions. Religious theorist Sandra Sizer asserts that within hymns messages were sent that "the individual by relying on Jesus achieves inward control to counter the turbulent world and his own evil passions; strength is generated internally by gaining control of emotions, turning them into positive forces by focusing them on Jesus alone" (1978: 34). It is this inner control (through Jesus) that the Church and Christian-themed businesses offer as being appropriate and proper. And, in many ways, this is what organizations such as *Focus on the Family*, through their youth oriented magazines and the numerous Christian teen and Christian women websites, want to see applied to physical control of the body and sex as well. If sex and the body are "turned over" to Jesus, then physical control can be had in the same way that inner, emotional control can be gained by focusing one's emotions on Jesus alone.

Mental images of Jesus' crucifixion, His pain on the cross, and His redeeming blood overlap with the idea of Jesus as lover to create a highly sensualized, eroticized space within the church. Indeed, Sizer argues that the lyrics of these hymns help to convey that "[t]he secret of [Jesus'] saving power lies in a movement inward, not only toward shelter and refuge with Jesus and/or in heaven, but to a realm of intimacy" (1978: 33). Tamke further explains, "images of wounds, blood, and pain are particularly frequent in the early evangelical hymnbooks because of the evangelical emphasis on the individual's personal relationship to God through the mediation of Christ's sacrifice" (1978: 140). One such hymn by William Cowper, "There is a Fountain Filled with Blood," tells believers that by bathing in the blood of Christ, or by accepting the sacrifice of Christ, they will be saved from damnation:

> There is a fountain filled with blood,
> Drawn from Immanuel's veins,
> And sinners, plunged beneath that flood,
> Lose all their guilty stains (Methodist Book Concern, 1935: 1-4).

This hymn, among others, may well have been one of those sung by Daniell, who mentions that, in church, "we sang hymns about the Blood of the Lamb and what worms we were" (1997: 47).

Images of sacrifice would, of course, be common experiences for women who have been and still are in many cases taught to sacrifice their own happiness and erotic fulfillment for the sake of their men. But within religious arenas, sacrifice was regularly tied to the image of the physical body.[1] The most obvious of these images is that of Christ's sacrifice through not only the crucifixion itself, but also the wounds and openings in Christ's body. Although Baptists have rejected overt iconography associated with the crucifixion, they continue to emphasize the importance of this imagery in hymns and biblical readings. Tamke explains that "the core of the gospel message… was the promise of salvation brought by Christ. The Cross was, therefore, an image of overwhelming importance in evangelical hymns. Evangelical hymnbooks are filled with hymns describing the crucifixion or adoring the crucified Christ" (1978: 37). These hymns, she continues, are filled with "emotional intensity" and "almost amatory physiological details". Even within the church service, with its "safe" hymns, people are offered salvation and redemption through what is, in essence, the physical body. Though, as we have seen, it is a physical body that must be controlled, limited and shaped towards only proper outlets and expressions, those outlets often being the ones that the Church itself offers.

This idea of "control" of the physical body leads us back to the Lord's Gym fitness club. In his groundbreaking *Discipline and Punish*, Foucault (1995) made the strong argument that authorities have increasingly attempted to assert authority over the populace through control of the body. With its ever-present but unseen "watchers," society has exerted the power to make individuals behave in certain ways for fear of being seen acting otherwise. Christian denominations and sects, particularly evangelical ones, provide a compelling example of this technique. Many studies have been carried out into the ways in which purity and chastity have been used, for centuries, to control females within society. In particular, feminist author Susan Bordo (1993) argues that, through advertisements and other visual forms of media, women have been convinced that their bodies are in need of control. In a Foucauldian reading of such media, she presents a history of women's relationships with their bodies that has led to such disorders as bulimia and anorexia nervosa. Furthermore, in a sociological reading of the history of women's "deviance," Edwin M. Schur (1984) shows how, historically, women have been trained to control their sexual urges and desires for fear of being "deviant." In addition, in Jagger and Bordo (1989) and Vance (1984), a number of writers including Susan Bordo, Carol Vance and Patricia Murphy Robinson have provided essays that trace the history of women's sexual repression as a result of societal and patriarchal pressure and the creation of feminine "norms" of sexuality.

Virginity has traditionally been highly prized and, in generations past, could bring a higher price to a family for their daughter. Controlling what a girl could do with her body allowed males to retain authority and dominance within society and within the family. The contemporary focus on chastity and physical control of one's body brings us full circle and back to the gymnasium. For what is a gymnasium's use if not to control and limit one's body? To enhance what is "good" and dispel what is "bad"? What is bad is what is out-of-control: fat, flab, loose muscles, these are bad. They show a lack of control over our own bodies. But muscles, slender proportions and strength – these show that we are in control of our own bodies. And if we are in control of our bodies, then we, presumably, can be in control of our thoughts and our actions, or so the argument would seem to go. Although chastity initiatives seem mostly aimed at females, the lessons of bodily control and strength would seem to appeal mostly to boys and men who are fostered to be "aggressive" and "strong." Even if we ignore evangelical culture for the moment and focus on secular culture, we can see that body-building has traditionally been aimed at males. But extrapolating from this, and looking at the Church's technologies of control, we can see that both women and men are, through differing rhetorical strategies, taught that the physical body must be controlled and restrained. Girls are taught, in magazines such as *Brio* and *Justine*, that being slender, looking pretty and wearing the right fashion and makeup are just as vital for Christian girls as they are for non-Christian girls. And, of course, the way to achieve these things is through Jesus, Christian worship and exercise.

Certain churches and faith-based businesses, much like their secular counterpoints, are attempting to corner mainstream consumers by appealing not only to sex, but also to anxieties concerning gender, the body and its connection to sexuality. By offering Jesus as both the premier example of the all-important control of the body and as the proper alternative to lust, these groups are appealing to both males and females via methods aimed at ensuring the sacralization of body-image, gender expectations and sexual desire. It is only by appealing to the sexual urges of people that they can even show that a Christian alternative for fulfillment of such urges even exists. The Interstate Jesus, the Porn-Star Bible, the books and magazines aimed at females in search of meaningful relationships, these are all ways and means through which churches and religious businesses make their "profit" (and such profit may be counted in both money and converts). Sex definitely sells, even, perhaps especially, when salvation is the product.

Notes

[1] What is interesting here, and certainly worth further study, is that, despite the previously mentioned articles, books and other attempts at "masculinizing" male Christians, these images and hymns still invite viewers/listeners to think of

Jesus as an erotic partner – a troubling idea when we consider that boys and men are given the same invitation within the church space. This is made more troubling, of course, by the Christian insistence that men will not find other men erotically appealing. Perhaps this is why, in the long run, such methods of control and sites of Christian meaning have ultimately appealed more to women than to men, and why more and more "masculine" outlets, focusing on improving one's own body, are being provided for the Christian male.

References

ABC News, "Mega-Churches Offer Prayer, Play, Shopping," http://abcnews.go.com/GMA/Business/story?id=617341andpage=1, accessed 18 February, 2007.

Althaus-Reid, Marcella, *Indecent Theology: Theological Perversions in Sex, Gender and Politics* (London: Routledge, 2000).

Bordo, Susan. "The Body and the Reproduction of Femininity: a Feminist Appropriation of Foucault," in eds. Jagger and Bordo (1989), pp 13-23.

_____, *Unbearable Weight: Feminism, Western Culture, and the Body* (Berkeley: University of California Press, 1993).

Brestin, Dee and Kathy Troccoli, *Falling in Love With Jesus: Abandoning Yourself to the Greatest Romance of Your Life.* (Nashville: W. Publishing Group, 2002).

Burrow, Lynn, "Marriage Choices for Single Women", *Christian Women for Jesus Ministries, Inc.,* http://www.christianwomen.net/marriage.html, accessed 10 March 2006

Coughlin, Paul T., *No More Christian Nice Guy: When Being Nice –Instead of Good—Hurts Men, Women and Children* (Minneapolis: Bethany House, 2005).

Daniell, Rosemary, *A Sexual Tour of the Deep South* (New York: Holt, Rinehart and Winston, 1978).

_____, *Fatal Flowers: on Sin, Sex, and Suicide in the Deep South* (New York: Holt, Rinehart and Winston, 1980).

_____, *The Woman Who Spilled Words All Over Herself: Writing and Living the Zona Rosa Way.* (Boston: Faber and Faber, 1997).

Dutton, Kenneth R, *The Perfectible Body: the Western Ideal of Male Physical Development* (London: Cassell, 1995).

Eisenman, Tom, *Temptations Men Face: Straightforward Talk on Power, Money, Affairs, Perfectionism, Insensitivity* (Downers Grove: Intervarsity Press, 1991).

Farnham, Christie Anne, ed. *Women of the American South: a Multicultural Reader* (New York: New York University Press, 1997).

Foucault, Michel, *Discipline and Punish: the Birth of the Prison,* trans. Alan Sheridan (New York: Vintage, 1995).

Gallup and Robinson, "Sex in Advertising," http://www.galluprobinson.com/tableofcontents.html, accessed 18 August 2007.

George, Jim, *A Husband after God's Own Heart: 12 Things that Really Matter in Your Marriage* (Eugene: Harvest House Publishers, 2004).

Hartford Institute for ReligionResearch, "Megachurches," http://hirr.hartsem.edu/megachurch/megachurches.html, accessed 10 March 2006.

Hendershot, Heather, *Shaking the World for Jesus: Media and Conservative Evangelical Culture* (Chicago: University of Chicago Press, 2004).

Jagger, Alison M. and Susan R. Bordo, eds. *Gender/Body/Knowledge: Feminist Reconstructions of Being and Knowing* (New Brunswick: Rutgers University Press, 1989).

Lacan, Jacques, *The Language of the Self: The Function of Language in Psychoanalysis* (Baltimore: Johns Hopkins Press, 1968).

Lewis, Johanna Miller, "Equality Deferred, Opportunity Pursued: the Sisters of Wachovia," in Farnham (1997), pp. 74-89.

Lord's Gym [for profit], http://lordsgym.biz, accessed 15 March 2006.

Lord's Gym [not for profit], http://lordsgym.org, accessed 15 March 2006.

Mathews, Holly F., ed. *Women in the South: an Anthropological Perspective,* Southern Anthropological Society Proceedings 22 (Athens: The University of Georgia Press, 1989).

Methodist Book Concern, *The Methodist Hymnal* (Nashville: Whitmore and Smith, 1935).

Moore, Stephen, *God's Gym* (New York: Routledge, 1996).

_____, *God's Beauty Parlor and Other Queer Spaces in and Around the Bible* (Stanford: Stanford University Press, 2001).

Peterson, Eugene H., *The Message: the Bible in Contemporary Language: Jesus Loves Porn Stars, www.xxxchurch.com, New Testament* (Colorado Springs: NavPress, 2006).

Pevey, Carolyn, Christine L. Williams and Christopher G. Ellison, "Male God Imagery and Female Submission: Lessons from a Southern Baptist Ladies' Bible Class," *Qualitative Sociology* 19.2 (1996), pp. 173-193.

Rambuss, Richard, *Closet Devotions* (Durham: Duke University Press, 1998).

Richardson, Miles, "Speaking and Hearing (in Contrast to Touching and Seeing) the Sacred," in White and White (1995), pp. 13-22.

Robinson, Patricia Murphy, "The Historical Repression of Women's Sexuality," in Vance (1984), pp. 251-266.

Rosenberg, Ellen M., "Serving Jesus in the South: Southern Baptist Women under Assault from the New Right," in Matthews (1989), pp. 122-135.

Schur, Edwin M., *Labeling Women Deviant: Gender, Stigma, and Social Control* (Philadelphia: Temple University Press, 1984).

Sizer, Sandra, *Gospel Hymns and Social Religion: the Rhetoric of Nineteenth-Century Revivalism* (Philadelphia: Temple University Press, 1978).

Smith, Lee, *Conversations with Lee Smith*, ed. Linda Tate (Jackson: University Press of Mississippi, 2001).

Tamke, Susan, *Make a Joyful Noise Unto the Lord: Hymns as a Reflection of Victorian Social Attitudes* (Athens, Ohio: Ohio University Press, 1978).

Thumma, Scott, "Exploring the Megachurch Phenomena: their Characteristics and Cultural Context," the Hartford Institute for Religion Research, http://hirr.hartsem.edu/megachurch/megachurches.html, accessed 10 March 2006

Vance, Carole S., ed. *Pleasure and Danger: Exploring Female Sexuality* (Boston: Routledge and Kegan Paul, 1984).

White, O. Kendall and Daryl White, eds. *Religion in the Contemporary South: Diversity, Community and Identity*, Southern Anthropological Society Proceedings

28 (Athens, Georgia: University of Georgia Press, 1995).

Wiggett, Lisa Ann, "Relationships: the Long Road," *Brio*, October (2005), pp. 14-17.

Wolfe, Margaret Ripley, "Waiting for the Millennium, Remembering the Past: Appalachian Women in Time and Place," in Farnham (1997), pp. 165-188.

Wolkomir, Michelle. "'Giving it up to God': Negotiating Femininity in Support Groups for Wives of Ex-Gay Christian Men," *Gender and Society* 18 (2004), pp. 735-755.

Websites

www.goldsgym.com
lordsgym.biz
lordsgym.com
www.xxxchurch.com

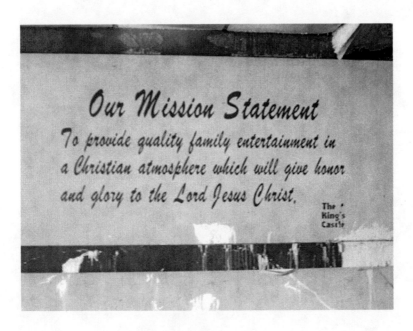

Fig. 19. Heritage USA, Mission statement.

Selling a "Disneyland for the Devout":
Religious Marketing at Jim Bakker's Heritage USA

Darren E. Grem

Televangelist Jim Bakker's Heritage USA opened in Fort Mill, South Carolina in 1978 and closed eleven years later along with the rest of his Praise the Lord (PTL) organization. Promoted as a Christian amusement park and resort, Heritage USA strived to "provide quality family entertainment in a Christian atmosphere" which gave "honor and glory to the Lord Jesus Christ" (fig. 19). Initially, this endeavor was a success. By 1986, it was the third most popular theme park in the nation behind Walt Disney World and Disneyland, attracting six million visitors per year. Between 1986 and 1988, however, Bakker's financial and sexual improprieties damaged the park's reputation, and, in 1989, it folded along with the rest of his PTL organization.

While the park was open, Bakker's critics cast Heritage USA as a particularly unfortunate example of religious kitsch. "Interesting that the same God who inspired the cathedral at Chartres, Westminster Abbey and the Sistine Chapel also inspired this," wrote humorist P. J. O'Rourke, "that Big Guy Upstairs can be a real kidder." The park made a similar impression on journalist Hunter James, who covered Bakker's downfall for the *Atlanta Journal and Constitution*. To James, the "fetid, cloying stench of PTL wholesomeness and good fellowship" was the park's defining characteristic. "You could tell instantly that it was no place for a fellow who wanted to be alone in a crowd." (O'Rourke, 1988: 93 and James, 1993: 8 and 14).

Curiously, scholars have been scarcely more insightful than these critics when considering the broader implications of Heritage

USA. The park receives mention in several studies of televangelism but has rarely been considered an important subject in and of itself. Only one essay examines Heritage USA in any meaningful detail, but this essay's focus on the park's "sacralization" of consumption overlooks its significance as a site of religious production and marketing as well. In turn, it presumes that Bakker's attempt at creating a "heaven on earth" mainly represented the intersection between "televangelism, neo-fundamentalism, and the religious right" (O'Guinn and Belk, 1989: 227). In its heyday, Heritage USA represented much more.

In fact, Bakker did not market Heritage USA as a place that strongly encouraged evangelicals to engage in a protracted political fight against "secular" American culture (a common goal of other televangelists, neo-fundamentalists, and the religious right). Rather, Bakker attempted to use Heritage USA to tap into another pervasive and long-standing desire among American evangelicals: the desire for conversions and spiritual refreshment through recreation, private space, and the consumption of "Christian" goods and experiences. Indeed, Bakker sold the park as *the* vacation destination for evangelical Christians, a theme park that outshined the rest because, from entrance to exit, it presented Christian values to the fullest and made them attractive to believer and non-believer alike.

Yet, as this essay shows, Bakker's marketing strategy did not always work as intended. Not all of Heritage USA's visitors consumed the park's amenities in an orderly or predictable fashion. Many walked away less encouraged in their faith and less willing to convert than Bakker might have liked; others found that Bakker's marketing program seemed to undercut the park's high ideals, excluding or suppressing elements that could not or would not adhere to its prescriptive list of Christian values. In light of these considerations, Heritage USA takes on new significance, seeming less like the peculiar venture of an eccentric televangelist and more like an especially revealing example of the uncertain process of religious marketing itself, a process that continues to inform much of contemporary evangelical culture in America.

In general, historians, sociologists, and other students of American religion see the two decades leading up to the 1980s as an era defined by a new evangelical impulse, one that engaged the nation's political culture head-on. According to the standard historical assessment, these years birthed the sentiments that would animate the political charges of the religious right and their supporters. But public engagement was not the only option available to American evangelicals at the time. During these years, evangelicals also built an alternative culture, one that allowed them to safely practice the values of family and faith that modern life seemed to question. By no means did evangelicals fully withdraw from "secular" culture; rather, many opted to sanitize America's "secular" consumer and recreational culture, to clean it of its seemingly sinful nature and reuse it to edify themselves and evangelize the "lost."

This attempt at sanitizing American culture had numerous expressions in modern evangelicalism. For instance, across the country after World War II, recreational facilities popped up behind countless evangelical sanctuaries. Fund-raising drives fueled the construction of these facilities, and evangelical churchgoers had no illusions about what their contributions were buying. As one southern Baptist at mid-century put it, evangelicals were not merely contributing to their church but buying "programs which hold high the ideals of the Christian faith. Recreation and entertainment, yes, but Christian recreation at its best – if you please" (Warren, 1956). This impulse also fueled the growth of the contemporary Christian culture industry, which grew from its meager origins in the 1960s and 1970s to become a billion dollar business by the 1990s, one that included Christian music, Christian book and magazine publishing, Christian film production, and even Christian tour bus lines (Hendershot, 2004). Of course, like Christian music itself, the contemporary Christian culture industry became remarkably splintered, as both its producers and its consumers approached it as entertainment, art, ministry and business (Howard and Streck, 2004). Still, regardless of its use and purpose, much of the Christian culture industry's commercial growth undoubtedly resulted from its ability to strengthen the faith of its evangelical audience in a way that secular culture – and sometimes, even their own churches – never could.

From the start, Bakker designed Heritage USA as yet another one of these Christian alternatives. Selecting land outside the small town of Fort Mill, South Carolina, just across the state line from the metropolis of Charlotte, Bakker broke ground on the first phase of Heritage USA in 1978. Bakker waxed hyperbolic during interviews about the park, calling it "the greatest project ever in the history of Christianity" (Shepard, 1989: 92). While in reality it was little more than a twenty-five acre campground, to Bakker, who participated in "almost every conceivable aspect of [its] construction and planning," it was a recreational park that brought "the Christian campground up to the 20th century" (Griffin, 1982: 5 and Woodward, 1986: 47). By casting the park in this way, Bakker attempted to meet the demand of American evangelicals for temporary withdrawal from the work-a-day world, a desire that had prompted the Christian summer camps and weekend retreats of many an evangelical Church for decades. And yet, "aware that lifestyle was changing in 20th century America," as one Heritage USA publication noted, "Jim knew that drab, outmoded campgrounds would no longer appeal to Christians who were taking their vacations in clean, modern, well-planned but secular theme parks and recreation centers" (*Heritage Village Church*, 1986: 91 and O'Guinn, 1989: 235). To keep up with the competition, Bakker intentionally made the grounds and buildings at the campground rustic in appearance while up-to-date and convenient in all other aspects. Cable television and phone hook-ups were available free of charge while an open-air tram offered guests an easy ride "to shady hiking spots, an Olympic-sized pool, eight lighted tennis courts… [and] a general store and gas station that [sold] PTL Frisbees, T-shirts and sun visors" (Yancey, 1979: 30). Bakker kept prices for tent sites and RV trailer spots to less than twenty dollars a night, but, for his more affluent guests, the campground also offered log chalets that overlooked a nearby lake and rented for $150 per night. By supplying the campground with such amenities, Bakker sold his fledgling campground-resort as a healthy, comfortable, Christian alternative to other, more "secular" vacation destinations, a retreat where evangelical visitors would not only be entertained and edified, but potentially encouraged to bring their non-evangelical friends to join in on the fun.

When Bakker began drawing up plans for the park's second phase in the early 1980s, the same sensitivity toward offering invigorating, Christian alternatives informed its conceptualization and construction. This time Disneyland, rather than outdated Christian campgrounds, served as his inspiration. "Why is it we can almost enshrine a Mickey Mouse or a Donald Duck?" Bakker asked, "Why can't we have something where young people will be connected to Jesus Christ?" Given the dearth of such places, Bakker wanted his park to become a "Total Living Center" because he believed "that the Christian family needs a place where they can not only have a good vacation, but their family's needs will be met, their marriages can be put together, [and] teenagers can find help with whatever problems they have" (Shepard, 1989: 291-292). As a Total Living Center, the visual and recreational experiences at his park would likewise serve the double purpose of evangelizing those outside the Christian fold. As Bakker put it:

> Jesus said, basically, that we were to be fishers of men. And with some of the bait that we have used in the church – I call it dill-pickle religion – I've never seen anyone catch a fish with a dill pickle and sourpuss religion... The thing that I have resented in the past is that somehow there is almost an unseen force that says religion has to be boring and dull and dreary. And I rebel against that. I think true religion is a relationship with Jesus Christ... It should be beautiful, it should be creative (ibid.).

Heritage USA – as Bakker now termed his Total Living Center – would thus be better than Disneyland, the supposedly "happiest place on earth." For non-evangelicals, it would ideally attract them to evangelical Christianity. For evangelicals, it would offer them what they had always wanted, a cleaned-up version of the all-American vacation. And, as they arrived at Heritage USA, many evangelicals found that the park offered sanitized versions of nearly everything else as well. As a result, as Heritage USA's Vice-President Neal Eskelin told Newsweek two years after the park's second phase opened, "Bible-believing, Christ-loving people think they've found nirvana here" (Woodward, 1986: 46).

Between 1981 and 1987, Heritage USA became the "Total Living Center" of Bakker's imagination. Funded by a Maryland savings and loan agency and contributions from PTL's television audience (and kept afloat by the shady accounting of Bakker and his associates), the complex grew from a modest campground site into a sprawling 2,300-acre Christian resort (Shepard, 1989: 255 and Schmidt, 1985: 8A). By 1986, it attracted six million visitors per year and had a full-time staff of two thousand, making it the second largest employer in the Charlotte metro area (Cran and Tepper, 1987). A central attraction, to be sure, was Bakker himself and the television studio on campus, from which PTL broadcast live nearly every day. But Heritage USA offered much more than just a chance to watch Bakker work his televangelistic magic. The resort also granted its visitors numerous recreational and consumptive opportunities, all intended to reaffirm their faith or invite them to convert and become "born again." Whether they walked down the concourse at Heritage USA's indoor mall, exercised at the state-of-the-art recreational facility, tubed down the slides at the Heritage Island water park, or strolled the park's Disneyesque Main Street, the park's visitors witnessed everywhere either visual reminders of their identity as evangelical Christians or visual arguments for the verity of evangelical belief and tradition (fig. 20 and fig. 21).

Fig. 20. Heritage USA, Main street shopping concourse, publicity material.

Fig. 21. Heritage USA, Heritage Island waterpark, publicity material.

Calling Heritage USA the "biggest bargain family vacation in Dixieland," one travel reporter noted that it was "an exciting moment when guests approach[ed] the... resort in its national park setting" (Mitchell, 1982: 78). Undoubtedly inspired by the simple entrances at various national parks, a rather unassuming wooden sign, cozily placed among a well-manicured and colorful flowerbed, welcomed visitors to the park. Admission was free, but visitors still needed to check in at the park's gatehouse for maps, parking passes, and other hospitality fare. One critic joked that the gatehouse looked like "a colonial Williamsburg turnpike toll plaza," but the gatehouse's design was purposeful and meaningful (O'Rourke, 1988: 92). Its placement at the park's entrance created a sense of security and exclusiveness that "secular" theme parks like Disneyland regularly invoked. As Megan Rosenfeld, a reporter for the *Washington Post*, noted, the gatehouse presented itself as the last stop before entering "a trash-free, profanity-free, sin-free zone" that intimated a "reassuring and comfortable atmosphere that comes from crowds of people secure in the knowledge that on most issues they think alike" (Rosenfeld, 1986: H1).

Once inside the park, visitors encountered additional examples of Bakker's extensive borrowing from Disney culture. For instance, Main Street Heritage USA, a twenty-five store shopping complex, was an unabashed copy of Disneyland's pastel-splashed, faux-Victorian Main Street USA. Though Heritage USA's Main Street included the additional attraction of a covered concourse, it differed little from Disney's original, at least at a glance. Both were a homage to idyllic small town life, which Bakker saw as a central part of his 1950s upbringing and many other evangelicals believed to be a casualty of the 1960s' social upheavals (Kopkind, 1987: 175-183). Both featured a litter-free, crime-free, worry-free downtown of years past, restored to its imagined former glory. As at Disneyland, the colors of the buildings – yellow, pink, green, purple – invoked a feeling of freshness and frivolity. Food and souvenir shops similarly dotted the Bakker's Main Street, inviting guests to sample "your daily bread" from Der Bakker Bakkery or take home a bottle of perfume from the Heavenly Scents shop. Each November, Heritage's Main Street even donned Christmas flair to rival Disneyland and Walt Disney World's annual holiday celebration, thereby signaling that Bakker's imitation of Disney culture was a year-round affair (English, 1987: 8A and Albert, 1998: 30).

Bakker, however, believed his Main Street trumped Disney's because it also took cues from modern American evangelical culture, thus making it, in the words of one reporter, a "Disneyland for the Devout" (Woodward, 1986: 46). Like an increasing number of shopping centers around the country, Heritage USA's Main Street concourse contained shops specifically aimed at a Christian clientele. At Heritage USA's Christian bookstore, Bibles in nearly every available size, color, and translation lined the shelves of the bookstore. Customers even had the chance to have their Bibles personalized with 24-carat gold lettering. Numerous selections from the Christian publication industry were also available for purchase. Jim and Tammy Faye Bakker's spiritual guides *You Can Make It!* and *I Gotta Be Me* received special display, but the Bakkers did not have a monopoly on the store's shelf space. Other inspirational literature was featured : notably *The Exodus Diet Plan*, the spiritual biographies of Roy Rogers and Dale Evans, and sermons by Billy Graham. Attentive to the growing market presence of contemporary Christian music, Bakker's bookstore sold tapes and records by Christian pop groups, Christian folk groups, Christian heavy-metal groups, and even Christian rap groups. Down the concourse, in Noah's Toy Shop, Christian alternatives to secular toys were on display for children, including Christian picture books, Christian action figures, and a selection of plastic weapons that ranged from the "shield of righteousness" to the "sword of truth" (Toner, 1987: 24; English, 1987: 8A; Woodward, 1986: 47 and O'Rourke, 1988: 94-95). Dolls in the store were packaged as "Praise Dolls" that sang "Jesus Loves Me" and cooed "God is Love . . . Plus five other sayings!" Lest these items encourage children to attempt a puerile tantrum, the store also sold "a spanking paddle emblazoned with the words 'YOU train YOUR CHILD'" (Rosenfeld, 1986: H1).

Other attractions also pressed the selling point of Heritage USA as a "Christian" world apart. Bakker had Billy Graham's two-story childhood home transported from Charlotte's suburbs to the grounds at Heritage USA. Guides offered tours of the home daily, granting visitors a unique chance to see, touch, and feel the birth-place of an evangelical icon. The layout and appearance of the park itself, which included not only the campground of Heritage USA's early years but also walking trails, tennis courts, and exercise facilities, sought to create opportunities for seclusion and spiritual reflection. Indeed, Bakker prided himself on the fact that Heritage USA was "laid out by hand and by the feel of the land. Not to destroy the hills. Too many times bulldozers cut in and they take all the quality and terrain and take all the stones that are naturally there, and we tried to save everything that was there naturally" (Albert, 1998: 19). As Nancy Hightower reminisced in her semi-fictional account of her childhood at Heritage USA, the park's grounds were indeed "beautiful" with "flowers everywhere and little shady spots with benches to sit down and feed the ducks," all connected by "smooth little paved pathways that take you everywhere." According to Hightower, the park's layout no doubt helped visitors feel "rested after fighting the great spiritual battles of their every-day life" (Hightower, 2005: 189).

For many visitors, one of Bakker's most impressive attractions was the park's 3,000-seat amphitheatre. The facility featured a $1 million replica of an ancient Jerusalem street as its main stage, but the amphitheatre's fixed design hardly limited its resourcefulness. Each summer, it played host to "Musical Heritage," a weekly presentation that depicted American history through song, dialogue, and costume, all the while forwarding a patriotic, city-on-a-hill thesis about the nation's God-blessed past. A week-long circus and Fourth of July celebration were likewise held at the amphitheatre, as were regular performances of various biblical stories and concerts by prominent Christian musicians. The highpoints of the amphitheatre's dramatic season, however, were the Easter Passion Play and Christmas nativity reenactment. The Passion Play had a cast of one-hundred and twenty actors, "all committed Christians." Bakker contracted freelance actor Gary Morris, a spot-on look-alike of the iconic, European, blue-eyed Jesus for his services, which included a PG-rated crucifixion. Fitting the celebratory mood of the amphitheatre's regular offerings, the Passion Play concluded with Jesus' resurrection and end-time victory over a red-suited, horned Satan, accentuated with strobe lights, lasers, and smoke machines. Beginning in November each year, the amphitheatre took on a decidedly more subdued tone, showing a nightly reenactment of Matthew and Luke's nativity stories. A common occurrence in evangelical churches around the country, this nativity drama had the same intention behind it – to draw believers and non-believers alike toward an appreciation for the true "reason for the season." Admission was, like many experiences at Heritage USA, only as costly as the gas to get there (Mitchell, 1982: 78-81; Fay, 1987: 87 and Anon., 'Fun and Games', 1985: 29).

Like the amphitheatre, Heritage USA's overnight amenities and long-term residential options aimed to impress. Located near the Main Street shops, the Heritage Grand Hotel could accommodate nearly five hundred guests for the middle-class price of fifty to ninety dollars a room per night. "With its combination of decorative grillwork [and] embossed metal painted to look like copper, balconies, columns and porticoes," wrote one critic, "it looks like a high-grade Holiday Inn with an overlay of Tara" (Rosenfeld, 1986: H1). A serious purpose directed every aspect of the hotel's design

and operation, however, namely Bakker's vision to construct a resort hotel that witnessed evangelicalism as fervently as every other
part of the park. Golden letters above the check-in desk proclaimed
"Jesus Christ is Lord," while morning wake-up calls began with
a rousing version of "This is the Day that the Lord Hath Made."
Housekeepers made sure that Gideon Bibles were not candidly
tucked away in bedside tables but prominently displayed. Bap-
tisms happened every Tuesday afternoon in the hotel's swimming
pool, and "Christian dinner theatre" was available in the hotel's
dining room. Even the doorman welcomed guests with a cheery
"God loves you" (Williams, 2000: 127-128; Woodward, 1986: 46
and Fitzgerald, 1990: 80). Those impressed enough with Heritage
USA's offerings to stay permanently also had the option of buying
a house or condominium in one of the resort's surrounding sub-di-
visions. To be sure, many who purchased these properties did so
for the sake of living near the Bakkers and their ministry. Yet, others moved permanently to Heritage USA because it offered more
security and homogeneity than a standard suburban sub-division
could; these properties were in a Christian community that guaranteed an additional layer of insulation for their families from "secular" elements. Thus, long-term residence at Heritage USA was the
American Dream made better.

Fig. 22. Heritage USA, Feature creature.

Fig. 23. Heritage USA, The King's Castle.

Since he wanted Heritage USA to be the nation's premier Christian resort, Bakker had a distinct interest in selling the park as a Christian alternative for children, teenagers, and young adults. As such, in addition to the toy store, children could explore the Christian petting zoo and farm on site. An enormous, twenty-foot tall sign with the words "Farming For Jesus" invited visitors to bring their children inside for up-close encounters with all kinds of farm animals and a ride on the park's feature creature, a Dromedary camel (fig. 22) (Fay, 1987: 87). Children could likewise wander over with their parents to one of the park's main attractions, the King's Castle. A focal point in the park, both because of its height and exterior coloring (yellow, green, and "royal" purple), the King's Castle mimicked the design of Sleeping Beauty's Castle at Disney's Magic Kingdom (fig. 23). Oddly enough, beyond positing in stone the centrality of King Jesus rather than Disney magic, the King's Castle offered relatively little in the way of entertainment. Only the quick service and square hamburger patties of Wendy's Old Fashioned Hamburgers, which operated "a king-size Wendy's" inside King's Castle, warranted a visit. Other attractions, however, offered much more for vacationing youth at Bakker's park (Woodward, 1986: 46).

After three years of construction, Bakker opened in 1986 a $13 million water park on Heritage USA property. Wrapping around an expansive lake and named Heritage Island, the water park was, according to one observer, "a dissonant mix of ornate Victorian out-buildings, intended to blend with the adjoining Partner Center and the centerpiece volcano of artificial rock that Bakker wanted." The volcano was "supposed to evoke images of old religious movies and serve as a stage for fireworks displays" (Shepard, 1989: 240). For Bakker, the water park was his most ambitious attempt at both marketing evangelicalism to non-believers and selling a safe space for evangelicals to find rest and relaxation. "Well, if the Bible says we are to be fishers of men, then a water park is just the bait," Bakker noted in an interview with *The New York Times*, "and I don't seen [sic] anything wrong in using some pretty fancy bait" (Schmidt, 1985: A8). Tickets for Heritage Island were a bargain – only $10 for adults and $7.50 for children – and visitors got a lot for their money. Featuring over forty different activities, Heritage Island was an attraction obviously designed for the diverse interests of each family member. Small wading pools were available for toddlers and children, while adolescents could enjoy rafting through the Raging Canyon Rapids or, if they were old enough, plummet sixty feet down the Typhoon drop slide. Bakker even installed the world's largest wave-making machine to ensure that the main pool's Caribbean blue water realistically lapped up on the shore. "The summers are so hot in Charlotte," explained Bakker in a 1989 interview, "that people coming from their vacations were sweltering in the heat, so we brought the ocean to Charlotte." Bakker saw Heritage Island's goal, however, as much more intentional. He undoubtedly envisioned a Christian seaside experience, intended to evangelize and edify those who paid admission for themselves and their families. Visitors had their hands stamped in red-ink letters reading "LOVE" before entering the water park, and all one hundred of Heritage Island's lifeguards were Bible school students, each just as ready to save a life for Jesus as they were to throw a life saver (Fay, 1987: 85; Albert, 1998: 25-26). Hence, Bakker's water park marketed more than just fun in the sun. It marketed evangelical Christianity itself.

Even into his last years at Heritage USA, Bakker continued to draft plans and raise funds for the park's expansion. Over the course of the park's history, Bakker had dozens of pet projects on the drawing board, including a Christian nursing home, a full-scale reproduction of first-century Jerusalem, a 30,000 seat convention center modeled after London's Crystal Palace, a "Heritage USA West" in California, and a Christian kids' park with such rides as The Shipwreck of the Apostle Paul and Jonah in the Belly of the Whale. Bakker also wanted to build at Heritage USA an attraction called A Ride to Remember. Keeping in mind that non-evangelicals might visit the park, "it was supposed to give people an experience of heaven and hell," explained one Heritage USA staff member, "Jim really thought people should know what to expect" (Fay, 1987: 87; Schmidt, 1985: A8 and Anon., 'Fun and Games', 1985: 25). The only one of these projects that Bakker oversaw before his departure from Heritage USA was the construction of the Heritage Grand Towers. A twenty story, five hundred room high-rise hotel, the Heritage Grand Towers continued the trend set by the Heritage Grand Hotel and, indeed, the rest of the park. As a part of Bakker's marketing strategy, the Grand Towers sought to provide its guests with all the finest amenities one might find at a five-star luxury hotel, albeit in a Christian setting. Bakker never had the chance to see how successful the Towers might have been at attracting vacationers. Construction on the Towers ceased when Bakker's financial misbehavior – linked in part to his fraudulent overselling of "free night stays" at the Towers to PTL's most earnest contributors – led to his resignation as Heritage USA's director and his later conviction in a federal court.

After visiting Heritage USA, one reporter remarked that Bakker's "marketing overkill gets visitors coming and going" (Fay, 1987: 85). It certainly did. From the moment visitors – evangelicals and non – entered the park, the marketing never let up. Even when leaving Heritage USA, visitors passed an exit sign reminding them that "GOD LOVES YOU. HE REALLY DOES" (James, 1993: 16). For many, the seclusion, beauty, and ambiance of Bakker's Christian playground created a favorable and lasting impression. "No matter how bad a week you had," observed one visitor, "once you hit the gates of this place it's like you're on a natural high till you leave" (O'Guinn, 1989: 232). For the most part, that high came from the knowledge that Heritage USA was a self-contained Christian world that offered many of the most pleasant experiences of the outside world without any of its complications. Poverty, crime, juvenile delinquency, sex, drugs – all were supposedly non-existent past the gatehouse. Disneyland and Walt Disney World, of course, offered the same type of experience, but whereas Disney's parks avoided religious references for the sake of broad appeal, Bakker's park reveled in them. As such, Bakker's Heritage USA cultivated a sense of Christian exclusion from the larger world and, by extension, a sense of Christian unity. As Margie Green of Ohio remembered, "maybe some people can't understand that, but when we walked in, there were Christians, I mean Christians all over the place and there was love, there was fellowship, there were all denominations that walked together and worshipped the Lord... We became brothers and sisters in Christ... That's what we went for" (Albert, 1998: 24). On her visit to Heritage USA, *New Yorker* reporter Frances FitzGerald observed that "the people I saw at Heritage USA seemed as diverse as most crowds at Disneyland, and the conversations I managed to strike up made it hard to imagine them all in a single church congregation" (FitzGerald, 1990: 80). In fact, despite its firm grounding in evangelical Protestantism, by 1985 Catholics visited Heritage USA as frequently as Baptists, spurring a feeling of spiritual unity and freedom around the park that was palpable and inviting (Albert, 1998: 27). "It's like you come into a whole different world," reflected one visitor, "you can come down here and you can open with your beliefs... It's an oasis... Here it is like one big family. It's like a whole different world with spiritual people" (O'Guinn, 1989: 231). Little wonder that another evangelical visitor commented, "at first, when you leave here, you feel all insecure, like leaving your mother" (Rosenfeld, 1986: H8).

However, by selling the park in this manner, as a "Christian" theme park, Bakker ran into several unintended consequences and ironies. First, Heritage USA's strategy for edifying "born again" Christians often undercut its evangelistic efforts. For as much as Bakker thought of his theme park as "fancy bait", his marketing strategy did not necessarily achieve the goal of all marketing strategies, namely to persuade the conversion of someone from one product or belief system to another. As one observer wrote, "Heritage

USA is all about salvation – nothing less than one's soul is on the line. But the people who come seem already saved, and only want to be blessed" (Hightower, 2005: 189-190). Another writer, remembering the park after its closing, agreed: "Heritage was self-contained and had everything from an indoor mall to endless recreation and cruise-ship caliber food. What it didn't have was non-believers who did not share their strict values" (Albert, 1998: 23).   Second, Bakker's marketing strategy failed to appeal to all Christians. Many found Bakker's park an aberration of Christian tenets rather than the embodiment of them. "Somebody spent an awful lot of money that had nothing to do with religion," related one Presbyterian after visiting the park, "I think [of] all the little people that listen to religion on television and send their very hard-earned money in, thinking that they will help spread religion and do good things for people. It's disillusioning." Bailey Smith, a former president of the Southern Baptist Convention, also questioned the necessity of Heritage USA since "Christians," he averred, "can go to Disneyland" (Watson, 1987: 62). Third, visitors did not always adhere to Heritage USA's preferred image of itself. The strict rules of the complex, intended to ensure squeaky-clean behavior, sometimes failed to do so. One reporter observed occasional scenes of rebellion, such as an exasperated father yelling at his teenage son to stop ruining their vacation. She also noted a twelve-year old boy smoking alone in a remote corner of one of Heritage USA's ponds. Even the park-wide ban on alcohol and other drugs could not keep Bakker's paradise free from the "occasional illicit beer can" or "telltale odor of marijuana." Furthermore, despite all the trumpeting by Bakker of the park's ethos of perfect community and mutual love, waiters in several of Heritage USA's restaurants complained that "Christians don't tip… They'll give you $100 if you need it, but they won't leave that 15 percent" (Rosenfeld, 1986: H1).

Given Bakker's tendency to present the park as a refuge for the needy and dispossessed, a similarly ironic, but more troubling, consequence of Bakker's marketing strategy was the segregation, exclusion, or suppression of those who might potentially ruin the sanctity of his Christian resort. For example, in 1984, Bakker opened Heritage House, a counseling center for unwed mothers who chose birth instead of abortion. The facility had first-class furnishings that "looked like they came straight from an Ethan Allan showroom." But that was not all: Heritage House also provided cooking and child-care classes, private rooms, and the Tender Loving Care Adoption Agency, which found Christian foster parents for unwanted children. Another facility, the People That Love Center, was located on the westernmost edge of Heritage USA and provided donated food, clothing, and furniture without cost to underprivileged families. In the southwest corner of Heritage USA, the thirty-acre Fort Hope complex offered housing, educational programs, and drug rehab to homeless men and women aged seventeen to forty. Fort Hope, however, did not accept all cases, admitting only those who were "serious about trying to learn a trade and the living skills necessary to lead productive lives." According to Bakker, these facilities displayed the commitment of his ministry and Heritage USA to servicing those in need; yet, since each of the facilities was hidden from the public view in a location far from the more pleasing attractions of Main Street or Heritage Island, it seems doubtful that Bakker wanted his visitors to encounter the disquieting realities of life represented by the people who used such facilities (Albert, 1998: 34-36).

Heritage USA's segregation of the unpleasant and difficult occurred elsewhere in the park as well. The park certainly attracted more than a few visitors who saw it as a place where all their various personal, medical, and financial problems might receive treatment if not resolution. "Underneath the cordial jollity," wrote one reporter, "dwells a free-floating mass of emotion. The pain of past lives and current troubles... All come spilling out in the ongoing effort to replace the anguish with an all-encompassing faith in Jesus." The emotional baggage that many visitors brought with them to the park varied widely. Some wanted relief from alcoholism, drug addiction, and the temptation to suicide. Others sought miraculous healing for crippling diseases and painful cancers. Still others desired counsel for their marital breakdowns or rebellious children. "We get a lot of widows coming here trying to deal with the change in their situation," reported Bill Ingram, a pastor who served in the Upper Room, the park's round-the-clock counseling center (Rosenfeld, 1986: H1). Yet, for as much as Bakker saw facilities like the Upper Room as exposing Heritage USA's evangelical and non-evangelical visitors to its advertised dedication to Christian love, the placement of these sites signaled that they were a unique, separate part of the park. By keeping the Upper Room from public view, Bakker was able to make its services an option for those who needed it, but also to maintain an atmosphere within Heritage USA that was positive, carefree, and uncomplicated.

At times, maintaining the sanitized environment of Heritage USA required the outright exclusion or suppression of unwelcome elements. On numerous occasions, the park's marketing worked too well, unintentionally attracting the poor and homeless to its gates. Standard protocol at Heritage USA treated these individuals to a free night's lodging but required them to move out the next morning. As a result, many ended up on the rolls of homeless shelters and social agencies in nearby Charlotte (Schmidt, 1985: A8). At other times, threats to Heritage USA's sanctity came from within and, on these occasions, Bakker took direct measures to ensure that the reality of the park matched its marketing as a safe, idyllic Christian environment. A thirty-person security force (six of whom were armed) regularly patrolled the grounds, looking for any signs of alcohol, drugs, or disorderly behavior. Anyone found breaking Heritage USA's long list of rules was immediately asked to leave. Bakker's handling of other threats, such as disgruntled workers, was likewise swift and direct. Since Heritage USA's early days, Bakker held the opinion that his employees "don't serve God for eight hours a day and then punch out." Accordingly, unpaid overtime and layoffs to "prod or punish those who balked" became standard operating procedure, especially as Heritage USA grew in size and popularity (Genet, 1978: 41). Indeed, according to one middle manager, labor relations at Heritage USA hardly operated under the Golden Rule:

> Upper management is so concerned with pleasing the partner that they forget about the front line employee who is "busting his fanny" every day in order to do a good job... As it now stands PTL views its employees as expendable and without individual merit. PTL's position is, "if they don't like what's going on, there's the door." Thus you have a high

turnover rate, huge discontent among the staff, and a real sense of disloyalty and dissension (Shepard, 1989: 330).

Such internal problems flew in the face of Bakker's public promotion of Heritage USA as a place where nothing but Christian love and devotion reigned supreme. Though everything from the Grand Hotel to the amphitheatre forwarded the notion that Heritage USA was an alternative world, a utopian Christian park cleaned of any sinful elements, this marketing could only go so far. It could not ensure that once on the property, visitors would always align themselves with this vision or that Christian principles would direct every part of the park's operation. Bakker thus promised a heaven on earth, but he repeatedly found that heaven was a hard promise to fulfill.

The difficulties that Bakker encountered reveal the limits of his particular brand of religious marketing. Despite his best efforts, Bakker could not make Heritage USA live up to his aspirations for it. Certainly, the park was a successful endeavor in one sense. While open, it attracted millions of like-minded Christians to an alternative version of Disneyland, effectively selling itself as a place where they could be not only edified but also encouraged that they had, as Bakker once put it, "a better product than soap or automobiles. We have eternal life" (Armstrong, 1979: 108). But as a marketing device aimed at converting others to evangelicalism, Heritage USA's successes were few. Heritage USA, in this sense, may have been fancy, but it was poor "bait" because few that visited the park walked away with a greater interest in becoming "born again." Likewise, as an experiment in Christian charity, Heritage USA had a mixed history. While many who came to Heritage USA found it a refreshing experience that could almost miraculously heal them of their most burdensome problems, the park's firm commitment to its sanitized "Christian atmosphere" often led to the compartmentalization of human need at best and its trivialization at worst.

Though Heritage USA fell into disrepair shortly after the departure of Bakker, its spirit continues to characterize much of American evangelical culture. The Christian culture industry operates on the same assumptions, offering myriad goods and services with the hope that they will spark devotion in Christians and non-Christians alike through de-secularized entertainment and amenities. Christian entrepreneurs of various backgrounds run Christian businesses, from bookstores to restaurants. Churches and mega-churches across America sponsor any number of Christian programs, from Christian marriage seminars to Christian yoga classes to Christian schools. In fact, although most of Heritage USA's facilities remain dilapidated, some currently house MorningStar Fellowship Church/Heritage International Ministries, a Pentecostal body that uses the former Grand Hotel as a retreat and worship center. Local building codes have condemned the Heritage Grand Towers to demolition, but MorningStar still plans to undertake a ten million dollar "restoration" of the Main Street complex, turning it into an all-in-one dormitory, shopping mall, and youth center, with "ministry meeting rooms" available for "equipping and training conferences" (Sulock, 2007: 1A and him.morningstarministries.org). Even Christian theme parks have become a viable option once more. Since 2001, Marv Rosenthal, a Messianic Jew, has run the Holy Land Experience outside Orlando, Florida. A "total immersion experience," this "Bible-based theme park" features reproductions of famous sites in first-century Palestine, including Herod's Temple, the Garden Tomb, and the Qumran caves. Like Heritage USA, the Holy Land Experience has a dual purpose: to edify the faithful and evangelize those considered outside the fold. As the park's web site notes, the "miraculous event" of Jesus's life, death, and resurrection "is… crucial for all humanity." Inspired by this "life-changing… revelation," the park aims "to demonstrate the living truths of the Bible in innovative ways through state-of-the-art exhibits, dynamic musical-dramatic performances, and insightful teaching presentations" (Labash, 2001: 22 and www.theholylandexperience.com).

Also like Heritage USA, however, many of these endeavors only end up preaching to the choir. While he watched a concert at the Holy Land Experience entitled "Revival in the Land!", one reporter found it hard "to see a non-believer being in serious jeopardy of conversion here unless he has a weakness for stiff choreography and melting pancake make-up" (Labash, 2001: 22). His response reiterates an important irony of this form of religious marketing. No matter whatever else it may promise or promote, it is hardly successful marketing in terms of converting others to evangelicalism. For those that fear a conservative, evangelical takeover of American culture and politics, this irony should grant them comfort. Despite all the posturing of the religious right and paranoia of their opponents, a significant portion of conservative, evangelical America operates in this mode, preferring private consumption of Christian goods and experiences to prolonged political engagement. For evangelicals in America, Heritage USA's other ironies should invite them to reconsider what they deem as acceptable Christian behavior. Though it may have the air of outward concern, the marketing and consumption of Christian goods, services, and experiences tend to limit another aspect of Christian identity, the consideration of human suffering as more than just an afterthought or platitude. In confronting and acting upon this consideration, American evangelicals might have to abandon their business of selling, and buying, the hope of a personal, custom-made heaven on earth. But in doing so, they may find themselves fully free to pursue the disciplined, selfless Christian life that, by all accounts, seems to be the true business of heaven.

References

Albert, James A., *Jim Bakker: Miscarriage of Justice?* (Chicago: Open Court, 1998).

Anon., "Fun and Games for Bible-Thumpers," *The Economist* 19 October (1985), p. 29.

Armstrong, Ben, *The Electric Church* (Nashville: T. Nelson, 1979).

Cran, William (director) and Stephanie Tepper (producer), *Praise the Lord*, Frontline, video recording (New York: Network Features, 1987).

English, Kathy, "At Heritage USA it's Pray and Play," *Toronto Star* 5 April (1987), p. 8A.

Holy Land Experience, "FAQs: The Holy Land Experience", http://www.the-holylandexperience.com/abouthle/faqs.html, accessed 4 May 2006.

Fay, Martha, "God's Country," *Life*, August (1987), pp. 84-87.

Genet, Harry, "PTL: Please Toss a Lifesaver," *Christianity Today* 13 (1978), pp. 41-42.

Griffin, Keith, "Jim Bakker Responds to Pressure," *Religious Communication Today* 5 (1982), pp. 5-7.

Hendershot, Heather, *Shaking the World for Jesus: Media and Conservative Evangelical Culture* (Chicago: University of Chicago Press, 2004).

Heritage Village Church, *Jim and Tammy Bakker Present the Ministries of Heritage Village Church* (Toronto: Boulton, 1986).

Hightower, Nancy, "When Satan Knows Your Name," Ph.D. Dissertation, University of Denver (2005).

Howard, Jay R. and John M. Streck, *Apostles of Rock: The Splintered World of Contemporary Christian Music* (Lexington: University of Kentucky Press, 2004).

James, Hunter, *Smile Pretty and Say Jesus: the Last Great Days of PTL* (Athens, Georgia: University of Georgia Press, 1993).

Kopkind, Andrew, "Jim Bakker's Lost America," *Esquire* December (1987), pp. 175-183.

Labash, Matt, "Holy Orlando! Jerusalem as a Theme Park," *The Weekly Standard* 5 March (2001), p. 22.

Mitchell, Mary "Biggest Bargain Family Vacation in Dixieland," *Saturday Evening Post* May-June (1982), pp. 78-81.

O'Guinn, Thomas C., and Russell K. Belk, "Heaven on Earth: Consumption at Heritage Village, USA," *The Journal of Consumer Research* 16 (1989), pp. 227-238.

O' Rourke, P. J., *Holidays in Hell* (New York: Atlantic Monthly Press, 1988).

Rosenfeld, Megan, "Heritage USA and the Heavenly Vacation; South Carolina Theme
Park Caters to Born-Again Christians," *Washington Post* 15 June (1986), pp. H1 and H8.

Schmidt, William E., "TV Minister Calls His Resort 'Bait' for Christianity," *New York Times* 25 December (1985), p. A8.

Shepard, Charles E., *Forgiven: The Rise and Fall of Jim Bakker and the PTL Ministry* (New York: Atlantic Monthly Press, 1989).

Sulock, Rebecca, "Too Late to Save Tower?" *The Herald, Rock Hill, South Carolina* 9 January (2007), p. 1-A.

Toner, Robin, "Bakker's Troubles Test Faith at Religious Resort," *New York Times* 29 March (1987), p. 24.

Warren, C. C., "Speech Given at the Southern Baptist Convention's Annual Meeting, Charlotte, N. C.," *Baptist Courier* 26 January (1956), n. p.

Watson, Russell, "Heaven Can Wait," *Newsweek* 8 June (1987), pp. 58-65.

Williams, Peter W., *Houses of God: Region, Religion, and Architecture in the United States* (Urbana: University of Illinois Press, 2000).

Woodward, Kenneth L., "A Disneyland for the Devout," *Newsweek* 11 August (1986), pp. 46-47.

Yancey, Philip, "The Ironies and Impact of PTL," *Christianity Today* 23 (1979), pp. 28-31.

Websites

him.morningstarministries.org
www.theholylandexperience.com

Marketing Performances

Evangelical Cartoons:
The Good News and the Bad

Harry Coverston

On any given day at most major college campuses in North America, it is possible to observe evangelizers distributing religious tracts to college students. Distribution of tracts is one of the primary ways in which North American Christians historically have sought to proselytize new believers. While a variety of materials are distributed ranging from the King James Version New Testaments distributed by Gideons International to leaflets appealing to reason peppered with proof-text passages of scripture, one popular type of tract commonly used on college campuses presents its message in much the same style as commercial comic books, offering highly simplified appeals to emotion and self-interest through stylized artistic depictions and a deft use of color.

In this essay I will examine tracts distributed in evangelical Protestant proselytizing efforts at a large state university in Florida. I begin with a brief history of the use of tracts in religious proselytizing and continue with an examination of a specific format of tracts used in evangelizing at the University of Central Florida. I continue with a comparison between the evangelistic project and consumer advertising and marketing techniques and understandings taught at the university. I conclude with an analysis of the tracts' content using Abraham Maslow's hierarchy of needs and Lawrence Kohlberg's stages of moral reasoning thus noting the connection between moral reasoning, consumerist advertising and proselytizing through evangelistic tracts.

A Brief History of Religious Tracts in American Culture

According to the *American Heritage Dictionary* (Houghton Mifflin, 2004), a religious tract is defined as a "leaflet or pamphlet containing a declaration or appeal, especially one put out by a religious or political group." The etymology of the word includes a Middle English word, *tracte*, treatise, which itself was probably short for Latin *tractatus*, from past participle of *tractare*, to discuss. Historically, a number of religiously oriented materials have been described as tracts. Early uses of this term within the Christian tradition referred to materials best described as either apologetic in nature, treatises seeking to explain a theological understanding, or polemical arguments seeking to distinguish a preferred set of beliefs from others. Such materials took the form of pamphlets, sermons or even whole books.

The American Tract Society was founded on May 11, 1825 for this stated purpose: "to make Jesus Christ known in His redeeming grace and to promote the interests of vital godliness and sound morality, by the circulation of Religious Tracts, calculated to receive the approbation of all Evangelical Christians." Within a few years of its founding, the society claimed to have produced millions of pieces of evangelizing literature; tracts, booklets, books, and even magazines (American Tract Society, 1825).

David Morgan's extensive study of religious iconography in America has found that the use of image laden tracts have served a variety of purposes in American history including the attempted construction of a national identity through a civil religion, albeit mainly in the evangelical Protestant image (Morgan and Promey, 2005: 223). American Tract Society tracts frequently targeted specific groups, usually those whom their creators held to be socially inferior: children, illiterate adults, Native Americans, slaves (and later freedmen) and immigrants. (Morgan, 2005: 223). Morgan observed that most tract campaigns were driven by what he described as a condescending "sympathy, compassion, or pity that was the emotional experience of benevolence par excellence" for the tract purveyor "which the tract reader vicariously imbibed." (Morgan and Promey, 2005: 57). Tracts were deliberately designed to "mobilize the heart-struck viewer." This approach would, by the turn of the twentieth-century, give way to themes of salvation and damnation (2005: 59).

Today, the use of tracts in Christian evangelistic efforts is observable worldwide. At the *World Christian Tract Directory* (2006) website 308 organizations are listed by the webmaster with a stated purpose of providing "information on the different ministries and organizations which publish evangelical Christian tracts." The directory lists tract producing agencies in every continent worldwide though the majority of the agencies listed are located in the South and Midwest of the United States (its famed Bible Belt). Tracts are offered in a wide range of languages ranging from Hebrew and Arabic to Russian and Japanese to Zulu and Afrikaans. They are also offered in a wide variety of formats from traditional booklet format, to comic books and web-based "digitracts" complete with videos. The Directory lists a number of the major players in American evangelical Protestantism: Focus on the Family, Moody Bible Institute, Billy Graham ministries, Jews for Jesus, Josh McDowell ministries, the afore-mentioned American Tract Society and Chick Publications.

According to the biography provided at the Chick Publications website (Chick Publications, 2006a), after Jack Chick's conversion experience following an evening of listening to Charles E. Fuller's *Old Fashioned Revival Hour* radio program, he sought to use his artistic talents to "wake Christians up" and evangelize those who were not Christians. Almost from the beginning, Chick focused on teenagers. Shortly after his first book, *Why No Revival?* was published, Chick recalls driving down the road, when his eyes were drawn to a group of teens on the sidewalk, a group that he, like his nineteenth-century American Tract Society forebears, saw as being socially inferior and in need of what he could provide them. He reports:

At the time, I didn't like teenagers or their rebellion. But, all of a sudden, the power of God hit me and my heart broke and I was overcome with the realization that these teens were probably on their way to hell. With tears pouring down my face, I pulled my car off the road and wrote as fast as I could, as God poured the story into my mind' (Chick Publications, 2006a).

Chick reports writing the story line in fifteen minutes for *A Demon's Nightmare* which he then illustrated with comic book style depictions to create his first tract. For forty years Chick has continued to create comic book tracts with the stated purpose of "producing easy-to-understand soul winning gospel tracts with a salvation message that anyone can understand."

According to Robert Harvey in his study of *The Art of the Comic Book* (1996), the literary genre of sequential narrative cartoons dates back to its nineteenth-century beginnings in newspaper comic strips. The original comic books were simply the compilation of newspaper strips into a single book. By the mid 1930s, the "visual-verbal graphic storytelling was entering its infancy. At the end of the decade, the comic book was a fact of adolescent American life." While the comic book was aimed at an adolescent readership, it found an important audience among the older brothers of those readers in those soldiers who read them between bouts of combat. Harvey reports that by the end of World War II, "the comic book was an established literary form. And before the end of the century, it would be aiming for adult readership with production values and story telling standards far more sophisticated than those that had governed its birth" (1996: 16).

Context of the Present Study

The University of Central Florida (UCF) is a sprawling state university of 46,000 students located fifteen miles east of the downtown center of Orlando, Florida. The Chronicle of Higher Education Careers Employer File (2006) lists UCF as the second largest university in Florida and the seventh largest university in enrollment in the United States. UCF has a diverse student body representing all 50 states and 136 countries, including China, India, Canada, Jamaica, and the United Kingdom. In terms of religion, UCF campus activities reflects that diversity. There are twenty two university-recognized religious organizations on campus ranging from the Roman Catholic chaplaincy, to the Baha'i Faith and the Hillel Jewish Student Union. The most visible religious presences on campus are conservative evangelical Protestant organizations such as Campus Crusade for Christ, whose national headquarters are located just ten miles south of the campus near the Orlando International Airport, the Fellowship of Christian Athletes and Intervarsity Christian Fellowship (UCF, *United Campus Ministries*, 2006).

A number of religious groups regularly visit the campus to disseminate religious materials and occasionally to engage in open air preaching, events which draw as many detractors as empathizers. The UCF Golden Rule (2006), which is the university's rules and regulations regarding campus activities, guarantees the right of anyone to use any or all of four designated "free assembly areas" on the campus for "political activity and other exercises of free speech and assembly" (16.F, Free Assembly Areas). One of these is the large brick-paved square in front of the student union. Because evangelizing organizations do not require payment for the materials they distribute, they are not covered by restrictions on campus vendors.

There is no prior announcement of the appearance of outside evangelizers on campus in student publications or posters at campus events announcement sites. To the outsider, there is no discernable pattern to such visits. This writer has observed various tract disseminators operating on campus on the average of three to four times per semester. The tracts discussed herein were collected on campus by this writer, a full-time instructor at the university present daily during regular sessions on campus, as well as by students during the 2006-7 school year. Because of the irregularity of the visits and the lack of prior notice of the same, interviewing the purveyors of these tracts has proven impossible. This discussion will instead focus on the text of the tracts distributed.

Among materials regularly disseminated on campus include the King James Version New Testaments from Gideons International, an evangelical Protestant organization (Gideons, 2007) as well as tracts from the Tract Ministry of Bible Believers Baptist Church in North Canton, Ohio. The most commonly distributed materials are the comic book tracts from Chick Publications which are offered in both English and Spanish. The primary site for distribution of these tracts is the plaza in front of the UCF student union, a site at the heart of the 1,415 acre main campus laid out in expanding concentric circles of sidewalks, grassy commons and buildings. Distribution tends to be interpersonal with distributors handing tracts to students willing to accept them. However, tracts are also left in highly visible locations in public restrooms on campus.

Analysis of Materials

The materials distributed on the UCF campus fall into three basic categories. The first category is a 3 ½ x 5 ½ inches booklet format, two pages front and back in length, which features a drawing or photograph on the cover superimposed by themes such as "Ballad of a Damned Sinner" and "Which Road Are You Choosing? Heaven or Hell?" The images feature prominent use of black and red used to depict blood and fire.

A good example is the tract "BALLAD OF A DAMNED SIN-NER" the cover of which features a drawing of two hands in chains reaching as to the sky surrounded by red flames. Its content is a poem which begins "I went to church and Sunday school, I kept the law and every rule," conduct that the tract's writer asserts to be insufficient to attain eternal salvation, the poem ending with the statement: "when I was alive all was well, Now I'm tormented, chained in Hell!" The back cover includes an exhortation entitled "DON'T LOSE YOUR SOUL" which features substitutionary atonement Christian theology ending with the promise: "we must receive His sacrifice and ask Him to cleanse us and come into our hearts. He will - all you have to do is ask." The tract provides a blank for the reader to supply their name and address and gives the address for the Bible Believers Baptist Church in N. Canton, Ohio, but, unlike the majority of the tracts studied herein, provides no further directions or connections to local churches.

A second category of tracts is more subtle and positive using photographs of clouds and butterflies superimposed with messages such as "God Cares for You" and "Born Again." These tracts, produced by Good News Publishers in Wheaton, Illinois, focus on issues such as loneliness which the tract writer explains as being the result of sin and unbelief and the concern for eternal life which can be allayed by being "born again." The Good News tracts did not provide transactional space, i.e., the reader was not invited to provide name and address and to return tracts to their producers, but they did provide the name, address and website of the Good News Publishers.

The third category of tracts utilizes a 3 x 5" comic book format which pictorially tells stories designed to convict the reader of their eternal damnation concluding with a set of propositions that one must accept in order to become saved, a specific prayer to evidence one's assent to the propositions, and a set of instructions as to what one must do to live out their "wonderful new life with Him." The back page of each tract includes the address and website for Chick Publications and reserves a large space for local church distributors to provide their location and phone number. It is this category of tracts upon which this chapter will focus. The analysis of three specific examples follows.

In *The Devil's Night,* the writer identifies Halloween as "the devil's" feast day celebrated by "pagan priests" worshipping Saman (sic) the Lord of death. It features a dour female public school teacher requiring students to celebrate Halloween as a means of covert evangelizing for witchcraft. One of her pupils is a little girl whose parents use Jesus' name only for swearing. A young friend of the pupil evangelizes her, relating an account of original sin, the western Christian doctrine that all human beings are sinners from birth which "stops us from getting into heaven." The young pupil finds the story frightening until her young friend relates the theological construct of substitutionary atonement: "the Lord Jesus shed His precious blood, cuz (sic) only God's blood could wash away our sins." The young pupil is converted on the spot at the direction of her young evangelizer friend, a decision which brings her existential security and happiness: "I'm not afraid anymore. I feel wonderful! I wish I could reach other kids for Jesus."

The tract ends with the young pupil pursuing her new calling through placing tracts in bags of Halloween candy to counteract the devil's plot: "Halloween pulls them into witchcraft."

Several aspects of the content are striking. The color scheme employed heavily features black with bright orange contrasts, colors frequently associated with evil and the flames of Hell. Yet, the tract repeatedly focuses on a theme: "how do I get into heaven?" with the word I boldfaced emphasizing the individualistic focus. It recounts the Christian understanding of Lucifer as the rebellious, fallen angel who is then identified with the serpent in the Genesis "fall narrative," tricking Adam and Eve "into disobeying God. That ruined their lives and ours. So now we are sinners and it stops us from getting into heaven." This version of the Augustinian theology of original sin is designed to create a perception of need for conversion on the part of the reader: "nobody else can save you." Hence, the predominant concern of the tract is how the individual reader can be saved and go to heaven.

It is also interesting to note that while the public school teacher is posited as engaging in evangelistic efforts for witchcraft, her now-converted pupil engages in counter-efforts, placing religious comics (presumably from] Publications) in the plastic bags among the candy doled out on Halloween night "cuz we're fighting for their souls." The young salvation fighter pupil does, however, disclose the presence of the comics among the candy which "show you how to go to heaven!," which her young witch-costumed trick-or-treaters accept with enthusiasm: "Cool! Thanks!" Ironically, while the teacher's depiction suggests an improper use of her position to proselytize diabolical converts, the pupil similarly uses a holiday context designed for childhood play as a means to proselytize for her own new religion (Chick Publications, 2006b).

The Chick website which contains this and numerous other tracts is somewhat ambiguous about the level of disclosure one might employ in disseminating the tracts. It speaks of how witnessing could not get any easier: "by dropping a Chick tract or two (along with some candy) into their bags, in one night you can give the gospel to hundreds of kids (and their families)...all without leaving your home." Such instructions suggest that surreptitious inclusion of tracts in candy bags would be appropriate, the ends justifying the means. But other pages of the site speak to placing stacks of different tracts with the candy given out to allow children to choose their own as well as distributing tracts to people in line entering haunted house attractions.

A second example, *Titanic*, uses a historical event as the vehicle for evangelism. Depicted in dark shades of blue, purple, gray and black, the story is told of a young couple on the ill-fated steamer. Chester, the husband, is the nephew of Aunt Sophie, his would-be proselytizer. Aunt Sophie does not come to see the couple off, sending instead a messenger who tells Chester that his aunt just wanted to make sure Chester's "name is in the Book of Life." Chester sums up the messenger as "nuts" and later rebuffs his wife's recounting of Aunt Sophie's "heaviness about us going on this trip." A final attempt to convert Chester comes when he opens his bags which Aunt Sophie volunteered to pack for him only to find she has put a note in his bags urging him to "admit you're a sinner, believe in Jesus and make him your Savior and Lord, then your name will appear in the Book of Life." Chester responds to this surreptitious evangelism by proclaiming his hatred for his aunt "and her Jesus" and wishing she was dead.

Chester is portrayed as a self-assured, successful businessman. He says of himself, "I've got it made, all the right connections" except, of course, the one vital connection that Aunt Sophie is so desperately trying to make. In the sinking of the Titanic, Chester's wife is allowed to enter a lifeboat but Chester remains behind, shouting "You can't do this to me. It's not fair. Just when I had it made. I hate You for this, God!" As his wife watches in horror, she echoes Aunt Sophie: "I pray he repented, dear Lord, and was saved." But, as Chester's lifeless body sinks to the bottom of the cold Atlantic, Chester's soul stands before a judging God. His name is not found in the Book of Life and Chester is ordered to depart "into everlasting fire, prepared for the devil and his angels."

Again, several aspects of the story are prominent. First, the strong focus on individual existential security, having one's name written in the Book of Life, an ancient idea which dates back at least to the ancient Egyptians. In the current context it connotes life after death but the tract's focus is clearly on eternal life in individual terms. A second aspect is the use of subterfuge, the inappropriate use of a given context to accomplish the business of evangelism. Aunt Sophie's offer to pack her nephew's bags provides her with a means of proselytizing and she even sends a messenger to see them off to get in a final word in that cause. A third aspect is the portrayal of those who reject the message of the evangelizer in inimical terms: "I hate her and her Jesus, I wish she were dead." Correspondingly, the evangelizer aunt is portrayed as suffering rejection and opprobrium for her efforts: "She's nuts…That old hen!" This is a familiar theme in Christian theology: "he was despised, rejected."

The third example is a tract disseminated in English and Spanish, *The Choice/La Decision* (fig. 24).This short story, depicted in stark reds and blacks, begins with the assertion "we always have to make decisions, sometimes good, sometimes disastrous. But there is one decision that is more important than all the rest." In the story, two middle aged men share a lunch and a conversation which begins with the assertion of the one who is the evangelizer that "it is vital that you make the correct decision before you die." When Jorge, the target of the evangelization, asks if his evangelizer means deciding between God and the Devil, his companion responds that "no, the majority of people will go to hell for thinking like you."

The evangelizer then spells out what such thinking means, beginning with an Augustinian interpretation of the Genesis 3 account of Adam and Eve's encounter with the serpent and the tree of knowledge of good and evil in the Garden of Eden, an encounter which Augustine sees as resulting in the inception of original sin. Ultimately, original sin "passes to all of us," an idea illustrated in the tract by a child with his cereal bowl on his head, cereal and milk dripping down his face, apparently acting out of original sin he has inherited from conception (fig. 25). Having defined the problem,

Fig. 24. Handing out *The Choice* (Chick Publications, 1999), cover, University of Central Florida, 2006.

Fig. 25. Handing out *The Choice* (Chick Publications, 1999), inside page, University of Central Florida, 2006.

the evangelizer points out that people who think like Jorge miss the point: "one of [the Devil's] favorite weapons is religion. He uses it to hold millions of people in slavery." Another factor in creating wrongful thinking is education which causes many people to "believe they are too intelligent to accept this truth." Though the tract writer is not clear exactly which religions are being referenced, given the evangelical Protestant bent of the tract, it could easily refer to any other religious understanding. The tract refers to social pressures seen as affecting the thinking of juveniles and some adults whose god is money or sports, but ultimately only "[t]hose who believe that Jesus Christ died for their sins and trust in him as their saviors are born again and are part of the family of God. They receive the prize of eternal life now and when they die they will go to heaven. You are already condemned and on the road to hell."

At this point Jorge reports that he is frightened and begins to inquire about the status of his family members: "they are good people. It is not possible that all of them are on the road to hell." The evangelizer gravely shakes his head and pronounces all of them condemned without Jesus Christ, the only who can rescue Jorge and his family members from "God's eternal condemnation to the lake of fire." The exchange ends with Jorge thanking his evangelizing lunch companion, who has paid the bill, thanking him for telling him about this decision to be made, expressing a desire to be saved at that very moment.

A couple of interesting aspects are observable in this tract. First, as in the other tracts, the focus is on individual salvation, here cast in terms of avoidance of eternal torment in Hell's lake of fire The individual aspect is emphasized by noting that one conversion does not cover a whole family, each individual member being required to make their own individual decision. Second, a strongly sectarian aspect marks this tract which distinguishes true beliefs and true believers from those Jorge's evangelizer judges as having bought into wrong thinking because of their religions and other social pressures. The evangelizer contrasts those who "believe they are too intelligent to accept this truth" with those who buy the simple dogma of Jesus dying for their sins and trusting in him as their Savior. The tract attributes such wrong thinking to tricks of the Devil who uses anything available to him to prevent people from escaping the road to perdition.

In looking at these tracts collectively, some broad patterns come into focus. First, the appeal in each of these tracts is highly individualistic. Each story features an individual with high levels of concern for existential security. The individualistic focus is accentuated by the repeated use of "I" statements by characters in the narrative, particularly those connected to heaven or hell, and by the directions aimed at the individual reader at the end of the tract. Second, all of the tracts feature individualistic utilitarian decision-making which turns primarily on concerns for avoiding pain (following the old Devil to hell, everlasting punishment, lake of fire) and correspondingly on concerns for attaining pleasure (going to heaven, name in the Book of Life, free gift of eternal life). The arguments offered by the tract writer(s) are an appeal to raw emotions of fear and desire.

Third, all of the concerns for existential security are actually induced by the evangelizer in the story. In all three cases, the targeting of the evangelizer is portrayed as naïve (young pupil), blinded by elitism (Titanic businessman passenger) or prone to intellectualizing (Jorge). In none of the cases is the person aware of the eternal existential danger they face until enlightened by the evangelizer and, in at least one case, even then the target of the evangelizer does not convert and faces eternal punishment. Fourth, the element of sleight of hand is common to two of the tracts. In *The Devil's Night*, the public school teacher is portrayed as subtly proselytizing disciples of Satan in the classroom, an inappropriate venue for such activities given the separation of Church and state in American law. However, her young pupil responds to this inappropriate proselytizing by using Halloween trick or treating as an opportunity to proselytize through tracts in candy bags. In *Titanic*, the evangelizing Aunt Sophie, realizing her nephew might avoid her if she comes to see him off, sends a messenger instead who is able to get past his defense system to deliver Aunt Sophie's concern about his name being in the Book of Life. But Aunt Sophie has the last word; having volunteered to pack her nephew's bag, an opportunity to slip a written version of her evangelistic message about the Book of Life into his bag destined to be opened once aboard ship.

Finally, in each tract, the procedure follows a similar pattern:

• Presenting the message in an image-driven, cartoon-story format
• Using striking colors (red, orange, black, dreary shades of blue and purple) and frequent depiction of human faces displaying anger, fear and suffering
• Concentrating on an individual character in the story as the object of evangelism with whom any reader could easily identify, substituting him/herself for the character in question
• Raising a question of existential security which, if accepted by the reader, then leads to a question about how to relieve the same
• Strong focus on individual, instrumentalist decision making which allows for hedonistic choices: avoiding pain, attaining pleasure

• Closure aspects which allow for a formalization of the decision made as a result of the tract's presentation of choices
• Prescribed ensuing conduct designed to help the reader "grow as a new Christian," two of the tracts suggesting purchase of their own publication *The Next Step*
• Information on how to connect with the local church which provided the tract complete with directions and website information

The tracts provide an interesting insight into evangelization of college-aged young adults but a number of questions arise from these presentations: who precisely are the targets of these tracts, why is the cartoon format used and what characteristics of these intended readers are presumed by the tract writers, artists and purveyors? How are those presumptions apparent from the content and approach utilized; how does the interaction anticipated by these tracts resemble other social interactions and how does it differ? A comparison of cartoon style tract evangelism to consumer advertising and marketing may provide some insights into those questions.

Selling Jesus—Evangelism and Marketing

It doesn't matter whether you're selling Jesus or Buddha or civil rights or "How to Make Money in Real Estate With No Money Down." That doesn't make you a human being; it makes you a marketing rep. If you want to talk to somebody honestly, as a human being, ask him about his kids. Find out what his dreams are - just to find out, for no other reason. Because as soon as you lay your hands on a conversation to steer it, it's not a conversation anymore; it's a pitch. And you're not a human being; you're a marketing rep [The film from which this text is extracted depicts a party at a sales convention in which the conflict between the religious beliefs of a young salesman and his cynical colleagues in the business comes to the surface] (*The Big Kahuna*, Universal Studios, 1999).

Traditional evangelism has often been an uncomfortable thing for me. In his book, *Blue Like Jazz*, Donald Miller talks about how Christians often feel the need to sell Jesus like a product, just as we would a vacuum cleaner or a new soap. I think this is true [TrueU.Org, from which this text is taken, is a self-described "community for college students who want to know and confidently discuss the Christian world-view"] (Denise Morris, 2006).

Within steps of the plaza in front of the UCF Student Union where religious tracts are distributed to passers-by lies the UCF College of Business Administration. The college offers a variety of bachelors and graduate degree programs which focus on how to advertise, market and sell goods and services including ideas. In one section of the UCF Marketing 3503 Customer Behaviors course, required for all business majors, the assigned textbook quotes Peter Drucker, "a world-renowned professor and perhaps the most influential writer among business executives," as saying "there is one valid definition of business purpose: *to create a customer*" (2001: 37). The text asserts that anyone marketing anything "must know consumers' needs - if they know where consumers 'itch,' they have a better idea of where to 'scratch' with new and improved products" (2001: 74).

The American Marketing Association describes consumer behavior as a "dynamic interaction of affect and cognition, behavior and environmental events" (Blythe, 1997: 2). Noting that consumers make decisions based upon product, place, price and promotion, marketers focus heavily on the promotion aspect asking themselves questions such as "What type of promotion will interest them? Which will encourage them to buy? Which addresses their needs, *in terms of activating the need* [emphasis mine] and offering a credible way of satisfying it?" Underlying these concerns is a major premise: "[Consumers] can be persuaded - by you, and by your competitors. In other words, they learn and thereby change their attitudes and behaviors" (1997: 4).

For marketers, two primary factors determine the likelihood of consumers changing their attitude and behaviors: affect (feeling responses) and cognition (thinking responses). Considered together with the environment in which marketing occurs and in light of the desired behaviors sought, most marketing strategies will include "a set of stimuli placed in consumers' environments designed to influence their affect, cognition and behavior" (Peter and Olson, 1999). Affective responses tend to be largely reactive with the strongest of responses coming from stimulation of emotions such as fear and anger. Cognitive response, on the other hand, function to interpret, make sense of and provide an understanding of significant aspects of personal experiences (1999: 38-40).

Consumer psychologists have long noted that a major means of activating affective response is through the use of color. Because affective responses tend to be immediate, unplanned and often experienced as outside the control of the individual, up to 60% of the individual's immediate response can be generated by colors utilized in the presentation of a product. While blue is the favorite color of 80% of Americans and yellow tends to command attention, it is the use of red that enhances strong affective emotions such as anger or fear (Wagner, 1990). Indeed, the Roman Catholic Church has long referred to "red letter days" on its calendar, the saints' feast days often commemorating martyrdom. Church fathers claimed that "the blood of martyrs is the seed of the Church" (Tertullian, 1842). On the other hand, black is often associated with death in the west (blacklist, black humor, Black Death) as well as fear connected with the unknown (black holes). While black is the business metaphor for business profits, it has only recently begun to be used in consumer advertising and, until recently it was seen as "taboo because of its funereal symbolism" (Alsop, 1984). A skillful use of color by marketers can manipulate the affective responses of potential consumers. With this in mind, it is important to recall the color schemes used by the creators of the tracts analyzed above: orange and black for the Halloween tract, representing an emphasis on death and fear; dark blues and black in the *Titanic* tract, emphasis on death and fear; and reds and blacks in *The Choice* tract, representing an emphasis on death, suffering and fear.

The ultimate goal of the marketer is the creation of a motivation in a targeted population to become consumers, people "motivated by a desire to satisfy their needs." Recognizing that human perceptions need to go beyond the merely physiological, marketers define need as "a perceived lack," a definition which recognizes that an actual lack of something does not create a need; it is an individual's perception that he or she lacks something that causes them to view that perceived lack as a need. The result of such perception is a "sense of unease", such unease being perceived as "an unfulfilled need" which in turn is likely to lead to a series of events taking place in a potential consumer's mind ultimately resulting in a transaction between marketer and potential buyer (Blythe, 1997: 11).

That advertisers, marketers and sales people have proven successful at creating a sense of unease perceived as unfulfilled needs is readily recognizable in today's western consumer world. Indeed, a persistent critique of modern societies by social scientists is that consumers have come to be constructed through "the manipulation of the group mind, the engineering of desires and needs" (Patterson, 2006: 50). Sociologist Jacques Ellul observed that: "one of the great designs of advertising is to create needs; but this is possible only if these needs correspond to an ideal of life that man accepts…Advertising goes about its task of creating a psychological collectivism by mobilizing certain human tendencies" (Ellul, 1964: 407).

In his critique of twentieth-century western culture, Frankfurt School scholar Herbert Marcuse observed a consumerist society powerful enough to create what he called false needs in consumers: "most of the prevailing needs to relax, to have fun, to behave and consume in accordance with the advertisements, to love and hate what others love and hate, belong to this category of false needs." False needs were defined as those which are:

> superimposed upon the individual by particular social interests in his repression: the needs which perpetuate toil, aggressiveness, misery and injustice... [N]o matter how much he identifies with them and finds himself in their satisfaction, they continue to be what they were from the beginning - the products of a society whose dominant interest demands repression (1964: 5).

Parallels between activities traditionally seen as related to consumerism - advertising, marketing and selling - and activities traditionally associated with religious evangelizing - witnessing, dissemination of tracts and other materials - have long been noted by those engaged in both enterprises. David Morgan's study of American religious iconography suggests that the young nation's framers' insistence upon the First Amendment's prohibition of an imposed national religion effectively created a consumer market for potential consumers of what were now strictly voluntary association religions. A primary method of engaging that religious consumer's market was the image laden tract: "many Protestants from the antebellum period to the present have used mass-produced images to compensate for the First Amendment's disestablishment of religion...The task of influencing Americans was premised upon regarding them as voluntary consumers of ideas and beliefs" (Morgan and Pomey, 2005: 225).

While some churches have seen themselves and what they offer to others in trademark, brand name consumerist terms, more frequently comparisons are drawn to the specific methods of evangelizing that are compared to advertising, marketing and sales techniques. The Methodist pastor Pamela C. Kinter (2003), in her sermon of Nov. 9, 2003 based on Rick Warren's *The Purpose Driven Life*, contrasted what she saw as effective evangelizing through building of relationships with approaches that churches have more frequently used: "a sales pitch, a conquest, a threat, and (sic) ultimatum, an argument - or even a show or entertainment."

Kinter's sermon included an analogy of evangelism to the apocryphal story of the door-to-door vacuum cleaner salesman who would dump a container of manure on the floor of potential customers' homes before they were able to stop him with the statement "Lady, this vacuum is so powerful, and I have so much confidence in its ability, that I believe this vacuum will pick up every speck of this manure or I will personally get on my hands and knees and pick up every speck by hand." The punch line of the story is perhaps obvious: "well, come right on in, young man. We don't have any electricity."

Kinter's sermon evidences a common perception among evangelizers that evangelism bears a striking resemblance to the consumer marketing process. The seller presumes that s/he has the ability and the duty to persuade the potential buyer that the seller has what the potential consumer needs. But, in order to insure the sale, an immediate sense of perceived need must be created. The strategy might well include the manipulation of emotions and strategic tactics that could be viewed as less than straight forward. At the end of the demonstration, the sale is closed through a formal agreement.

What might such a business model plan by evangelizers to win souls at UCF look like? Begin with a presumption that the seller has what the buyer needs, making the case in the tract contents and concluding with contact information at its conclusion. Create an immediate sense of need by manipulating existential security through fear tactics including the use of dread-inducing colors (red, black, orange) and a story line that employs both carrot (existential security on an eternal basis) and stick (failure to accept the religious beliefs of the tract-writer results in eternal damnation). With the first three rules of successful sales in mind - location, location, location - choose the unrestricted free assembly area in the Student Union, an area more known for its handouts advertising nickel beer, spring break getaways and wet t-shirt contests than religion. Leave tracts in public toilets on campus amidst the leaflets for happy hours at local clubs and calls for roommates where students sitting on toilets would read them (fig. 26). Finally, close the sale by encouraging the reader to sign a page of the tract indicating their acceptance of its contents and returning it to the tract publisher. Provide them with local franchise contact information to encourage ongoing connection to the organization.

It is uncertain to what degree tract evangelism is representative of evangelistic efforts of churches today. The tracts distributed at UCF include the name and contact information for local evangelical Protestant churches, many bearing the word "Bible" in their names. Tracts like the ones under consideration here are used around the world, given their translation into many languages. While this approach has numerous supporters, particularly among evangelical Protestant "Bible" churches, it is also clear that this approach draws much criticism from other Protestant churches. This is particularly true with advocates of the emerging church movement, a post-modern grassroots movement among evangelical and mainline Protestant churches marked by a focus on experience, belonging, and wrestling with traditional understandings of the faith, rather than accepting pat answers (PBS, 2005). Brian McLaren (2002), pastor of the Cedar Ridge Community Church in Spencerville, MD, is a particularly vocal critic of the commodification of evangelism, which he describes as his "great love" but a word which has become "so bastardized I can hardly bear to use it...a word with a good heart, in spite of its dirty reputation". He asserts that:

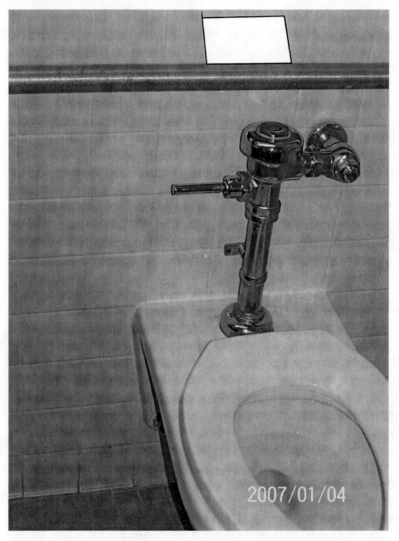

Fig. 26. Evangelizing a toilet cubicle, tract excised (due to absence of copyright permission), University of Central Florida, 2006.

On the street, evangelism is equated with pressure. It means selling God as if God were vinyl siding, replacement windows or a mortgage refinancing service. It means shoving your ideas down someone's throat, threatening him with hell if he does not capitulate to your logic or Scripture-quoting. It means excluding everyone from God's grace except those who agree with the evangelizer (2002: 12).

McLaren lays much of the blame for this approach to evangelism on what he calls "the whole career of modernity," a power-based approach in which "winning people for Christ" becomes an activity consonant with modernity's historical imperatives of conquest, crusades and obedience to laws. While McLaren's emerging church alternative emphasizes relationship and community as the matrix in which healthy evangelism can occur, he contrasts that with the approaches arising out of modernity in which the Christian gospel becomes an argument in which evangelism has become "located... rhetorically somewhere between courtroom prosecution and door-to-door sales or cable TV informercials, complete with clever closes ('is there any reason, Mrs. Jones, why you *wouldn't* want to buy our new Dirt-B-Gone Household Vacuum System?')" (2002: 25).

Ironically, while Christian evangelizers disagree among themselves about the value of traditional evangelistic approaches which use the tactics of the business world, business approaches to advertising, marketing and sales have recently begun utilizing the jargon and tactics of Christian evangelism. A new approach to selling, Customer Evangelism, seeks to not just sell products to consumers but actually to convert them to true believers in the product who, in turn, become committed individual evangelizers for that product.

McConnell, Huba and Kawasaki make the claim in *Creating Customer Evangelists: How Loyal Customers Become a Volunteer Sales Force* (2003) that customer evangelists are effective in creating demand for a given product. Citing case studies of a series of corporations including Southwest Airlines, Krispy Kreme Doughnuts, IBM and the Dallas Mavericks, the authors connected the success of those companies with a base of customer who "believe in" the particular product or service the company offers. The publisher of the book explained the goal of this strategy as being to "[l]earn how to develop evangelism marketing strategies and programs that will create communities of influencers who can expand and drive sales for a company." The authors define evangelism marketing as "the process of getting buyers to believe in a product or service so much that they are compelled to tell others about it" thus creating "communities of influencers who can expand and drive sales for a company." This approach has been called the "new mantra for entrepreneurial success" by the New York Times and the book from which it springs "an absorbing read" by the Harvard Business School (Dearborn Publishing Company, 2006)

All approaches to selling are premised on understandings of who the potential buyer is, what their potential needs might be perceived to be and how to reach that perceived need. Given the approaches evidenced in the content and dissemination process of tract evangelism efforts among the students at the University of Central Florida, what presumptions about the targets of such efforts might be discernable? To answer that question, two social science analytical models will be employed: Maslow's hierarchy of needs and Kohlberg's stages of moral reasoning.

Analysis

In the chapter on "Drive, Motivation and Hedonism" in *The Essence of Consumer Behavior,* Jim Blythe, a business professor from the University of Glamorgan, devotes a significant portion of the discussion of the perceived needs of consumers to humanist psychologist Abraham Maslow (1954) and his hierarchy of needs. Blythe suggests that Maslow's hierarchy of need is "widely used to explain motivation in such areas as human resource management and sales management" (Blythe, 1997: 17)

According to Maslow's system, a five tier pyramid of human needs are met in a specific order of importance beginning with physiological needs (food, shelter) followed by safety and security needs, love and belonging needs, esteem and respect needs and concluding with what Maslow described as "self-actualization... achieving one's goal in life, to become all that one can be." Maslow's system was sequential and progressive in that each higher stage of needs included and subsumed all lower stages. Just above the most immediate human needs for survival, Maslow ranked "security needs," ensuring that immediate physiological needs will continue to be met in the future (1954: 17).

One of the many aspects marketers of consumer goods and services consider is the notion of products as "values satisfiers." In a textbook used in another section of the "Marketing 3403 Consumer Behaviors" course at UCF (Peter and Olson, 1999: 71) consumers are seen as seekers of "personal, symbolic values that products and brands help them satisfy and achieve." Values are defined as "broad life goals (*e.g.*, I want security)" and often involve "emotional affect associated with such goals and needs." Broken into instrumental values (preferred modes of behavior) and terminal values (preferred end states of being), the textbook authors recognize "salvation (eternal life)" as a terminal value of security. Hence, a belief system which would provide an individual assurance of eternal life, salvation, would meet a perceived need for survival after death, i.e., ongoing existential security. The purveyor of a belief system who was able to draw into question the eternal existential security of a potential consumer might readily find a willing customer for a system which could then supply assurance of the same.

The tracts distributed to UCF students on campus all utilize a strategy of drawing existential security into doubt. For example, in *The Titanic* tract, the unsuspecting passenger is headed to his doom, deluded with the widely shared belief that the ship was unsinkable. But in all tracts, the security of one's eternal soul is the subject of the discourse which begins with the assertion that all human souls are at least initially in danger because of original sin. Existential security is drawn into question from the very onset.

Maslow ranks "belonging needs" as the third stage of the hierarchy once survival and security needs have been met. It is interesting to note that the tracts in question all contain a closure of sale provision in which the convert is conducted step by step through a formulaic process which ends with a recommendation to read *The Next Step* from Chick Publications for further guidance. All Chick tracts disseminated to UCF students concluded with information on how to contact a local church, presumably that which sponsored the tract dissemination. For the new believer, once existential security needs have been met, belonging needs can be addressed by potential membership in a new church community.

Another possible analysis of the understanding of the evangelized by the evangelizer can be found in the work of ethicist and social psychologist Lawrence Kohlberg (1984). Much like Maslow's sequential stages of needs, Kohlberg observed that human beings develop moral reasoning in three broad levels which he broke into six specific stages. The pre-conventional level, found predominately in pre-high school aged youth and prison inmates, featured almost exclusively self-focused reasoning where one's avoidance of punishment by those stronger than the individual (stage 1, what must I do to avoid punishment?) or attainment of pleasure and avoidance of pain (stage 2, what's in it for me?) formed the basis for moral decision making. The conventional level, the level at which most adults function, featured bases for moral decision making determined almost exclusively by authority figures outside the decision maker. Stage 3 moral reasoning (Good boy, nice girl) tends to be determined largely by trusted authority figures, frequently significant others, a tribal approach. Stage 4 moral reasoning (law and order) tends to be determined largely by submission to social institutions and conventions.

Kohlberg found that most human beings developed as far as conventional stages but no further. However, his research found that a relatively small number of individuals developed into post-conventional stages, stage 5 the social contract and individual rights stage at which questions of justice begin to critique the presumed valid law and social order of conventional authority and stage 6 moral reasoning, the Universal Principles stage where the understanding of duties to others expands to include all of humanity if not all living beings (Colby, 1983: 28)

In the tracts under consideration here, the exclusive focus of the message is the individual's post-death existential security, i.e., eternal salvation. The repeated use of first person pronouns such as "I" and "my" indicate that the focus of the tract writer and disseminator is on the individual. Moreover, the appeal of the tract is strictly individual in nature: "when *I* die, what will happen to *my* soul?" From a Maslowian perspective, the focus is on a very low level of needs, existential security, ranked only above survival needs. From a Kohlbergian perspective, the focus is pre-conventional in nature- How can I avoid eternal damnation? (stage 1, avoiding punishment) How can I achieve eternal salvation? (stage 2, what else is in it for me?).

Perhaps more importantly, while the focus of the tracts seems to presume a "buyer" at basic levels of need as well as low levels of moral reasoning at the inception of the interaction, the goal in both cases appears to be to move the consumer to the next level of need (belonging) and the next higher level of moral reasoning (conventional, stage 3, tribal) by virtue of the transaction. In short, while the evangelized might begin at lower levels of need and moral reasoning, the ultimate goal of the evangelizer is to move the evangelized to a higher level of belonging to the sectarian religious community. What might this have to say about the project of tract dissemination at UCF? Who seems to be the perceived target of such tracts? Who sees them as the targets? And what presumptions are being made about the needs of the individuals and their moral reasoning which the tracts, and the religious belief system they offer, embody?

Given the prevalence of Chick Publications in evangelistic efforts targeting college aged young people, it is helpful again to review Jack Chick's accounting of his own sense of calling - a sudden experience of the "power of God" which caused his heart to break "with the realization that these teens were probably on their way to hell" (Chick, 2006a). For Chick, it is the alienated teen, in need of salvation and presumably of religious community providing the same, who is the target of Chick's pity. Such targets might well be found in a college population such as that at the University of Central Florida. UCF Students come to a sprawling state university with 46,000 students. Some are away from home for the first time. Apart from significant others from whom connection and moral reasoning might well have previously come, feelings of alienation could readily be expected in such a crowd. A loss of existential security resulting from disruption of home life and the cognitive dissonance resulting from understandings of reality brought into question in college classes might well provide a ready made customer for the evangelizer. Some potential consumers might well be the academically struggling student experiencing a question of his or her own adequacy in the face of intellectuals, who like Jack Chick's Jorge, find that their intellect prevents them from seeing the simple truths revealed to children. For the student experiencing existential insecurity and alienation, a religious transaction is offered in which the student is reassured of existential security and provided with a religious community which offers a sense of purpose and belonging.

A study by social psychologists Altemeyer and Hunsberger (1997) of the religious lives of more than 4000 Canadian college freshmen suggests the strategy of targeting existentially insecure college students might prove effective in limited cases. The 1994-5 study of two cohorts of freshmen at the University of Manitoba and Wilfred Laurier University found that the vast majority of students held essentially the same religious beliefs to which they had been exposed as children. However, the study located a small number of students, 0.8% of the total studied (1997: 30), who had been raised in essentially unreligious or anti-religious homes who by the time of entering college had become fervent believers, the vast majority of them choosing fundamentalist Protestant churches "that had reached out to them" (1997: 198). The study's intensive interviews of these "Amazing Believers" identified a common pattern in their conversion paths:

> If you want a one word explanation of what started the fif-
> teen [Amazing Believers] just mentioned down the road to
> religion, we would say it was fear. It struck from several di-
> rections: fear of what would happen to them if they did not
> overcome their problems, fear of death itself, fear of what
> might happen to them after they died. If you wanted a sec-
> ond-place cause, it would be loneliness, often accompanied
> by the depressing feeling that their life was empty (1997:
> 195).

The study indicated that most of the Amazing Believers had "serious personal problems at the time they began to convert," chief among them alcohol, mental health problems and an overwhelming sense of alienation from others (1997: 194). Thus, evangelistic efforts like those evidenced in the tract-based campaign among UCF students - fostering perceptions of need based in existential insecurity and offering the means of restoring a sense of security - might well find potential "buyers." On the sprawling campus, the chances are that the troubled teenager Jack Chick pledged to reach; lonely, atomized, perhaps battling newfound problems with the maladaptive use of alcohol and/or drugs, might well find a message of hope and connection through the message of the tracts that offered him or her a welcome relief. The seller might well have found a willing buyer.

The ideal types that have been constructed here of the participants in efforts to evangelize UCF students may well exist in fact, as the study of Canadian university freshmen suggests. However, to know if this theoretical analysis describes actual types of both evangelizers and the potential evangelized, it would be necessary to survey and interview the actual participants in this process, a possibility that may be more tantalizing than realistic given the relative anonymity of these particular evangelizers. Whether "Turn or Burn" tracts are successful in creating "Amazing Believers" at UCF is an interesting question whose answer awaits the empirical data of another study.

Clearly similarities exist between business practices of marketing and some practices of evangelism. But such similarities hardly exhaust a discussion of either practice. What more might be said about the motivation of evangelizers than what the mere accumulation of yet another "sale" might suggest? What might be said about the economic considerations of a cost-benefit analysis of evangelism efforts which appear destined to ultimately attract few buyers? How do such efforts represent evangelism generally and how representative is the experience at UCF of college campuses generally? Finally, darker questions must also be considered; questions about what might be seen as the predatory aspects of seeking out troubled youth with sales techniques which appear to manipulate existential insecurities for the purpose of creating a new member of one's flock. Yet, lest this discussion be seen as peremptorily making such a judgment, as Altemeyer notes in his response to the question of whether zealous evangelizing should be condemned, "suppose you had discovered the perfect way to live life, a way that solved all your problems and promised you an eternity of happiness. Would it not be selfish to keep the news to yourself?" (1997: 51)

References

Alsop, Ronald, "Color Grows more Important in Catching Consumers' Eyes", *Wall Street Journal* 29 November (1984), p. 1.

Altemeyer, B., and B. Hunsberger, *Amazing Conversions: Why Some Turn to Faith and others Abandon Religion* (Amherst: Prometheus Books, 1997).

American Tract Service, "Statement of Purpose" [1825] from "American Tracts: Early History," http://www.atstracts.org/readarticle.php?id=4, accessed 2 January, 2007,

Blackwell, R., and P. Miniard and J. Engel, eds., *Consumer Behavior,* 9th ed. (Fort. Worth: Harcourt College Publishers, 2001).

Blythe, J., *The Essence of Consumer Behavior* (New York: Prentice Hall, 1997).

Chick Publications, *Titanic* (Ontario, California: Chick Publications, 1983), http://www.chick.com/reading/tracts/0100/0100_01.asp, accessed 10 August 2006.

_____, *The Choice* (Ontario, California: Chick Publications, 1999), http://www.chick.com/reading/tracts/0100/0100_01.asp, accessed 10 August 2006.

_____, *Biography of Jack Chick* (Ontario, California: Chick Publications, 2006a), http://www.chick.com/information/authors/chick.asp, accessed 2 January 2007.

_____, *How to Make Halloween a Soul Winning Night* (Ontario, California: Chick Publications, 2006b), http://www.chick.com/seasonal/halloween/howto.asp, accessed 10 August 2006.

Chronicle of Higher Education, *Chronicle Careers Employer Profile: University of Central Florida,* http://chronicle.com/jobs/profiles/842.htm?pg=i, accessed Jan. 2, 2007.

Colby, A., Longitudinal Study of Moral Judgment, Monographs of the Society for Research in Child Development 48.1/2 (Chicago: University of Chicago Press, 1983).

Dearborn Publishing Company, *Promotion* (Dearborn: 2006), http://wisdomtools.com/scenarios_readymade.html#scenarios_offerings_mcconnellhuba, accessed Aug. 15, 2006.

Drucker, P., *The Practice of Management* (New York: Harper and Row, 1954), p. 37 quoted in Blackwell, Miniard and Engel (2001), p. 25.

Ellul, J., *The Technological Society* (New York: Vintage Books, 1964).

Gideons International, *About Us,* http://www.gideons.org (Gideons, 2006), accessed 2 January, 2007.

Harvey, R., *The Art of the Comic Book: an Aesthetic History* (Jackson. University of Mississippi Press, 1996), p. 16.

Houghton Mifflin, *The American Heritage® Dictionary of the English Language,* 4th ed. (Boston: Houghton Mifflin, 2004), http://www.answers.com/topic/tract, accessed 10 August 2006.

Jacobson, Susan, "In Orlando, tourists and locals mix to ring in '07," *Orlando Sentinel* 1 January (2007), p. 1.

Kinter, Paula, *Purpose Driven Life #5 – MISSION* (St. Paul's United Methodist Church: Chalmersburg, 2003), http://www.gbgm-umc.org/spumc-pa/fls11092003.html, accessed 2 January 2006.

Kohlberg, L., *The Psychology of Moral Development: the Nature and Validity of Moral Stages* (San Francisco: Harper and Row, 1984).

Marcuse, H., *One-Dimensional Man: Studies in the Ideology of Advanced Industrial Society* (Boston: Beacon Press, 1964).

Maslow, A., *Motivation and Personality* (New York: Harper and Row, 1954).

McConnell, B., J. Huba and G. Kawasaki, *Creating Customer Evangelists: How Loyal Customers Become a Volunteer Sales* Force (Chicago: Dearborn, 2003).

McLaren, Brian D., *More Ready Than You Realize, Evangelism as Dance in the Postmodern Matrix* (Grand Rapids: Zondervan, 2002).

Morgan, D., *The Sacred Gaze: Religious Visual Culture in Theory and Practice.* Berkeley, CA: University of California Press, 2005).

_____, and Sally M. Promey, eds. *The Visual Culture of American* Religions (Berkeley: University of California Press, 2005).

Morris, Denise, "Apathetic Urgency", www.TrueU.Org, accessed 2006.

Patterson, M., *Consumption and Everyday Life* (New York: Routledge, 2006).

Peter, J. P., and J. Olson, J, *Consumer Behavior and Marketing Strategy*, 5th ed. (Irwin: McGraw-Hill, 1999).

PBS, *The Emerging Church, part 1*, episode 845 Religion and Ethics Newsweekly 8 July (2005), http://www.pbs.org/wnet/religionandethics/week845/cover.html, accessed Jan. 2, 2006.

Reuff, Roger, *The Big Kahuna*, dir. John Swanbeck (Hollywood: Universal Studios, 1999).

Tertullian, *Address to the Martyrs* (London: J. H. Parker, 1842).

UCF, *Golden Rules 2006/7* (Orlando: University of Central Florida, 2006).

_____, *United Campus Ministries* (Orlando: University of Central Florida, 2006), http://www.ucm.sdes.ucf.edu/ministries.html, accessed 2 January 2007.

Wagner, C., "Color Cues", *Marketing Insights*, spring (1990), pp. 42-46.

World Christian Tract Directory, http://www.serve.com/Tracts/CTD.html, accessed 10 January, 2007.

Fig. 27. Millennium Theater, Sight and Sound Ministries,
Strasburg, Pennsylvania, 2006, photograph by Chelsea Fleeger.

The Passion and the Profit:
Evangelical Christianity and Media Space in Amish Country

Jennifer Fleeger

During a recent trip to Lancaster County, Pennsylvania, I attended a production by a successful area theater company, fully expecting to see a play about local history or the values of country living, themes emphasized by the region's attractions I had already experienced. Upon arriving at the theater, however, I realized that my knowledge of the county's large Amish population had caused me to assume that Lancaster's tourist industry would work merely to celebrate the past, forgetting the ways in which the construction of history intersects with the technologies and ideologies of the present. The area's guides, covered with photos of austere silos, vast fields, and wagons pulled by horses on winding silent roads, offer visits to Amish farms and one-room schoolhouses, sites that operate, according to Amish regulation, without electricity or other appliances that foster connection to the outside world. While these promotional materials use the lifestyle of a conservative and separatist religious group to signify the heritage of Lancaster County, they also transform the simple practices of the Amish into spectacular attractions by combining new media with traditional values. Visitors to the area can select a package that offers a tour of "authentic" farmlands and a reenactment of an Amish wedding ceremony alongside trips to the location where the movie *Witness* (1985) was filmed and tickets to a production that presents the "Amish experience" complete with multi-media special effects. I situate my visit to Sight and Sound's Millennium Theatre in this setting.

Though surrounded by rolling hills and horse and buggy traf-
fic, the Millennium, with its oriental façade, 2,000 seat interior, and
wraparound stage is not an Amish tourist site. Owned by Sight
and Sound Ministries, an evangelical Christian corporation that reported earning $26 million in 2004, the Millennium is often filled
to capacity three times a day and draws an estimated 800,000 customers each year by staging theatrical productions of biblical tales
(*D and B*, 2004 and Anon, "Area Theater", 2002). Sight and Sound
Ministries uses the same strategic blend of tradition and spectacle
employed by Lancaster's promotion of Amish attractions to establish a space that sets evangelical Christianity apart from modern
American consumer culture while at the same time replicating its
procedures. This paper reveals how the theater's fusion of recognizable aspects of both church construction and mall architecture
results in a place in which its visitors convert to Christianity by
purchasing products. I examine the hybrid structure of the Millennium Theatre and its anachronistic placement in Amish country
in order to position Sight and Sound Ministries within a history of
Christian marketing and explore the corporation's impact on the local tourist economy. I then turn to Louis Althusser and Slavoj Žižek
as well as film theorists Christian Metz and André Bazin to demonstrate that the Millennium produces this space of conversion by
relying on a mode of identification specific to Christian narratives
and dependent on the tradition of the Passion play and its recent
cinematic incarnations.

The Church of Sight and Sound

Sight and Sound descends from a tradition that appropriates popular spaces and procedures for evangelical pursuits. In this essay I
will use the term "evangelical" to indicate a goal-oriented program
of Christian interests engaged with the mechanisms of modernity
in order to distinguish it from the separatist ideology often associated with the idea of "fundamentalism" (Ammerman, 2003 and
Marsden, 1991). While one could certainly argue that the notion of
separatism is inherent in the creation of entertainment for a Christian demographic, my use of "evangelical" follows from Heather

Hendershot's employment of the word to emphasize the proliferation of Christian products in order to proclaim and spread faith (Hendershot, 2004: 17-34). Sight and Sound's mission statement makes its evangelical objectives clear: "Our purpose is to present the Gospel of Jesus Christ and sow the Word of God into the lives of our customers, guests, and fellow workers by visualizing and dramatizing the scriptures through inspirational productions, encouraging others and seeking always to be dedicated and wise stewards of our God-given talents and resources" (InSight, 2005: 3). The organization's stated goal stresses the infusion of religious influence that continues once the audience leaves the space of the theater, the potential for which is central to evangelical beliefs. The Millennium Theatre, in fact, facilitates all five of the tenets of evangelical Christianity identified by religious historian George Marsden (Marsden, 1991: 4-5). The first two of these, belief in the concrete reality of the Bible and acceptance of its role as unmediated truth are made evident by the Millennium's use of capitalization ("Word of God") and its efforts to authenticate biblical stories by "dramatizing the scriptures". The conclusion of each performance asserts that Jesus is the route to salvation and invites the uninitiated to share in this knowledge, fulfilling Marsden's third foundational principle, that Christ alone opens the door to eternal life. Fourth, Marsden stresses the necessity of evangelical outreach. The Millennium's cultural positioning allows it to serve as a space for mission work in a region ripe with tourism. Finally, in answer to Marsden's fifth requirement, the Millennium's printed objective demonstrates the theater's hope that the lessons derived from its productions will be applicable to the daily decisions of its visitors, emphasizing the spiritual transformation it attempts to bring about for those who attend its performances.

The distinction between fundamentalism and evangelicalism in relation to the public sphere after the 1925 Scopes "Monkey" Trial is historically untidy. Although the jury decided against Scopes and legally enforced the prohibition on teaching evolution in the state of Tennessee, the publicity surrounding the trial itself ultimately turned public opinion against an exclusively creationist doctrine. Faced with perceived public censure, Christians constructed their own brand of educational and cultural training fueled by the acquisition of radio and television stations, bookstores, publishing houses, and schools. Yet even before the initiation of the "Moral Majority" in 1979, fundamentalist activities muddied the waters between isolationism and mission work. The most influential Christian pursuit involved building a relationship to the mass media, beginning in the 1940s with radio, a move that sustained an alternative community but at the same time provided the potential for Christian ideals to reach millions of additional listeners. Although estimates indicate that the percentage of secular listeners to Christian radio was and likely remains quite small (Schultze, 1990), the actual number of radio stations devoted solely to Christian programming increased rapidly, expanding from approximately one in thirty-seven in 1945 to one in eight by 1995 (Hamilton, 2000: 120). These stations do not just provide traditional sermons or even those infused with Pentecostal excitement, but also call-in advice shows, radio dramas, songs, interviews and news. This variety allows the evangelical mission to affect both personal and political concerns directly, providing a sphere for the kind of interactivity promoted by Sight and Sound's Millennium Theatre that aims to influence the lives of visitors or listeners apart from their encounter with the text. The success of a radio program has often relied upon its integration with the community within reach of its signal. The contemporary situation, however, demonstrates that shows like Focus on the Family, Dr. James Dobson's hugely influential daily Christian radio address broadcast in over 160 countries (FF, 2006), have found a way not only to engage the local, but also to construct a virtual community of listeners who, in addition to tuning in to the radio, read the same books and watch the same films, which are in turn made available through donations to Focus and other like-minded organizations. The relationship of evangelical Christianity to the mass media and consumption continues with televangelists like Pat Robertson, whose 700 Club website links to an online store that sells books, videos, and apparel (CBN, 2006). While Focus on the Family and The 700 Club certainly speak directly to a self-constituted group of Christians, they nevertheless embrace the evangelical potential of the media by transforming listeners and viewers into consumers, by both encouraging the purchase of goods from the station or its associated website and informing their audiences of how to share religious insights with their physical communities.

The mission statement of the Millennium Theatre requires that one interpret everything onstage as coming from God, read it through the lens of "inspirational production", and relate it to one's personal experience. Christian radio shows and televangelists like Robertson also provide interpretations of biblical events, often updated to suit the contemporary American political scene. All these supposes an inherent passivity on the part of the spectator in accepting the message's validity. Christian radio and televised sermons posit the listener as participant in a congregation of sorts, a group of people whose ideological similarities are confirmed each time they tune in. In order to gain access to this network, the evangelical must disconnect from a particular location and adopt a symbolic position as part of the on-air congregation. Slavoj Žižek's notion of "interpassivity" may be useful in explaining the efficacy of this arrangement. A typical example of interpassivity is canned laughter, where the television laughs instead of the viewer, both anticipating her appropriate response and covering over for her genuine silence. With this idea Žižek explains a specific negotiation that takes place between the subject and the "big Other" (the symbolic order, the invisible community of listeners/viewers into which the member of the electronic church is inscribed) (Žižek, 1998). Canned laughter affirms my "activity", keeping me from acknowledging the otherwise overwhelming fact that I have affected nothing. The societal problems outlined by the radio and television church are generally submitted alongside evangelical solutions that each parishioner can work individually to implement. For example, Focus on the Family encourages listeners to contact their state representatives, use specific parenting methods, or monitor academic materials in their local schools. The stability of this situation arises from the lack of impact spectators have on the actual source of the information, the symbolic order constituted by this imagined public. This radio and television audience is denied access to correlative action; instead, it reacts in a space detached from the one with which it is audio-visually engaged. Thus listeners make up for their own passivity by seemingly becoming active, yet only in ways directed by the electronic church itself.

Sight and Sound's Millennium Theatre operates within the context of Christian radio and televangelism, "communities" built upon a lack of social contact between "members". Like Christian programming broadcast over the air, the theater depends on a particular mode of reception in which the audience consents to receive religious instruction in addition to entertainment. The Millennium makes this relationship explicit by bracketing the play itself with the address of an energetic minister who articulates an appropriate range of responses that visitors may have to the performance. His brief sermon at the play's conclusion encourages those who do not yet identify themselves as Christians to come to the stage and learn how join the faith. By the time conversion becomes possible, however, this particular audience has already disbursed. A relationship with Jesus must be personal, the play's closing speech informs us, something to be nourished at home not experienced *en masse*. Yet a Christian community, while no longer physically accessible at the Millennium, can be accessed virtually through radio and television programs that mimic the theater's ideological mission.

The Millennium Theatre's presentation of authorship further replicates the procedures of the digital church. The program book for the production I attended, a Passion play titled *Behold the Lamb*, cites the name of no actor, writer, composer, or director, with one exception: an entire page of this full-color brochure is given over to Dave Craun, the Design Group Engineer for Sight and Sound's creations. While not an author as such, Craun becomes designer of the message, translator of the Word, a figure that affirms the truth of heavenly authorship by explicitly placing his own body in the position of transmission. The program claims that Craun possesses "such a rare blend of skills that only God could have put him in this job" (InSight, 2005: 11). Thus Craun's achievements are framed within a predetermined narrative originating with God himself. By including a section on the making of the play's storm sequence, a particularly spectacular moment of the performance that makes Jesus appear to walk on water, the program book also works to expose the special effects Craun produces, a revelation that solidly places control of media technology at the Millennium in the hands of a Christian. This model characterizes the media as a neutral force that can be appropriated to communicate both

Christian and secular philosophies. Quentin J. Schultz notes that historically, "American evangelicals championed a rhetoric of the media that emphasized the power of such technologies to change people, especially to convert them to the evangelical faith" (Schultze, 2003: 48). Indeed, in the eyes of many evangelicals, adopting the familiar practices of secular marketing may be the fastest road to salvation. The success of films like *The Passion of the Christ* (2004) and *The Chronicles of Narnia: The Lion, the Witch, and the Wardrobe* (2005), the promotion of a flood of Christian video games from the relatively mild "Timothy and Titus: Saints, Martyrs and Heroes" to the rather gruesome "Left Behind: Eternal Forces", and the use of megachurches, whose congregations number in the thousands, as screening spaces for these and other entertainments demonstrate a belief in the validity of turning to media technology to achieve Christian goals. This approach is elegantly summarized by megachurch minister Lee McFarland in an interview in *The New York Times*, "we want the church to look like a mall. We want you to come in here and say, 'dude, where's the cinema?'" (Mahler, 2005). McFarland's hopes depend upon the strength of new media as an attraction that creates a Christian substitute for a pleasurable secular experience.

A belief in a media with the capability for salvation is essential for the production of the Millennium Theatre as a space of conversion. The power of new technology, mixed with the forces of capital, has proven an effective tool for persuasion since evangelicals began employing the entrepreneurial model of Dwight L. Moody in the late nineteenth century. Moody boldly sought the resources of both corporate and individual sponsors and regularly drew large crowds by carefully planning revivals to generate interest, using temporary or newly built spaces, and featuring the singing of modern hymns (Frankl, 1997 and Hamilton, 2000). New media, whether in the form of a hymnal or in the computer-generated graphics at the Millennium, function as a lure, drawing in audiences on the brink of salvation. An advertisement for an upcoming Sight and Sound show demonstrates how essential technology is to the theater's identity: "join the celebration [for] the most memorable account of the Nativity you"ll ever see—with spectacular staging, special effects that include flying angels, a variety of exotic animals, and beautiful music sung by live accomplished actors" (InSight, 2005: 16). This invitation highlights the construction of the spectacle while at the same time assuring the reader of the truth of the performance: while there may be flying angels, the actors are accomplished, their singing is beautiful, and the animals, however exotic, are real. Sight and Sound's theatricality is dependent on up-to-date digital technology because the stories it tells are miraculous. Rather than emphasize the historical veracity of a biblical event, the theater suggests its very improbability by calling attention to the difficulty of its reconstruction. However, this same move allows the Millennium to proclaim the ultimate truth of its message. By revealing the mechanisms through which Dave Craun constructs his magic, Sight and Sound demystifies the process of theatrical creation. The biblical tales become conceivable, both on stage and in reality. In privileging the role of the special effects engineer, Sight and Sound announces its dependence on new media as a means of saving souls. Yet this is certainly not the only evangelical space to engage this practice; the Millennium builds upon a history of Christian outreach that views media technology as the fastest route to conversion by using special effects both to sell tickets and, paradoxically, to confirm the authenticity of the Word.

Filling the Shelves with Jesus

In addition to providing its visitors with a religious encounter, Sight and Sound substitutes for a particular secular event. The creation of Broadway-quality productions exclusively for Christian (or would-be Christian) audiences allows for the same pleasurable experience structured by the "correct" moral code. This replacement of secular products with similar (and sometimes almost indistinguishable) Christian ones is not exclusive to Sight and Sound's Millennium Theatre. In her *Shaking the World for Jesus: Media and Conservative Evangelical Culture*, Heather Hendershot identifies apparel, toys, rock music, movies, magazines, television programs, radio shows, books, and entire retail outlets aimed at a specifically Christian demographic (Hendershot 2004). This wide range of products varies as to its overt proclamation of Christianity, nonetheless, each item or experience, while taking the place of a secular equivalent, is also necessarily integrated into a culture of consumption. These products and performance spaces like Sight and Sound's Millennium Theatre permit Christians to keep a distance from mainstream culture while maintaining the purchasing power of their secular peers.

Fig. 28. Entrance, Millennium Theater, Sight and Sound Ministries, Strasburg, Pennsylvania, photograph by Chelsea Fleeger.

Fig. 29. Lion and Lamb, Millennium Theater, Sight and Sound Ministries, Strasburg, Pennsylvania, photograph by Chelsea Fleeger.

Sight and Sound's visitors pay nearly as much as their secular counterparts for theatrical entertainment. With the average adult seat priced between $40 and $53, it is perhaps surprising to learn that the company is not funded by ticket prices alone. Customers wait for the theater's doors to open in an ornately designed lobby replete with concession stands and gift stores. With no place to sit, not much room to move about, and little else to do, the visitor is drawn toward these areas as a way to avoid interaction with a congregation of strangers. Despite the scale and religious dogma that differentiates the theater from many of the tourist attractions in Lancaster County, Sight and Sound makes one concession toward community integration: the hallways providing the route to the gift shops are plastered with advertisements for the local outlet mall. In fact, the Millennium's lobby shares many of the architectural attributes of a mall that move the visitor through space and prepare him for the experience of shopping comfortably. The theater's two small gift stores and concession stands are set back considerably from the main entrance on either side, giving the customer adequate time to become familiar with the requirements of the new space. In fact, the Millennium Theatre becomes less exotic as one approaches the building (figs. 27, 28 and 29). Upon leaving the enormous parking lot and nearing the entrance, the spectacular pastiche of "oriental" architecture disappears from view and is replaced by a large sculpture of a lion and a lamb, an image laden with symbolic Christian capital. The animals sit atop a rocky waterfall (replaced by poinsettias for the holidays), surrounded by green shrubbery and rusted red stone. While displays of water and plant life are common additions to the indoor shopping center, the Millennium's visitors would presumably have a more direct relationship to this iconography than the average consumer and thus more immediately identify with the figure of purification suggested by this pastoral scene. The overt symbolism plasters over any direct perception of Sight and Sound's status as a private company. While the inclusion of a recognizable corporate logo would differentiate the Millennium from other similar theaters (as its three golden domes clearly attempt to do), the lion and lamb monument instead connects the building to other familiar religious locations. This association unites the customer with the idea of Christianity as such,

masking the building's inauthentic historical references and inco-
herent spatial context.

The theater brings together a strange collection of artifacts that
at first appear to contrast starkly with the quaint farmhouses of rural Pennsylvania, but upon closer examination prove to be assembled out of everyday materials. Thus the creamy white stones of
the footpath are in reality lines etched into the concrete and the sky-
scape on the interior dome is undoubtedly airbrushed. The placement of this painting on the lobby's ceiling quotes the frescoes of the
Renaissance cathedral and in so doing, exemplifies the fragmenta-
tion and citation characteristic of postmodern space. Certainly the
indoor sky works to demolish the difference between inside and
outside as required by Fredric Jameson's definition of postmodern
architecture (Jameson, 1991: 98). One cannot but read the sky as
one of the religious articulations of the theater and link it to the lion
and lamb on their waterfall just beyond the Millennium's doors.
While each of these objects carries with it specific historical associa-
tions, its signification has been appropriated by the contemporary
shopping experience such that the very evocation of history makes
possible what David Harvey calls "the architecture of spectacle" in
places like Baltimore's Harbor Place and perhaps especially, Disneyland (Harvey, 1989: 91). The revelation of the actual lack of exoticism in the Millennium's construction prepares the visitor to take
on a new status as consumer by associating the space with similarly
extravagant retail environments that employ the shift from the ar-
resting to the accessible. Those who study the habits of shoppers
realize the value of this transition. In the words of Jon Prahl, malls
"*disorient* us, by using natural and religious symbols and spatial
patterns...and then *reorient* us toward one or another of the purveyors of goods" (Prahl, 2003: 71-2). The Millennium aids the process of reorientation by exploiting the sense of smell. Between the
entrance and each gift shop stands a cart selling vanilla roasted
almonds, reminiscent of those commonly found on the streets of
nearby cities Philadelphia and New York. Arriving at the almond
stand puts one in full view of other edible options as well as the
Christian merchandise on display, which ranges from generic angel
statues to shirts and mugs advertising the theater and its productions. In designing the space of the theater as a movement from the

ornate to the commonplace, from a structure evoking the exoticism of ancient Christianity, through modern symbols of the religion, and into a setting where comfort is available by purchasing familiar snacks and household objects, the theater presents religion as a spectacle to be consumed by acquiring Christian commodities.

Sight and Sound's dressing up a Christian message in postmodern clothing is a characteristic move for evangelical retail sites. As the mandate to convert grows ever stronger, the boundary between an adherence to biblical principles and the demand for market participation withers away, until a particular mode of spending becomes a requirement for Christian living. Many evangelicals feel that the point of sale is equally as important as the product itself. One online source for religious merchandise, Spread the Word, takes issue with the secular middleman: "[the] mission of Spread the Word [is to]... redirect dollars spent on Christian products away from secular companies and into the hands of Christian families, ministries and Churches" (SWM, 2006). It is implicit in the location of this exchange within twenty-first-century capitalism that some receive a healthy economic benefit from the production and sale of Christian products. Pyramid schemes like Spread the Word ensure that profit remains in the hands of Christians. The ideology behind this equation is an extension of that once touted adamantly by televangelists: God wants his followers to be rich, thus augmented personal wealth is the heavenly reward for monetary contributions to Christian organizations, a formula aptly named "sacrificial economics" by Susan Friend Harding. Harding explains the procedure in her examination of Jerry Falwell and the language of fundamentalism: "Men and women sacrificially give money to God, and God gives money to men and women, above all to great men of God such as the Reverend Falwell: that is the gospel economy" (Harding, 2000: 122). The equation of faith with financial gain makes a handy solution for televangelists desperate for both economic stability and a consistent audience. It also accounts, in part, for the willingness of tourists and residents of rural Pennsylvania to pay increasingly high prices for evangelical entertainment. The combination of its impressive stature and religious ornamentation only adds to the impression that Sight and Sound's fortune is a reward for devotion. In order to be recognized as "successful" in an evangelical marketplace, the theater must present evidence of remuneration for doing God's work. The spectator can therefore realize three functions for the cost of her/his ticket: a donation ensuring the longevity of a company that engages in mission work, a righteously earned compensation for its entrepreneur, and a means of securing her/his own financial future by reading her/his purchase in terms of a tithe.

The model of "sacrificial economics" was employed by another (now-defunct) Christian retreat, Heritage Village, USA, Jim Baker's 2,300-acre entertainment center and home to his PTL (Praise the Lord) ministry before the organization was adversely affected by fiscal and ethical scandal. In their study of the resort, Thomas C. O'Guinn and Russell W. Belk found that its religious connotations infused the commodities available there with a sacred value based largely on the conception of reward outlined by Harding. The authors noted the centrality of a mall to the geographical and social organization of the resort, despite the location of a renowned church on the premises and the evangelical orientation of its visitors. They further identified the ritual of shopping as culminating in what many understood to be a pilgrimage; visitors bought something because they wanted to identify themselves as participants - as having *arrived*. Moreover, their purchases were made on Disneyfied streets, trash-free zones of nostalgia lined with turn-of-the-century facades. While it worked to reproduce an idealized past, consumption in Heritage Village simultaneously provided for the future: many of its visitors considered themselves partial owners, having paid $1,000 to obtain a "Life Partnership" in the resort (O'Guinn and Belk, 1989: 231). Much like the audience at Sight and Sound, tourists in Heritage Village became part of an imagined collective upon entering its gates, their membership in this sanctified community reified by the purchase of commodities. Sight and Sound's excess is less a justification for inflated pricing than an insurance plan for the effectiveness of its mission—the visible confirmation of abundance at both Heritage Village and the Millennium signifies the blessings of God.

O'Guinn and Belk's description of Heritage Village matches the perceptual organization of Sight and Sound's Millennium Theatre, a place that also tries to evoke a past, though of a different order.

The sense of nostalgia here is predicated on a mishmash of Christian heritage, a conglomeration that echoes the productions themselves, which whittle biblical tales down to their most accessible elements and insert these into fictionalized frame narratives. While Heritage Village relied on a notion of a distinctly American past, albeit with bits of old Jerusalem thrown in for good measure, Sight and Sound's history is potentially universal. Perhaps this framing is a conscious response to recent criticism of the connections drawn politically between Christian heritage and U.S. history. Evangelical author Darius Salter makes historiography one of his goals for reforming the relationship between evangelism and technology. "Religious television has been far more concerned with returning to an American primitivism and nationalism than a primitive Christianity. It is not fully appreciated that Christians need to pay more attention to what Jesus thought than what Thomas Jefferson and James Madison thought" (Salter, 1996: 370). By avoiding the Americana aesthetic of Heritage Village and most of Lancaster County's tourist attractions, the Millennium appears politically neutral and economically inoffensive. Perhaps the Millennium's architecture and performances reflect a shift in viable representations of Christianity and consumption after the Swaggart and Baker scandals. Sight and Sound's owner Glenn M. Eshelman maintains a low profile, representative of the fact that very few *individual* conspicuous Christian consumers have emerged since the televangelism crisis of the late 1980s. Instead, the bonds between Christianity, the middle class, and corporate ideals have grown stronger, resulting in hierarchical organizations like Spread the Word, tourist destinations like Sight and Sound, and the enormous proliferation of megachurches like Lee McFarland's, all of which are particularly if not primarily concerned with the defining mission of evangelical Christianity, conversion.

The Tourist and Technology

Sight and Sound's reordering of Lancaster County's tourist landscape is enabled by its location. The Millennium Theatre is conveniently situated near Route 30, a highway linking Astoria, Oregon to Atlantic City, New Jersey and bringing large numbers of travelers through the county since the 1960s. Lancaster's tourist profile solicits visitors that seek history, nostalgia, and retreat by exploring the vast countryside and Amish farms, as well as local restaurants and inns. Since the construction of Sight and Sound's first theater, however, the region has had a different focus. The company's influence in Lancaster began over two decades before the Millennium's initial production, with multimedia Christian tours of area churches and schools conducted by Eshelman, a native of the region, and culminated in the opening of the Sight and Sound Auditorium in 1976. The Sight and Sound Entertainment Centre, a larger version of the Auditorium, began giving performances in 1991, but was destroyed in a fire and rebuilt as the Millennium in 1998 (SSM, 2006). Sight and Sound's Millennium Theatre now takes in more tourist income than any of the county's other destinations (Gerhart, 2000) and appears predominantly on many advertisements for the region. Furthermore, the theater offers "getaway packages" which integrate a visit to its premises with trips to Amish and other rural sites. Other tourist attractions echo the Sight and Sound mode of engagement. While the Millennium utilizes technology to emphasize traditional values, promotional literature for the nearby Amish Experience F/X Theater, constructed in 1995, boasts that with the latest media devices it presents *Jacob's Choice*, a "dramatic tale of an Amish family's effort to preserve a lifestyle and a culture… unforgettably told through a high-tech, multi-media production conceived in the finest tradition of Hollywood or Orlando themed attractions" (PDCWC, 2006). The application of technology to tell the story of a community whose rules prohibit its use demonstrates both the influence of Sight and Sound on Lancaster's historical presentations and the incredible flexibility of tourist capital. In its reorganization of major local attractions around its own production and religious values, however, the Millennium Theatre has met with implicit opposition. Lancaster County supports a "Heritage Tourism Plan" which aims to "save [the] region's heritage, share it with its visitors, and reap the economic benefits of tourism" (Route 30 CIS, 2005). Sight and Sound appears nowhere in the promotional materials for the plan, and it is even strikingly absent from the "Freedom of Religion Walking Tour" (County of Lancaster, 2003). Of course, many of those who travel to the county due to the popularity of Heritage Tourism will be likely to visit the theater as well, despite its neglect by efforts that work to construct an "authentic" version of Lancaster's religious history. Thus the theater's presence generates further income for both the area in general and its own interests in particular and in so doing, complicates the stories Lancaster tells about its birth by projecting an evangelical vision of the past onto the region's future.

The goal of the Amish Experience F/X Theater is to "break down the barrier of audience and movie screen or stage... to allow you to 'experience' the action along with the characters" (PDCWC, 2006). This promise is equally integral to the execution of Sight and Sound's productions. Aside from exploiting the wraparound stage to draw the audience into the show, the Millennium Theatre relies heavily on the mobility of actors and the use of technology to accomplish this task. The combination of these efforts intensifies the story's emotional impact on the viewer, resulting in what I claim is a historicized primary identification of sorts. Film theorist Christian Metz outlines the distinction between primary and secondary identification with regard to the cinema. For Metz, these processes are rooted in the Lacanian mirror stage; "secondary identification" indicates the connection between spectator and character, and the "primary" type refers to the identification with oneself as the viewing subject, accomplished by identifying with the camera's look (Metz, 1982: 45-52). Thus primary identification, both in the mirror stage and in the cinema that reproduces it, constitutes a fundamental misrecognition of oneself as a unified subject with a degree of control over the action on "screen". Louis Althusser provides some essential assistance in rounding out this inquiry. According to Althusser, "there are no subjects except by and for their subjection" (Althusser, 1971: 182). The condition of subjectivity is submission to an authority capable of designating this status. When paired with Metz and applied to this theatrical setting, Althusser's examination of the subject makes it impossible to view this play without first recognizing the passive position of the spectator required by the performance. Yet recognition always errs. Metz's patron at the cinema, like Lacan's child in the mirror, reads himself as an individual in control while failing to acknowledge the means of subjection to which he must surrender in order to take up the look. Psychoanalytically, the spectator is always in the process of constructing barriers and breaking them down. Identification only works because, even if for a moment, the viewer forgets the film is just a film, ignores the existence of the intermediary, and wills himself to accept that what he sees is everything. Ideology exists in the relation, in the mirror, between the subject and the screen.

At Sight and Sound, identification is produced through a route that insists upon conversion. In order to elicit the emotional response necessary to provoke spectatorial action and make conversion the end result, The Millennium Theatre needs to transgress the border between spectator and stage. In his consideration of the relationship between the cinema and the theater, André Bazin provides an illustration of the reason behind the Millennium's efforts with his claim, "Tarzan is only possible on the screen" (Bazin, 1967: 99). Bazin's route to explaining the failure of theatrical secondary identification moves through the notion of a mass audience. In the cinema, the desires of each individual spectator are united in the figure of the hero: his conquest becomes ours as well. The theater, however, eradicates this happy scenario. The physical presence of the actor provides competition for the spectator's acquisition of what is now a very real Jane. For Bazin, identification with the hero is further prevented by the increased importance of primary identification: the theater is dependent on me. My passivity is thus necessary for the performance to continue; were I to stand up and shout, I would call the bluff, the play would come to an end. The goal of Sight and Sound Ministries, to "sow the Word of God into the lives of our customers" (InSight, 2005: 3), requires a direct physical and emotional response on the part of the viewer. The theater demands passivity from its audience while the story is taking place, yet action upon its conclusion—a tricky procedure. The play I saw at the Millennium, *Behold the Lamb*, makes identification with its hero doubly impossible by framing the narrative within the story of John's relationship to Christ. This distance puts the performance on a par with recent filmic representations of Jesus. As I demonstrate below, the contemporary Passion narrative, whether on stage or screen, imposes a taboo on secondary identification with Christ. To subvert this forbidden misrecognition would be to undermine the subjection necessary for conversion; one cannot be a subject in Christ unless one recognizes Christ as Subject. Identifying with Jesus, then, would conflate the relation between subject and Subject and shatter the ideology that makes sense of the story. These Passion narratives permit me to "experience the action along with the characters" as the Amish F/X Theater insists, but only as John or Mary, or better yet myself, striving to be *like* Christ, but never mistaking myself *for* him.

The film *The Passion of the Christ* avoids the possibility of misrecognizing oneself as Jesus by neglecting to award him a musical leitmotif. While both Mary and Satan (arguably the two key supporting roles in this version of the Passion) are each given a melody to identify their respective characters (Satan's played by the erhu, a Chinese stringed instrument, and Mary's a vocal lullaby), to the extent that he can be located in the soundtrack, Jesus *is* Western tonal harmony. As the film progresses closer to Jesus' death, the music becomes more Western, both in orchestration and instrumentation. Not coincidentally, the film's most corporeal moment coincides with its most beautiful sound. The radiant chorus that bursts forth as the blood from Jesus' newly pierced wound rushes over Cassius is illustrative of the film's association of corporeality with tonality. To identify with this very physical representation of Jesus would be to lessen the recognition of his status as Subject. Paradoxically, even as *Passion* highlights the manifestations of Christ's suffering, the excess of his mutilated body paired with the overdetermined score prohibits direct recognition of Jesus' humanity. The film responds to the danger of cinematic identification by eliminating the potential for the individuation of Christ. Sonically, Jesus has no discrete melodic representation. Visually, his body circulates among a metonymic chain of cinematic action heroes whose texts refuse to contain them.

In a reversal of *The Passion of the Christ*, which uses flashbacks to insert moments of Jesus' life otherwise excluded by a film focused primarily on his final days, *Behold the Lamb* is a Passion play framed as a flashback related years later from the perspective of John, one of Jesus' disciples. The flashback form generally sets a tone for audience passivity; nestled deep in the memory of one of the characters, a story unfolds, from which we are assured (with a few exceptions) the narrator will emerge unscathed. The audience can then safely explore a world that carries its own limits. *Behold the Lamb*, however, quickly rips away the guise of comfort by putting technology on display. After a brief introduction by John, now an old man recalling the time he spent with Christ, the curtain rises to expose a bustling Jerusalem, complete with computer-generated backdrops and a musical recording playing over the surround-sound speaker system. This revelatory move is repeated throughout the program, which at times replaces the staged story of Jesus' ministry and crucifixion with short films of events difficult to reproduce theatrically (for example, the multiplication of the fish and loaves of bread to feed a large crowd) and at other moments integrates this projection with onstage action (most impressively, allowing Jesus to walk on water). The modern-day Passion play, even more reliant on a filmic past, produces a unique arrangement of characters. There exists no object of desire for whose attention the spectator competes with Jesus to attain. Unsurprisingly then, only Jesus remains to be desired, but like a theatrical Tarzan, he stands before us in the flesh while only significant as an idea. By remaining undifferentiated from the apparatus of the theater, however, Jesus the character avoids the dangers of consumption. Represented by the Western tonality that regulates the cinematic *Passion*, Jesus, a figure both within the film and outside of it, is unified with the means of presenting his story. As Sight and Sound's *raison d"être*, Jesus makes the performance possible both by providing the material for the narrative and by empowering the actors and technicians with the inspiration and skills required to spread the Word. In this theatrical setting, authorial and technological excess prevent us from (mis)recognizing the humanity of Christ. If this were any other play, the hero might stay entrenched within it. But *Behold the Lamb* is a production that invades the space of the spectator, forcing upon him a participatory role that, due to the regulations of polite behavior, can only be deferred. Breaking the boundary at the end of the footlights disables the passive spectator hailed by André Bazin; the need to keep Jesus at a distance disappears when the flashback comes to an end. If desire has been channeled correctly, then action, in the form of conversion, is the only result.

Filmed versions of the Passion story, such as *The Passion of the Christ*, and even to an extent the allegorical *Chronicles of Narnia*, solicit a particular kind of spectatorial investment. As a compassionate subject, the viewer calls for an end to the pain caused by events leading up to the crucifixion, but as a filmic spectator, she desires its persistence in order that the production may culminate in a guaranteed spectacle of death and resurrection.   In effect, these films construct the spectator as a reluctant voyeur through the persistence of the soundtrack. Both *The Passion* and *Narnia* rely upon constant rhythms and tones to lull the audience into accepting even the most violent of scenes. In each case, the source of the indiscernible otherness of these sounds—whether vocal chants vaguely Eastern or drumming patterns that hint at African styles—remains unseen. What stands visually in its place are figures, people or creatures that mimic the motion of the music. The indistinct, yet frightening mumblings of the crowd are all but ubiquitous in *The Passion*'s final hour, erased only to emphasize a particularly brutal lashing. As a film for children that translates the story of Christ into a tale about a sacrificial lion named Aslan, *Narnia* employs most of *The Passion*'s effects with less emphasis: the horror of Aslan's "crucifixion" is matched by the screeching and roaring of fantasy woodland creatures.   In both films the music that accompanies death is regular, even comforting—drums, low drones, chanting that seems situated safely in the distance—and yet those who watch from within the diegesis understand the directionality inherent to sacrifice. Primary identification lets us know that we are watching too, caught up in a relentless drive of visual violence that the steady soundtrack gives us permission to observe.

Sight and Sound's production *Behold the Lamb* provokes a spectatorial positioning similar to that of these filmed Passion narratives by projecting both characters and special effects into the audience space. At several points throughout the production, actors run through the auditorium shouting, "crucify him", a phrase that the audience finds reprehensible due to the operation of secondary identification within the play itself, but with which it is nevertheless forced to agree in order to resolve the story satisfactorily. This procedure mimics what Slavoj Žižek calls the "perverse core of Christianity". Žižek asks, "if it is prohibited to eat from the Tree of Knowledge in Paradise, why did God put it there in the first place?" (Žižek, 2003: 15). For him, the answer to this question is identical to the reasoning behind Judas' act of betrayal. The proof of Judas' love for Christ, and the means for the salvation of mankind, is his own unfaithfulness. The theatrical devices in *Behold the Lamb* that surround the spectator with treacherous chants, bathe them in a frightening thunderstorm, or induce terror by wrapping the theater in low green pulsating lights work to situate them in an uncomfortable historical position in which the only way out is through a similar contradictory act of devotion. This escape is provided by the production itself in the form of a conversion that takes place by identifying with oneself as the subject of the look. While no camera appears in this schema to unify the view, the sense of completeness is provided by the idea of the past. The spectator identifies with themselves as historical subject, united with the apparatus of the theater in the decision to crucify Christ. Only by first adopting the role of Judas can they prove themselves worthy of the place of Mary. While secondary identification pulls them to understand the story in terms of pain and injustice, the reaction required by their historical positioning effects a self-loathing that can only be effaced by their acknowledgement and subsequent reconstitution as a subject defined by the parameters of the play. To acknowledge us as theatrical viewers in the present, *Behold the Lamb* insists that we answer to the historical conditions that make this story possible. The spectator must submit to reading themselves as the executioner of Christ (thus the persistent chanting of "crucify him") in order to come out on the other side as a legitimate viewer of the play who looks upon these moments with horror and eventual repentance. Thus Sight and Sound anticipates conversion by exploiting the boundaries of identification and allowing the spectator to be resurrected as a subject only by defining themselves as a Christian.

The spectacle of the Passion maintains the spectator's distance from Jesus until the completion of the performance and makes Christianity available for purchase and individual consumption thereafter. Through its exploitation of media technology, *Behold the Lamb* announces that this display has been assembled for me, by an author transmitting through the designer of the performance and residing in the theater and its products. With the Millennium Theatre Sight and Sound creates a place far more complex than the community of the sacred commodity founded in the evangelical shopping experience of Jim Baker's resort. The theater, functioning as both church and shopping center, channels spectatorial libido through the purchase of goods. Here, money replaces wafers and wine as symbolic of the incorporation of Christ. *Behold the Lamb* demands participation in the form of conversion, both by the construction of identification within the production and by a speech given at the end of the play that informs us about where to buy commemorative products and tickets for future events. Sight and Sound is a commercial enterprise whose members are initiated when they spend money, either on the premises, at its associated gift store, or in the form of a donation to a megachurch that mimics the spectatorial arrangement of the theater. Thus the evangelical theatrical experience modifies the procedure of incorporation, marking it in the literal language of investment that identifies the spectacular space of conversion.

In a sense, my own investment in Sight and Sound's Millennium Theatre is demonstrated by the existence of this essay. As I write these words, a Hollywood version of the Nativity story has just been screened at the Vatican, Mel Gibson is poised to release another epic, and Sight and Sound Ministries is constructing a new theatrical complex in Branson, Missouri. While products situated at the intersection of religion and popular culture are certainly nothing new, the growing influence of the evangelical movement in places like rural Pennsylvania has important political implications. The strength of evangelical Christianity at the beginning of the twenty first-century impacts not just patterns of consumption, but the construction of community and the comprehension of history. In positioning itself as economically successful, architecturally significant, and religiously motivated, the Millennium Theatre restructures the landscape of Amish Country on its own terms. Rather than remain an anachronistic monument, the theater provides the region with a new sense of history by asking that we read both the Millennium and the Amish farms that surround it as signifiers of nebulous Christian heritage. The nostalgia that unifies Lancaster County coincides with the political project of many evangelical leaders who tell the story of a Christian American past intended to shape our present approach to both global and local concerns. Evangelical Christians have begun to demand that the culture industry adapt to their interests, and as scholars, it is imperative that we examine the results. Sight and Sound's Millennium Theatre may be an exceptional place that stages seemingly incongruous productions, but it is symptomatic of an evangelical movement that combines merchandising with religion, constituting a Christianity that requires market participation in order to abide by the Word.

Acknowledgements

I would like to thank Mark Andrejevic, Corey Creekmur, Ofer Eliaz, Dennis Hanlon, Joseph Klapper and Linda Mokdad for reading and commenting on earlier versions of this essay.

References

Althusser, Louis, "Ideology and Ideological State Apparatuses (Notes Towards an Investigation)", in *Lenin and Philosophy and Other Essays*, trans. Ben Brewster (New York: Monthly Review Press, 1971), pp. 127-186.

Ammerman, Nancy T., "Re-awakening a Sleeping Giant: Christian Fundamentalists in Late Twentieth-Century US Society", in eds. Gerrie ter Haar and James J. Busuttil, *The Freedom to Do God's Will: Religious Fundamentalism and Social Change* (London: Routledge, 2003), pp. 89-110.

Anon.,"Sight and Sound Seeking to Increase Storage, Parking", *Lancaster New Era*, 26 January (2002), p. a8.

Bazin, André, "Theater and Cinema", in *What is Cinema?* vol. 1, trans. Hugh Gray (Berkeley: University of California Press, 1967), pp. 76-124.

CBN, *The 700 Club* (Virginia Beach, The Christian Broadcasting Network, 2006), http://www.cbn.com, accessed 30 October 2006.

The Chronicles of Narnia: The Lion, the Witch, and the Wardrobe, film, dir. Andrew Adamson, (USA: Walt Disney, 2005).

Country of Lancaster, "Lancaster County Heritage" (Lancaster, Penn.: County of Lancaster, 2003), http://www.lancastercountyheritage.com, accessed 27 August 2006.

D and B, *North American Million Dollar Database 2004* (Short Hills: Dun and Bradstreet, 2004), http://www.dnb.com/us, accessed 1 April 2005.

FF, *Focus on the Family 1999-2006* (Focus on the Family: Colorado Springs, 2006), http://www.focusonthefamily.com, accessed 4 November 2006,

Frankl, Razelle, *Televangelism: the Marketing of Popular Religion* (Carbondale: Southern Illinois University Press, 1987).

Gerhert, Ann, "Act of God; Lancaster County's Christmas Story: A Miracle at the Box Office Too", *The Washington Post*, 25 December (2000), p. C1.

Hamilton, Michael S., "More Money, More Ministry: the Financing of American Evangelicalism Since 1945", in eds. Larry Eskridge and Mark A. Noll, *More Money, More Ministry: Money and Evangelicals in Recent North American History* (Grand Rapids: William B. Eerdman, 2000), pp. 104-138.

Harding, Susan Friend, *The Book of Jerry Falwell: Fundamentalist Language and Politics* (Princeton: Princeton University Press, 2000).

Harvey, David, *The Condition of Postmodernity: an Enquiry into the Origins of Cultural Change* (Oxford: Blackwell, 1989).

Hendershot, Heather, *Shaking the World for Jesus: Media and Conservative Evangelical Culture* (Chicago: University of Chicago Press, 2004).

InSight, *Behold the Lamb* (Lancaster, Penn.: Sight and Sound Theatres, 2005).

Jameson, Fredric, *Postmodernism, or the Cultural Logic of Late Capitalism* (Durham: Duke University Press, 1991).

Mahler, Jonathan, "The Soul of the New Exurb", *The New York Times*, late ed., 27 March (2005), sec. 6, p. 30.

Marsden, George, *Understanding Fundamentalism and Evangelicalism* (Grand Rapids: William B. Eerdman, 1991).

Metz, Christian, *The Imaginary Signifier: Psychoanalysis and the Cinema*, trans. Celia Britton, Annwyl Williams, Ben Brewster and Alfred Guzzetti), (Bloomington: Indiana University Press, 1982).

O'Guinn, Thomas C., and Russell W Belk, "Heaven on Earth: Consumption at Heritage Village, USA", *Journal of Consumer Research* 16 (1989), pp. 227-238.

The Passion of the Christ, Film, dir. Mel Gibson (USA: Icon, 2004).

PDCWC, "Amish Experience" (Leola: Pennsylvania Dutch County Welcome Center, 2006), http://800padutch.com/z/amishexperience.htm, accessed 11 November 2006

Prahl, Jon, *Shopping Malls and Other Sacred Spaces: Putting God in Place* (Grand Rapids: Brazos, 2003).

Route 30 CIS, "Heritage Tourism", Route 30 Corridor Improvement Study (2005), http://www.route30corridor.com/Heritage.html, accessed 27 August 2006.

Salter, Darius, *American Evangelism: its Theology and Practice* (Grand Rapids: Baker Books, 1996).

Schultze, Quentin J., *Christianity and the Mass Media in America: Toward a Democratic Accommodation* (East Lansing: Michigan State University Press, 2003).

_____, "The Invisible Medium: Evangelical Radio", in ed. Schultze, *American Evangelicals and the Mass Media: Perspectives on the Relationship Between American Evangelicals and the Mass Media* (Grand Rapids: Academie Books, 1990), pp. 171-195.

SSM, *Behold the Lamb* (Strasburg, Penn.: Sight and Sound Millennium Theatre, 2005) [first performance, 1987].

_____, *Sight and Sound Company History 2002-2006*, (Strasburg, Penn.: Sight and Sound Millennium Theatre, 2006), http://www.sight-sound.com/WebSiteSS/gethistory.do, accessed 17 November 2006.

SWM, *30 Fold* (Phoenix: Spread the Word Ministries, 2006), http://www.30fold.com/Mission.php, accessed 27 August 2006.

Žižek, Slavoj, "Cyberspace, or, How to Traverse the Fantasy in the Age of the Retreat of the Big Other", *Public Culture* 10.3 (1998), pp. 483-513.

_____, *The Puppet and the Dwarf: The Perverse Core of Christianity* (Cambridge, Mass.: MIT Press, 2003).

Pursuing *The Passion*'s Passions

Kent L. Brintnall

On the Sunday following the opening of *The Passion of the Christ*, Michael and Krista Branch had an experience that led them to praise Mel Gibson's film for reasons other than its breath-taking cinematography and violent verisimilitude (Eldred, 2004: 49-59). Like many who saw *The Passion*, the Branches identify as conservative evangelicals and looked forward to attending the film as an expression of their faith. *The Passion* opened February 25, 2004, Ash Wednesday of that year. Ash Wednesday marks the beginning of the season of Lent, a forty-day period of reflection and preparation in the Christian liturgical calendar historically tied to the training of candidates for baptism. Lent precedes and culminates in Holy Week, the ritualized remembrance of the arrest, crucifixion, death and resurrection of Jesus Christ. By releasing a film depicting the central events of Holy Week on Ash Wednesday, Gibson was marking the film as a liturgical implement designed to assist Christians in their spiritual development. Many fans of the film acknowledged the liturgical and meditative significance of the timing of the film's release. Several commented on how the film prepared them for Lent and made the experience of Holy Week more meaningful; many returned to see the film as a way of commemorating Good Friday or Easter. Both Michael and Krista had a powerful emotional reaction to the film, experiencing it as a window onto the events of Jesus' death, thereby gaining, in their own words, a richer understanding of their prior belief that Jesus had suffered and died on their behalf.

On the Saturday night following their viewing of the film, Michael had a conversation with his brother-in-law about the film's depiction of Mary, Jesus' mother, and how he was "really struck" by the grief and sorrow she must have experienced at the death of her son. The next morning, while the couple's sons were finishing breakfast and Michael was working on the computer, Krista put their eleven-month-old daughter, Kenna Beth, in the tub. Contrary to habit, Krista failed to take the drain-stopper out of the tub, but merely set it to one side. Called away by her husband to help him with a computer problem, Krista left Kenna Beth, who was playing excitedly, alone for a few minutes. When Krista returned to the bathroom, she saw water on the floor and her infant daughter floating face down and motionless in the tub.

Krista screamed for her husband and thrust her daughter's limp body into his hands when he raced to her. As Michael recalls, "there was no life in her. From the moment I touched her, call it a spiritual thing or whatever, I knew she was not in her body... she was gone." Krista dialed for an ambulance and shouted the dispatcher's instructions to her husband; at the same time, with complete confidence that God did not intend for Kenna Beth to die, she began expressing her gratitude for healing power proleptically, repeatedly saying, "thank you, Jesus; thank you, Jesus," as evidenced by tapes of the emergency call. Michael was also certain that this was not an expression of divine intention: "I realized right away this was an attack of Satan.... The thief came into my house to steal, kill, and destroy." Kenna Beth was not to be stolen that day, however. Rushed to the hospital, she recovered fully with no indication of brain damage from the lack of oxygen, much to the surprise of the medical staff.

Later, the Branches realized that a single image had supported their respective faith that their daughter would not die; both Krista and Michael were remembering the extremely brutal flogging scene from *The Passion* during this crisis. Michael recalls that the verse "by His stripes we are healed" from Isaiah, which appears as a textual prologue to Gibson's film, kept repeating in his mind. On the Branches' understanding, those stripes – Jesus' suffering and victimization – had been experienced so that neither they nor Kenna Beth would have to suffer. As Michael explains, "by those stripes we have authority to take back what was ours." Although both Krista and Michael are clear that it was God's power, and not movie magic, that restored their daughter, they are equally certain that *The Passion* had a role to play. Krista explains that the film's realist aesthetic gave her a new confidence in Jesus. "I don't think I would have been so confident about praying for Kenna if I had not had those images in my mind." Her husband expressed a similar sentiment: "Had this happened a week before I'd seen the movie, I would not have been so on edge and ready to defend my family spiritually."

This "miraculous occurrence" may strike those who do not share the Branches' religious heuristic as incredible. To some readers, the Branches may appear less like courageous spiritual warriors and more like frighteningly careless parents. To others, they may seem like the beneficiaries of incredibly good fortune who choose to interpret the positive outcome as the work of divine intervention. To still others, the couples' story may be accepted as evidence of divine favor, with the Branches mistakenly crediting a film rather than God for the restoration of their daughter. Whatever gloss the reader places on the Branches' account of the significance of *The Passion* for their lives, the couples' interpretive interaction with the film is remarkably typical for fans of the movie, even if their Sunday morning near-misadventure is not. Their experience of the film was sufficiently rich for them to assign it efficacy in their workaday lives. While undoubtedly shaped by their Christian faith commitment, the power ascribed to the film depended also on its cinematic specificity; according to their account, the film's power stemmed, at least in part, from its graphic depiction of violence. Both *The Passion*'s content and form, then, gave it power in the Branches' lives. This engagement with *The Passion* exceeds anything like typical audience pleasure, typical fandom or even typical cult fandom. After all, even if a dedicated, repeat viewer of *The Rocky Horror Picture Show* claims that her life has been saved by finding a community of like-minded sexual and social misfits and even if a committed, multiple watcher of the *Star Wars* trilogy takes a character from the film as his model for behavior, these fans and those who study them generally understand the language and performance of their devotion as only analogous to religious adoration. What does it mean when audience members, because of their religious/cultic commitments, become devoted/cult fans of a film?

Are fans of *The Passion*, like the Branches, a cult audience? How do their responses to this film compare to the behaviors of other cult-film audiences? What features does *The Passion of the Christ* share with other cult artifacts?

This essay examines *The Passion of the Christ* as a cult film and its fans as a cult audience to understand how conservative Christians interacted with this artifact to establish and solidify the boundaries of their community identity.[1] While making reference to the film itself, the pre-release controversy surrounding the film, the criticisms leveled against the film and the marketing of the film to sympathetic Christian audiences, the focus of the inquiry will be on favorable, non-institutional audience reactions. I have focused my attention in this way for several reasons.

First, most of the commentary concerning *The Passion* has related to questions of its violent imagery, its possible anti-Semitism and its biblical and historical accuracy. There has been intense discussion of the pre-release controversy (Boyer, 2004; Fredrickson, "Preface,"
2006; Levine, 2004 and Silk, 2004), the marketing of *The Passion* (Caldwell, 2006 and Maresco, 2004), the film's faithfulness to the historical and biblical record (Corley and Webb, 2004), and its purported anti-Semitism (Landres and Berenbaum, 2004). These interrogations of the film are purely textual in their focus. At the same time, these textual analyses generally treat the film as a narrative-in-pictures without necessarily thinking carefully about how films make meaning in a way distinct from written texts, how *The Passion* might be related to other films and film genres, or how it might reflect Gibson's prior work. In other words, although numerous biblical studies, cultural-studies and religious-studies scholars have written about Gibson's film, they rarely, if ever, have considered how the conceptual tools of film studies might inform, deepen, sharpen or transform their understanding of Gibson's film *as a film*. The majority of essays that devote any attention to the cinematic context of Gibson's film discuss it solely as the latest installment in the long history of Jesus films (Baugh, 2004; Fuller, 2006; Gilmour, 2005; Leone, 2005; Reinhartz, 2006 and Tatum, 2004). Although journals devoted to film have discussed *The Passion*, these pieces have generally echoed the concerns of scholars of religion rather

than offering any unique contribution from the perspective of film analysis (Grace, 2004; James, 2004; Kermode, 2004; O'Brien, 2004 and Whalen, 2004; but see also Bailey and Pizzello, 2004; Duncan, 2004; Prince, 2006). Although many reviewers compared *The Passion* (unfavorably) to films from the horror or action genres, most commentators did this in a superficial or even condescending way (see, for example, Thislethwaite, 2006); careful examination of the film's cinematic roots and dependencies is rare (Aitken et al., 2005; Brintnall, 2006; Márquez, 2006).

Second, although critics of *The Passion* produced a voluminous literature in response to the film, very little has been written on audience reactions to the film and no qualitative analysis of audience reaction has been done, although we do have a very informative compendium of data on *The Passion*'s audience (Woods et al., 2004). My interest in *The Passion*'s audience is in line with a growing awareness in film studies of the importance of the audience and its reactions to understanding how cinematic artifacts make meaning and influence the culture of which they are a part. This focus on the audience has recently been championed by leading scholars of religion and film (Lyden, 2003 and Marsh, 2004).

Third, as will hopefully be apparent in the discussion of cult audience's "boundary drawing" especially, there are significant parallels between how cult audiences construct themselves in relation to mainstream moviegoers and how conservative Christians construct themselves in relation to mainstream culture. In this most recent battle in the on-going "culture war," conservative Christians negotiated and solidified their sense of a distinctive and oppositional identity in relationship to a film. Investigating the behavior of *The Passion*'s fans can illuminate more fully not only the cultural moment the film generated, but may also provide insight into how certain religious communities create, understand and maintain their sense of identity in and through their consumptive practices.

Comparing details of the Branches' story with elements of the general fan reaction to *The Passion* will provide a helpful overview of the central features of positive reaction to the film. First, like most champions of Gibson's film, the Branches' spectatorial engagement was informed by a theological pre-understanding remarkably similar to the film-maker's. The Branches identified as Christian, assigned Jesus' death an important role in their religious worldview and interpreted that death as an atoning sacrifice prior to seeing *The Passion*. Although there are instances of non-Christian and non-religious audience members having such a strong reaction to Gibson's film that they felt convicted of their sinfulness, desired to learn more about Jesus or even converted to Christianity, the overwhelming majority of those who had a positive reaction to the film expressed their response in terms of a renewal, deepening or intensification of an already existing Christian faith.

Most fans with such prior theological commitments, however, demonstrated no awareness of how these commitments affected their viewing of the film. For example, fans often responded to criticisms of the film's graphic violence by stating that the enormity of the violence illustrated the magnanimity of God's love, as if the connection between brutality and compassion would be – should be – obvious to all viewers. Supportive viewers posted numerous messages expressing incredulity that anyone could watch the film and not be moved by its depiction of God's mercy without acknowledging to the slightest degree that such an interpretation of the film was both pre-ordained by and required a certain set of theological lenses. Many fans went so far as to claim that anyone who failed to receive a positive message from the film must be spiritually deformed in some way; such fans failed to acknowledge, in this context, that this film was a Christian text with Christian presuppositions designed for a Christian audience.

This appeal to transparent and univocal meaning extended beyond the film itself to interpretations of audience reactions to the film. One fan posted a story about watching several young boys running through the theatre to a screening of *The Passion*. This commentator interpreted the boys' enthusiasm as a sign of religious fervor rather than as a sign of bloodthirstiness; one has to wonder what meaning would have been assigned to the boys' behavior if they had been running to a screening of one of Gibson's prior action-adventure films. Numerous fans, along with Gibson and members of pre-release audiences, commented on the audience silence that followed any showing of the film. To a person, all observers interpreted this silence as evidence of reflection, thought and contemplation; not a single commentator wondered whether this silence might be indicative of shock, trauma or emotional paralysis. In *Changed Lives*, Jody Eldred's documentary about miracles attributed to *The Passion*, the director, a former CNN correspondent in Iraq, includes footage of *Passion* audiences recorded with "night vision" technology. What the footage shows is people wincing, flinching, crying, covering their eyes and doubled over; what Eldred observes is people experiencing spiritual transformation. While fans' interpretations of the film's text and the reactions of its audience could be plausibly defended, these interpretations are certainly not incontestible and rely heavily on the supportive audience's experience of the film. Although some fans did recognize that certain moments in the film might not be fully comprehensible to the non-Christian viewer, the overwhelming majority of supporters treated the film's overall message as being clear and obvious to any viewer, regardless of religious background.

In addition to experiencing the film as a reflection of their Christian faith, the Branches, like fans generally, praised the film for its realist aesthetic. The film not only inspired and transformed its viewers by giving them a sense of having "been there," but enhanced their emotional connection to these events by doing so. Several fan postings described how they saw Jesus, rather than Jim Caviezel, while watching the film. Others explained how they had heard and read the story on numerous prior occasions, but only now understood it because they had seen it. Many viewers reported crying throughout the entire length of the film (with several noting that they never cry at movies), due in large part to having finally realized, because having finally seen, the enormity of Christ's sacrificial love for fallen sinners such as themselves. Other viewers stated that they felt every blow of the whip in their own bodies while watching Jesus being flogged. Many viewers expressed their desire to shout at Jesus' tormentors to stop what they were doing, while a few reported actually shouting at the movie screen. Given the frequency with which fans discussed their physical reactions to the film and the frequency with which reviewers characterized the film as horror or pornography, I am reminded of Linda Williams' argument (2003) that the genres of horror, pornography and melodrama should be grouped together as "body genres" because each aims to elicit both an emotional – fear, arousal and sorrow – and a corporeal – screaming, orgasm and crying – response in the spectator.

Many viewers made the viewing experience intentionally devotional by praying, saying the rosary or kneeling while watching the film. For the few viewers who confessed a desire to leave the theatre because of the level of violence, most reported that they worked up the courage to stay because they needed to endure watching Jesus' torture because Jesus had actually undergone such torture for them. For these viewers, enduring the displeasure of the viewing experience was understood both as somehow analogous to the suffering of Christ and as a mark of faithful discipleship. The insistence by the film's defenders prior to release that it was biblically and historically accurate, the film's use of period costumes and ancient languages as well as Gibson's repeated observation that he was merely a conduit for the Holy Spirit in making the film, worked to blur the lines between movie, biblical text, historical event and theological interpretation. The film was not experienced by its fans as a depiction or re-telling of the events that comprise the Christian narrative; it was, for the vast majority of fans, both experienced and described as an unfolding of the events themselves. In fact, reading fan postings is disorienting: it becomes quickly unclear whether the writer is discussing the film, Gibson, the Bible, history, Jesus or God. Far beyond mere claims of biblical and historical accuracy, then, fans of the film reported having had an *experience* of Christ's Passion by watching the film. This slippage caused many supportive viewers to assign the film enormous importance in their religious imagination and spiritual lives. This experience of boundary blurring helps explain why *The Passion*'s fans perceived criticisms of the film as attacks on Christianity itself.

This ambiguity with regard to *The Passion*'s status is illustrated in the Branches' assignation of power to the film in the restoration of their daughter. Although the Branches were clear that God, and not Gibson's film, was ultimately responsible for the miracle in their daughter's life, they were also quite willing to assign *The Passion* a pivotal role. To paraphrase their comments, *The Passion* was a necessary but not sufficient cause of their daughter's recovery. At the same time, their narrative of their daughter's drowning accident highlights the importance of emotional reactions as evidence: according to the Branches, Kenna Beth was not merely revived (a sufficient reason for gratitude), she was resurrected; the sole evidence that she was dead is Michael's spiritual sense that "she was not in her body". *The Passion* is assessed favorably by most of its fans because it made them cry, made them feel angry, made them feel guilty, made them feel peaceful, made them feel loved or some combination thereof. The centrality of affect in the assessment of *The Passion* is fully consistent with the importance assigned by evangelicals to the personal experience of God through a relationship with Jesus Christ, the faith-insights gained through other believers' testimonies of spiritual struggle and the guidance offered by conviction of the believer's spirit by God's Spirit. The positive value assigned to the experiential dimension of the film is also remarkably similar to Catholic practices of meditating on physical or mental images from the Passion narrative as a means of placing oneself within the events thereby deepening one's spiritual connection to God. The importance assigned to affective response, similar to the importance of theological pre-understandings, prevented many viewers from reflecting on how or why they were having particular reactions or why other viewers might be having markedly different ones.

The conflation of faith and film, coupled with martial images of cultural war and spiritual battle, generated a *frisson* around *The Passion* and critical responses to it unsurpassed by most films of Hollywood vintage. As will be discussed more fully below, *The Passion* highlighted themes of spiritual and cultural warfare, both as text and event. Michael's understanding of the struggle to save his daughter's life as a form of spiritual battle is consistent not only with understandings of what transpires between Jesus and Satan in *The Passion* (Bartunek, 2005: 17-18), but also what transpired between defenders and denouncers regarding *The Passion* (Fredriksen, 2006; Juergensmeyer, 2004; Levine, 2004 and Silk, 2004). Language of fighting, struggle, preparedness, conflict, combat and battle abound in discussions of *The Passion*, both those that occurred prior to the film's release and those that have occurred in the wake of the film's success. Fans were also quick to link the battle between the "secular minority" that decried the film and the "silent majority" that flocked to see it to struggles concerning abortion, the rights of gays and lesbians, school prayer and other volatile social issues (see King, 2004; Prothero, 2006; Smith, 2004). In a book entitled *The War on Mel Gibson: The Media v. The Passion*, Gary North (2004: ix-xii, 6-10, 175-89) identifies *The Passion* as a decisive turning-point and definitive opportunity in the cultural war between a Hollywood elite and a Christian mainstream and calls his readers (understood as belonging to the latter group and hostile to the former) to action.

The rhetorical drawing of battle lines by the film's defenders make it appear as if the camp of the film's critics is populated solely by non-Christians and that all Christians, as well as many non-Christian allies, have rallied to the camp of supporters. The actual fault lines in this cultural skirmish are, of course, much more complicated. Christians, Jews, Muslims, agnostics and atheists can be found among the ranks of those who had, at the very least, strong reservations about Gibson's *Passion*. By the same token, secular cultural critics, Muslims, Jews and Christians raised their voices in support of the film. The boundaries are further complicated by the fact of the film's Catholic content and its primarily evangelical audience. Michael's reaction to the film, as evidenced by his Saturday night conversation with his brother-in-law, highlights the fallout from the fact that this profoundly Catholic film was championed primarily by a conservative evangelical audience. As a Protestant family, the Branches most likely assigned Mary, Jesus' mother, only a peripheral role in their religious imagination, confining her to Christmastide and the narratives of Jesus' birth. For Gibson, a Catholic film-maker who rejects the reforms of Vatican II as a misguided concession to modernism (Boyer, 2004; Lawler, 2004 andIain Noxon, 2003), Mary was at the heart of his project. As he told *Christianity Today*, a periodical written by and for evangelicals, he was "amazed" at how Evangelicals were responding to *The Passion* precisely because "the film is so Marian" (Neff, 2004. See also Miller, 2005: 13-29). Almost all commentators on the film have noted the centrality of Mary to *The Passion* (Linafelt, 2006; Morgan, 2004; Ortiz, 2004 and Prothero, 2006). Her point-of-view serves as the audience's primary source of information; her reactions serve as the audience's primary emotional cue; Maia Morgenstern's portrayal of her is one of the richest performances in the film. The prominence of Mary was celebrated by Catholics and greeted as a welcome surprise by most Protestant viewers. This convergence of an evangelical audience on a cinematic artifact with Catholic over-tones may have more do with alliances in the political arena than with a shared theological vision (Ingersoll, 2004).[2]

As this overview demonstrates, *The Passion* generated a strong reaction in its audience and a deep commitment in its fans. This fan reaction was generated both by the film's textual features as well as by the cultural context in which the film appeared. Fans interacted with the film, with their world and with each other to define and strengthen their sense of identity. In the following sections, I will examine how this artifact and audience compares to other cult films and fandoms.

Before proceeding to a more detailed consideration of the textual features and audience reactions that might justify classifying *The Passion of the Christ* as a cult film, I want to specify my understand-ing of the key features of a cult film and the typical behaviors of a cult-film audience. Because it has often served as a starting point for discussion of cult films and fandoms, I begin with Umberto Eco's essay, "*Casablanca*: Cult Movies and Intertextual Collage" (1986).

In delimiting the range of movies that can be classified as cult films, Eco focuses primarily on textual features. Eco emphasizes that the cult film "must provide a completely furnished world" (1986: 198). This world must be presented in familiar narrative structures that "display some organic imperfections." The cult film, then, is structured as a collage of well-known, oft-repeated narrative *topoi* that give it an already-seen feel. Moreover, it cannot ascend to the status of masterpiece; it must falter, fall, fail to some degree. One such failure is "glorious ricketiness." According to Eco, "one must be able to break, dislocate, unhinge [the cult film] so that one can remember only parts of it, irrespective of their original relationship to the whole." This allows the cult audience to disassemble the film, breaking it into quotable, repeatable, memorable pieces. Finally, the cult text should appear virtually authorless.

> Its addressee must suspect it is not true that works are cre-ated by their authors. Works are created by works, texts are

created by texts, all together they speak of each other inde-
pendently of the intention of their authors. A cult movie is
proof that, as literature comes from literature, cinema comes
from cinema (1986: 199).

Although chiefly concerned about the textual features of cult
object, Eco also provides insight into the behaviors of the cult audience. As his description of typical behavior for a *Casablanca* audience indicates, the cult fan has a strong emotional attachment to
the cult object and an in-depth familiarity with the details of the
cult object; these feed and are fed by repeated viewings of the film
and the intense pleasures provided by the film for the cult fan (Eco,
1986: 198; see also Kawin, 1991: 19-20 and Telotte, 1991: 6-7). This
audience behavior is intimately linked with the textual features of
the cult film. The "complete world" presented by the film gives rise
to cult behaviors:

> Its fans can quote characters and episodes as if they were
> aspects of the fan's private sectarian world, a world about
> which one can make up quizzes and play trivia games so
> that the adepts of the sect recognize through each other a
> shared expertise (Eco 1986: 198).

In his discussion of fan activities, John Fiske elaborates on the
productivity of fans in relation to the cult object. Like all those who
engage with cultural artifacts, fans produce meaning (Fiske, 1992:
37). Cult fans, however, often produce meaning in external, textual
forms: letters to stars, fan fiction, or, more recently, fan-generated
web-sites (1992: 37-40). Fans engage in these behaviors – repetitive
viewing, quotation of textual material, generation of extra-filmic
materials – as a way of creating a recognizable sect of adepts (1992:
41-42). As Eco's observation about "recognition" makes clear, these
fan activities are often related to the creation and definition of a
community of like-minded individuals in relationship to a particular text. In other words, as many commentators have noted,
fan practices are often a form of border patrol (Fiske, 1992: 34-35;
Kawin, 1991: 20 and Telotte, 1991: 7). Departing from Eco's emphasis on the cult film's textual features, the editors of *Defining Cult*

Movies insist that it is the peculiarity of the cult audience's behavior that marks a film as a cult movie. On this account, cult films come in many forms, use a variety of narrative structures and transcend traditional genre classifications; they are identified primarily by the consumptive practices of their audiences (Jancovich et al., 2003: 1). The most important element of this consumptive behavior, however, is the conferring of value on the film and its audience as well as the recognition of the film's and the audience's oppositional status (2). Cult audiences gain "a certain degree of group identification and... a sense of being somehow validated by the film, as if it acknowledged their values" (Kawin, 1991: 20). The cult audience, then, uses the film as a mechanism by which to identify, demarcate and consolidate itself as an identifiable, unique, separate and – often – superior group.

In virtually all discussions of cult objects and audiences, including the very brief summary given here, religiously inflected language seeps into the description. Cult audiences watch films in a ritual context; they venerate their adored objects; they become a group of adepts. Cult texts are considered sacred; certain texts are given canonical status within the cult. While some authors have challenged the meaningfulness of the religious analogy with respect to cult fans (Le Guern, 2004: 5-6), when thinking about *The Passion*'s fans, the appeal to religious categories and religious language is not only appropriate, we may need to think of these terms outside of their usual function of analogy and evocation. *The Passion*'s audience does, indeed, revere the film; they do use the film to organize a group of adepts; the film deepens, supports and sustains their faith commitment. Viewing the film became, for many fans, a spiritual practice that supplemented or replaced meditating on the stations of the cross or saying the rosary. *The Passion* works in conjunction with social, institutional, ritual and narrative structures outside the film to support a solidification of a particular communal identity. *The Passion*'s fans are, in many ways, a cult audience *par excellence*. The remainder of this essay is a more detailed consideration of this claim.

For the overwhelming majority of fans, the power of *The Passion of the Christ* stems from its realistic portrayal of Jesus' arrest, trials, flogging and crucifixion. To describe *The Passion* as realistic, how-ever, serves mainly to highlight the problematic territory delimited by the adjective. On the one hand, Gibson's film uses costuming, set design and dialogue to create a cinematic image that feels an-cient, from another time. The characters, while portrayed in rather broad gestures and therefore somewhat flat and unidimensional, behave in ways that resemble the psychology of normal human beings: they get angry, they cry, they offer one another comfort, they wince in pain. The narrative, although broken by periodic flashbacks, operates according to the cause-and-effect principles of the audience's non-filmic lives and unfolds in predominantly linear fashion. Gibson's skill in crafting an ancient diegetic world allows the audience to feel its solidity, its completeness, its separateness from their non-filmic lives. In this way, *The Passion of the Christ* is a world of images parallel to the audience's lived reality: the audi-ence can enter this world and imaginatively move around in it pre-cisely because it is as "completely furnished... [as] the fan's private sectarian world" (Eco, 1986: 198).

At the same time, this is a world with a palpable supernatu-ral dimension: demons appear on-screen, the presence of God off-screen is strongly implied, resurrection occurs. Moreover, as many commentators observed in denouncing the level of violence in the film, no one but a super-human figure could survive the brutality Gibson's Jesus undergoes during his flogging (Cardullo, 2005: 622; Crossan, 2004: 23; Meachum, 2006: 5; Wallis, 2006: 123-24 and Wi-eseltier, 2006: 256-57. See also Prince, 2006). As the film's fans point out, this is precisely the point: as the incarnation of God, Jesus was indeed a super, or at least more than, human figure. This defense demonstrates, however, that fans' sense of the film's reality has as much to do with their theological sensibilities as it does with the film's aesthetic character or fealty to the historical record.

Supportive fans describe how their understanding of the enor-mity of Jesus' sacrifice has been profoundly deepened due to the richness of Gibson's cinematic vision. The film is frequently de-scribed as a window on the past or as a time-machine; audience members repeatedly describe the sense of having been there, hav-ing "seen" the events they had previously only read about in the Gospels or heard about in church. The familiar story, then, becomes more meaningful or even real for the first time. For some, this is keyed to Jim Caviezel's performance, especially the expressivity of his eyes. When discussing his performance, Caviezel, a devout Catholic who insisted that Mass be celebrated on-set every day and constantly prayed the Rosary during the making of the film, stated that he wanted audience members to see Jesus when they looked at him (Eldred, 2004: 94-98; Neff, 2004: 30). Many fans, when discussing Caviezel's portrayal of Jesus, explicitly referenced his comments and reported that he had succeeded and that when looking at him in the film they saw Jesus. At the same time, fans also displayed very typical behaviors regarding Caviezel: trading pictures, posting links to fan web-sites, seeking contact information, trading stories about seeing or meeting Caviezel and alerting other members of the fan community as to when and where Caviezel would be making television or public appearances. Because Caviezel and Gibson are the only performers in the film to be generally known to a popular American audience, they are the virtually exclusive focus of "star" attentions.

Like *Star Wars* and *Star Trek* fans before them, *The Passion's* devotees accept Gibson's vision of first-century Jerusalem and the execution of Jesus as "the world" in which the events depicted transpired. As with the failure to consider how their theological commitments might shape their interpretation of the film, fans of *The Passion* generally do not reflect on the distinction between the realist aesthetic that Gibson used and the purported factual, historical, documentary value of the film he has made. In an article praising the film for its ability to show the horror of violence and thus profoundly influence the emotional life of the viewer, Robbert Veen (2004) describes the emotional power, intimacy and realism of *The Passion of the Christ* as compared to the coldness, distance and seeming unreality of the videotape recording of the attacks on the World Trade Center. Veen makes this comment and moves on without ever reflecting back on how Gibson's film is, quite unlike the images of the towers' collapse, at most a fictional representation of an historical event, its evidentiary power stemming from its aesthetic stylization rather than its indexical function. Veen does explicitly state, however, that it is precisely the style of violent movies generally, and *The Passion* specifically, that allows the viewer to understand the meaning and significance of the violence depicted, as opposed to the detached, "factual" style of the twin-tower video that keeps the viewer at a distance. In his discussion of the film's supposed realism, film historian Stephen Prince focuses both on the film's historical "mistakes" as well as its reliance on digital technology and asserts that its realism depends on its similarity to prior cinematic representations of violence rather than the viewer's familiarity with real world violence (Prince, 2006). For *Passion* devotees, the film's aesthetic qualities and theological perspective make it seem familiar, which gives it a sense of being real, true and accurate. Fans rarely acknowledged that the film would not seem as transparently real to viewers who did not share the same theological and aesthetic touchstones.

Not only did viewers of *The Passion* come to the theatre with theological understandings of Jesus' death and resurrection, but like afficionados of *The Lord of the Rings*, the *Harry Potter* books and, most recently, C.S. Lewis' *Narnia* chronicles, the audience for *The Passion* viewed the film with a prior set of texts in mind. Gibson's film was going to be measured, by supporters and critics alike, by the extent it adhered to or deviated from the biblical text it was adapting. The adhesion of *The Passion* to Scripture is a common topic in fan discussions of the film. Given the fairly striking ways in which Gibson's film adds details to the gospel narrative from Catholic visionary texts, a surprisingly large number of fans, including self-identified Protestants, comment that they observed no instances in which Gibson deviated from Scripture. A small group of Christian critics, as noted above, denounced the film precisely because of these emendations. The largest number of fans to address this question observe that Gibson clearly took some artistic license with the biblical text, but since his deviations are consistent with the spirit of the text, they have no problem with his additions. In fact, many of the fans in this group find these additions – the depiction of Satan, the expanded role of Mary, the portrayal of Simon of Cyrene, the introduction of Veronica – helpful for their understanding of and emotional attachment to the story of Jesus. At the same time, connected to the notion of community formation to be considered more fully below, fans were quite clear that Gibson's film, whatever its deviations from Scripture, was so far superior to most Hollywood biblical epics that Christian audiences should support the film.

Although those who write about cult films and cult audiences rarely address the issues arising from the transformation of a cult text into a cult film, the problem of adaptation seems related to Eco's notion of unhingeability. According to Eco, the cult text – whether written or visual – is constructed from a number of memorable episodes, quotes and characters. The text can be broken up – and reconstructed – in a variety of ways. Like the verdict that Gibson's reconstruction of the Passion narrative is acceptable because it stuck sufficiently close to the spirit of the Gospels, cult fandoms generally seem interested in this problem of respecting the spirit of the adapted work. If Gibson had omitted an important character – Judas, say – this may have been one deviation too far. On the other hand, Gibson may have been able to omit Jesus' appearance before Herod without causing controversy among fans of the adapted text. Gibson's most (in)famous "omission" is the "blood libel" from the gospel of Matthew (Matthew 27:25). Although this statement remains in the Aramaic dialogue on the film's soundtrack, it does not appear in the English subtitles. Gibson made this change to appease critics who contended the film was anti-Semitic; explaining this change in his interview with Peter Boyer (2003: 61) for *The New Yorker*, Gibson stated that "they'd come kill [him]" if he failed to do it. Although a small number of fans criticized Gibson's choice to remove this language, most fans supported the change, explicitly referencing how the verse had been used to justify violence against the Jewish people. Overall, it seems to me that it is possible to think through issues of adaptation in light of Eco's notion of the unhingeability of texts. Insofar as the adaptation "gathers up" a large number of the adapted text's most memorable and important features, it will likely be considered a faithful, and thus successful, rendering by cult-fan communities.

The Passion is "gloriously rickety" in at least one other sense. As David Goa (2004) observes in an essay discussing *The Passion*'s dependence on static visual art:

> *The Passion of the Christ* is not a film in the normal sense. Rather, Mel Gibson has carefully crafted a set of *tableaux*

vivants (living pictures) of the Stations of the Cross, a Roman Catholic devotion that began in the twelfth century as a way of accenting the humanity and suffering of Jesus (2004: 152).

Other commentators have noted that Gibson's dependance on and quotation from prior Christian art gives *The Passion* an "already seen" quality that adds to the sense that it is a real, authentic and faithful adaptation of the biblical text (Miles, 2006: 11-20 and Morgan, 2004: 85-86). Although all movies are composed of scenes, many of the scenes of Gibson's film have a kind of stillness and stability that makes them seem much more like celluloid paintings. The most brilliantly executed example of this is the film's penultimate scene: Mary, Mary Magdalene, and John are cradling Jesus' corpse at the foot of the cross in a pose clearly dependent on *Pièta* and Deposition type-scenes. Mary looks directly into the camera and holds out her hand to the audience in a gesture both pitiable and accusatory. This scene takes up a good twenty seconds of screen time with the only change being the slow backward movement of the camera. This *tableaux* – like Jesus' prayer in the Garden, the encounter between Mary and Pilate's wife, the flashback of the woman caught in adultery, the "*ecce homo*" scene where Pilate presents a beaten Jesus to the crowd, the encounter between Jesus and Veronica, and the Resurrection scene – could be separated from the film as a whole and retain their intelligibility and affective resonance. Thus, while obviously having a through narrative that lends a cumulative emotional effect to each scene, Gibson's film is easily separable into its constituent pieces. Paula Fredriksen, a biblical scholar who wrote a number of essays strongly criticizing the implicit theology and biblical inaccuracies of Gibson's film, observes, in terms strikingly similar to Eco's discussion, that the fact that *The Passion* "is actually a series of biblical-movie set pieces... [may be] what makes it so effective as a commercial interdenominational hit" (Fredriksen, "No Pain," 2006: 94-95). These *tableaux*, unlike more typical movie scenes "filled out" with dialogue, allow "viewers of quite various theological orientations" to "find... whatever message they want, because they are the ones filling in all the blanks that [Gibson] left" (2006: 95).

In some ways, the film's reliance on the stations of the cross or the five sorrowful mysteries of the rosary to shape its narrative and inform its visual content may seem to undercut Eco's notion of unhingeability. After all, the stations and the rosary are rituals: unlike quotable, fragmentary texts, they are intended to be experienced as a whole, moved through from beginning to end as a piece. The same, of course, is true of most films – a narrative film is intended to be experienced as a single arc, beginning to end, in one temporal direction, rather than as snippets of dialogue, costume, gesture and setting. What *The Passion* shows is that ritual expressions are also susceptible to the disassembling intervention of audiences. Just as audiences have their favorite moments from *Mommie Dearest* and *Gone with the Wind*, audiences also have their favorite moments from the stations and the mass. Rituals – cinematic and liturgical alike – are susceptible to the vagaries of audience attention, passion, memory and imitation.

The Passion's devotees demonstrate this when they discuss and debate which scene in the film is their favorite. Although the fans obviously consider the film as a whole and as a religious experience, a number of threads on MyLifeAfter.com are dedicated to singling out moments from the film and discussing, in great detail, their features. The *Pièta* tableaux described above is often mentioned. The most loved scene in the film, however, is one of the episodes of Jesus falling under the weight of the cross as he walks from Jerusalem to Golgatha, the site of his crucifixion. As the adult Jesus falls, the adult Mary runs to comfort him; these moments from the present are cross-cut with a younger Mary racing to catch an infant Jesus who has fallen while running up stairs. With this scene, Gibson powerfully and economically portrays the extent of maternal love for the dying Jesus. It should be noted, especially in light of fans' insistence that the film either did not deviate from the biblical text or that it remained faithful to the spirit of the text, that neither of these "favorite" scenes appears in the gospel accounts. In other words, despite the defenses of Gibson's film as a visual record of the familiar Passion narrative, the most moving and memorable features of his depiction are a product of his creative initiative, not his faithful adherence to the canonical text.

Other scenes in the film are singled out so that the fan community can come to a shared consensus as to what they mean. Here, the image most frequently discussed is the "satan baby" scene. During Jesus' flogging, Satan appears three times, wandering through the crowd, observing – perhaps even officiating over – the proceedings. In Satan's final appearance, s/he holds a deformed, wizened, hairy-backed baby in her/his arms. Fans expressed great confusion as to what this image signified. Some fans appealed to Gibson's explanation that his understanding of evil is that it always "apes" what is good and beautiful; thus, the distorted image of mother and child (Neff, 2004: 32. See also Powell, 2004). Other fans, with Gibson's explanation in mind, note that Satan is often parallel to Mary in Gibson's film and that the Satan-with-baby image is a direct distortion of the mother-child relationship between Mary and Jesus. Finally, a small group of fans identify the ugly baby as the anti-Christ of the Christian apocalypse.

As evidenced by fans' appeal to Gibson's statements in their efforts to make sense of the Satan-baby image as well as the direct address of many postings to Gibson himself (and even more powerfully by the ThankYouMel.com website) Mel Gibson's presence as the director and promoter of *The Passion of the Christ* was a key element in the film's success. As Gibson screened the film for church audiences prior to its release in commercial venues, evangelicals responded strongly to his testimony of having encountered God and having been led to make *The Passion* as a sign of his gratitude for having had his personal wounds healed by the wounds of Jesus (Caldwell, 2006: 216, 219 and 223 and Fredriksen, "No Pain," 2006: 95-96). In his testimony before such crowds, Gibson demonstrated an astonishing ability to translate a traditional Catholic piety focused on the bodily wounds of Jesus as a site of redemptive power into the language of an Evangelical sensibility that focuses on the believer's experience of being born-again into a relationship with Jesus Christ. Because of Gibson's ability to make his religious self-understanding appear comprehensible and familiar to his audience, fans linked Gibson's statements about his personal faith not only to the accuracy, insight and power of the film, but also cited it as evidence for why the film succeeded: because Gibson is a God-fearing Christian who made a God-centered film, God made the film succeed. At the same time, many of *The Passion*'s fans linked their enjoyment of Gibson's most recent offering to their devotion to Gibson's work overall. Fans most commonly mentioned *Braveheart* and *The Patriot* when speaking of Gibson's larger body of work, but they sometimes mentioned *Signs* and *We Were Soldiers* as films in which Gibson showed his faith. Some fans, however, spoke of loving all of Gibson's films, with a few specifically referencing the *Mad Max* and *Lethal Weapon* series. Although Gibson's (most recent) public persona is markedly different from other cult-film directors (e.g., John Waters, George Romero, David Lynch, Russ Meyer) *The Passion* audience demonstrates the importance of the personality behind the film to the film's cult audience. How, if at all, can this be squared with Eco's notion that the cult film must appear authorless?

Eco glosses the notion of "authorless" texts by observing that "works are created by works, texts are created by text… as literature comes from literature, cinema comes from cinema" (Eco, 1986: 199). Eco's point is not so much that the authorial personality for the text is invisible, but that the object which the author creates borrows in obvious ways – or, in ways obvious to its cult following – from other cultural artifacts. In other words, the John Waters cult can demonstrate a slavish devotion to Waters as a director while still experiencing his films as authorless in Eco's sense by acknowledging the ways Waters' films borrow from, quote, parody, ridicule and twist other cinematic offerings. Although *The Passion*'s fans do not describe Gibson's film as borrowing from previous films, they celebrate the film as borrowing from – in fact, as replicating – the biblical text. Gibson, while acknowledging his hand as the film's creator and shaper, often characterized himself merely as a conduit for the work of the Holy Spirit in fabricating the movie. In their praise of the film as biblically accurate and/or spiritually insightful, fans vociferously agreed with Gibson's self-description. In this way, Gibson is present as an authorial personality – a God-fearing personality that was attractive to the evangelical audience which most staunchly championed Gibson's film – as well as absent. The film is applauded not because it is an expression of Gibson's artistry as a film-maker, but because of its relationship to a larger set of cultural texts and practices.

The relationship between *The Passion* and the offerings of the secular entertainment media was the most frequent topic of conversation among fans, second only to their descriptions of their emotional reactions to the spiritual power of the film. This distinguishing of the cult object from mainstream offerings is, as noted above, the most typical feature of cult audience behavior. This boundary-drawing took various forms in relationship to *The Passion*. From the moment that Mel Gibson told Fox News commentator Bill O'Reilley in January 2004 that "certain forces" were trying to prevent him from making a film about Jesus, the controversy over the film was characterized by Gibson and his defenders as a battle between Christians and their secular foes (Boyer, 2004; Caldwell, 2006; Fredriksen, "Preface," 2006; King, 2004; Levine, 2004 and Silk, 2004). *The Passion*, then, was understood by conservative Christian audiences as an important – perhaps decisive – moment in the culture wars (Buchanan, 2004; King, 2004; North, 2004). This charged context is evident in the postings on SeethePassion.com. This website, created by Women Influencing the Nation (WIN), was part of an effort to combat "enemies" of the film who wanted to censor and deform it. Fan postings reacted strongly to notions of censorship, citing the First Amendment, the controversy over *The Last Temptation of Christ* and the Jewish monopoly in Hollywood, in their calls that Gibson's film should be allowed into theatres untouched. Although WIN did not identify the enemies they were combatting, there were no public attempts to censor Gibson's film. Abe Foxman, leader of the Anti-Defamation League, and other Jewish leaders had cited concerns about possible anti-Semitism in the film. An ad hoc committee of biblical scholars organized under the auspices of the United States Conference of Catholic Bishops sent Gibson a confidential report on a script of the film expressing their concerns about anti-Semitism and biblical and historical inaccuracies. Neither group of critics expressed the intention or had the power to censor or change Gibson's film. In fact, unlike events surrounding *Last Temptation*, no group ever called for a boycott of Gibson's film. The use of charged terms like "enemies" and "censorship" structured perceptions around the film's importance and its place in the larger cultural struggle.

In addition to the vituperative terms used by both the film's supporters and detractors to characterize their opponents and their opponents' views, *The Passion*, as a cinematic text, works to generate an us-them boundary in its audience. First, in its most simplistic rendering, the film depicts a battle between good (Jesus) and evil (Satan). The opening scene in the garden of Gethsemane has Satan verbally taunting Jesus and Jesus crushing the head of Satan's serpent. After his betrayal of Jesus, Judas is tormented and eventually driven to suicide by demon children. During Jesus' flogging, Satan circulates among the witnesses. And, most tellingly, when Jesus dies on the cross after uttering, "it is accomplished", the audience sees Satan, alone in a barren desert, howling in an agonized defeat. The film, then, delineates a clear and sharp contrast; its viewers are either on the side of Jesus or the side of Satan.

Second, the film assumes a high-level of Christian literacy from its audience (Beal, 2006: 200-03 and Jordan and Brintnall, 2006: 83). The most frequently cited example for this assertion relates to one of the film's flashbacks. After Jesus' flogging has concluded, Jesus' mother and the woman accompanying her, begin mopping up Jesus' blood with the cloths provided by Pilate's wife. While she is bent down on the ground, the woman assisting Mary flashes back to a scene of a dusty street: a crowd of men are in the distance, a sandaled foot stomps in the foreground, the foregrounded figure's finger draws a line in the dirt, rocks fall to the ground, the woman's hand worms shakily into the frame toward the foregrounded figure and the figure reaches down and pulls the dirt-stained woman to her feet. For the Christian viewer, the flashback will most likely be interpreted as a memory of the woman caught in adultery saved from stoning by Jesus (John 8:1-11. See also Schaberg, 2006). For the uninitiated, the non-biblically literate, the outsider, however, the events depicted in this flashback would most likely be indecipherable. Most of the film's flashbacks have a similar quality; in other words, they are comprehensible only to the Christian in-crowd to which the film is primarily addressed. The "limited" address of the film is sometimes noted by its fans. A number of fans note that the film's primary effect will be a strengthening of those who are already Christians and perhaps a reigniting of the hearts of "lukewarm" Christians. At the same time, without any consideration of the intelligibility of the film to a non-Christian viewer, the majority of the film's supporters see the film as an invaluable evangelical tool. This evangelistic hope seems to have gone unrealized. While 60 to 70 percent of Christian viewers thought the film would be a good way to introduce non-Christians to the gospel and planned on recommending the film to their non-Christian friends, only 15 percent of non-Christian viewers saw the film because they had been encouraged to do so by a Christian friend (Woods et al., 2004: 172-73).

In addition to the high degree of biblical literary required by the film, *The Passion* also demands that its audience have a Christian perspective on the biblical texts. As noted earlier, in the film's opening scene, Jesus stomps the head of a serpent that has slithered from beneath Satan's robe. Although this event is not relayed in the gospel texts, it is consistent with a Christian interpretation of Genesis 3:15: namely, Jesus, as Messiah and Redeemer, will remedy the problem of original sin. Non-Christian (as well as some Christian) readers of that Hebrew sacred text might flinch at the meaning Gibson assigns to Jesus' forceful stomp. Even more telling, however, is Gibson's textual prologue to the film. At the film's beginning, the following words appear on the screen, "He was wounded for our transgressions, crushed for our inequities . . . by His wounds we are healed" (Isaiah 53:5). This text has been interpreted by many Christians as a prophecy about Jesus, confirming his identity as the Messiah. Jewish readers of this text, however, interpret the passage as relating either to the historical Israel, contemporary Israel, the Jewish people as a whole or the awaited Messiah. Gibson's use of this Scripture to summarize the theological viewpoint of his film, and his supporters' citation of this Scripture to defend his film as a comprehensible tool of evangelism, demonstrates that the "we" and "our" of the cited passage are not accidentally invoked. The film goes even further than requiring a Christian approach to Scripture by assuming and rewarding a Catholic perspective on the events. Evidence of an "ideal Catholic reader" can be found in the depiction of Mary, the structuring according to the stations of the cross, the reliance on the nineteenth-century German mystic Anne Catherine Emmerich's writings to embellish the narrative, the establishing shots for the preservation of relics and the introduction of Veronica and her veil. The sense of disorientation and exclusion felt by Protestant viewers when witnessing details that were not familiar to them is evidenced by comments and discussions on the film's web-sites.

The textual and extra-textual rhetoric of inside and outside generated a passionate embrace of the film as a marker of (conservative) Christian identity. Understanding attendance of the film to be "an act of religious commitment", evangelicals bought out entire theatres for *The Passion*'s opening week (Caldwell, 2006: 221 and Beal and Linafelt, 2005: 3). Not unlike the ritual performances of *Rocky Horror Picture Show* audiences, conservative Christian viewers used *The Passion* as an opportunity to solidify their identity, to connect with other like-minded citizens and to distinguish themselves from critics of the film. If cult fandom is fundamentally characterized by a desire to generate a separate and oppositionally defined community, then *The Passion*'s audience certainly qualifies as a cult audience. From Gibson's star persona while marketing the film, to the construction of the discussion of the film during pre-release publicity, to the content of the film itself, to the terms of its reception in fan discourse, *The Passion of the Christ* served as a means to mark the boundaries of a "Christian" community and its enemies.

The construction of an intense separation between Christian and secular communities in relation to *The Passion* created an interesting problem for fans of the film with respect to secular markers of the film's success. The intense devotion to *The Passion*, as well as the controversy generated by pre-release publicity, made the film a box-office sensation. The film, which cost approximately $30 million to produce, grossed over $600 million (King, 2004: 160). This figure needs to be supplemented by revenue generated by the sale of the soundtrack (50,000 copies sold on the first day of release), VHS and DVD copies of the movie (4.1 million copies sold on the first day of release), the official book of photography (650,000 copies in the first printing) and various other items of licensed merchandise, including t-shirts, key chains, coffee mugs and New Testaments with Jim Caviezel's photograph on the front (Maresco, 2004). The film's commercial success generated a range of responses among its fans. Some fans enthusiastically reported the film's mounting financial success and noted with glee each revenue record broken.

Other fans decried this attention to the film's commercial success, noting that neither Gibson nor "true" fans of the film's spiritual message should be concerned with secular markers of success. A smaller group of fans went so far as to take issue with the idea that Gibson would make money from the film. Relying on their assessment of the film as a spiritual experience and Gibson's desire to make the film as an expression of faith, these fans felt that making a profit was inconsistent at least and repugnant at most. They suggested that Gibson donate proceeds from the film to charity or use them to establish a fund for other Christian filmmakers. Although Fox News, who had championed Gibson throughout the pre-release period, reported that Gibson donated $10 million dollars to two children's hospitals and $5 million to help build a traditionalist Catholic church, this certainly accounts for far less than the movie generated in terms of net income.

A similar controversy was sparked by the film's recognition by the movie industry. Almost immediately following its release, fans and press pundits began to speculate on the film's chances to secure an Academy Award nomination or victory. As with fan discussions about the film's financial success, they were split on this issue. The majority claimed that the film should definitely receive awards for direction and acting with a minority noting that this should not be a concern of fans of this particular film. Other fans claimed that the film should receive such awards but that a secular Hollywood would most definitely ignore the movie. PassionforFairness.com was launched to petition the Academy of Motion Picture Arts and Sciences to give the film its deserved accolades. When the film received Oscar nods only for cinematography, makeup and music and failed to secure a single victory, fans felt snubbed and expressed their anger. Many fans responded that the more important victory was the People's Choice Award for favorite movie drama. The award from an organization controlled by "the masses" rather than the Hollywood elite only fed the Christian-majority v. secular-elite narrative that the fans were telling each other in regard to the movie. Although such a narrative could have been troubled by Jim Caviezel's nomination for an MTV movie award, no fan posting noted the nomination.

The Passion's supporters, however, are not univocal in their defense of the film. The one issue on which the fan community engages in earnest debate is whether the violence in the film went too far. On one side are those who contend that flogging and crucifixion were remarkably cruel and inhumane forms of torture and execution and that the film's violence is either true to what it seeks to represent or not sufficiently gruesome. On the other side are those who contend that the violence is too extreme and extensive and that the film could have been just as effective – if not more so – if the violence had been toned down a bit. This debate was especially joined over the release of *The Passion Re-cut* and the question of whether it was appropriate to take children to the film. On the issue of violence, then, the fan community seems willing to consider whether or not Gibson faltered in bringing his vision to the screen. Although the issue of the film's violence – whether it is excessive, how it relates to competing strains within Christian theology, what possible pleasures it might provide and meanings it might have for the audience – lies outside the scope of this essay, the fan community's discussion of the film's violence is relevant to the question of how they acted to police their boundaries.

The question of the film's violence did not appear in coverage of the film until after its release. In the fourteen months of squabbling prior to the film's release, the dominant concern was whether *The Passion* would generate anti-Semitic sentiment through its depiction of the Jewish leadership with some attention given to whether the film was biblically and historically accurate. On these questions – questions that had shaped and been shaped by the Christian v. secularist culture war context – fans tended to be univocal. As to the allegations of anti-Semitism, fans were emphatic: there was no anti-Semitism in the film and the portrayal of Jews was simply a reflection of the gospel accounts which should be understood as what really happened. On the question of biblical accuracy, fans were willing to acknowledge that there were embellishments of the biblical text, but supported the film as consistent with the spirit of the biblical accounts. These defenses paralleled Gibson's pre-release characterization of his directorial vision. Unlike the film's purported anti-Semitism or supposed biblical inaccuracy, fan communities could allow themselves to consider the question of the film's violence in more expansive and open-ended ways because they could disagree with each other on this question without violating the markers of devotion and support that had been established by the pre-release controversies. To state the point in yet another way, a *Passion* fan could criticize the film's level of violence and still be considered part of the supportive, appreciative, "Christian" community surrounding the film. To break ranks on the issues of accuracy and anti-Semitism, however, would align the viewer with the secular media and academy.

The same dynamics of permissibility are evident in the ways the fan communities sought to interpret the film's images. On the one hand, unlike most other cult communities, fans of *The Passion* do not seek to interpret or interact with this film by producing ancillary texts extending or embellishing the story. Although there is a section of MyLifeAfter.com dedicated to art and poetry produced in response to *The Passion*, these works are exclusively meditations on the cross of Jesus and the grace of God; they do not supplement, expand or comment on the text like traditional fan fiction. In fact, some postings on the web-site were deleted because they were considered inappropriate additions to authoritative representations of Jesus, based primarily on their depiction of Jesus as a sexual being. Given the phenomenon of fans writing narratives of sexual encounters between characters in other cult communities, the limitation here based on the religious and theological identity of the community is all the more striking. Because *The Passion* was understood by its fans as a visual adaptation of the gospel text and because the gospel text is understood by these fans as literally true and unchanging, *The Passion* acts to prevent, on its own terms, the typical forms of fan productivity.

This structural limitation can also be observed in fan struggles to interpret enigmatic moments in the cinematic text. Two of these enigmatic moments have already been discussed – the Satan-baby image and the woman-caught-in-adultery flashback. Both of these scenes are discussed on fan web-sites. The range of interpretations and the level of disagreement allowed with respect to the former is much greater than that for the latter. The former image, however, is not part of the biblical text, but is a creation of Gibson's reliance on "authoritative" Catholic visionary texts. With respect to the flashback, interpretation of the scene is controlled by a reference to the biblical text. Once John 8 is cited, there is no further discussion as to what the flashback intends to represent. At the same time, fans are able to offer their own understandings of what Jesus wrote in the dirt (a list of the accusers' sins, the Ten Commandments, an invisible barrier to protect the woman from stones) because this detail of the story is not specified in the biblical text. In sum, like most fan communities, a canon of authoritative texts circumscribes interpretive options for "legitimate" members of *The Passion*'s fan community. Unlike most fan communities, however, the identification between the artifact of fan adoration and the relevant canon, and the strict limitations on modifying the canon for *The Passion*'s supportive audience, leaves virtually no room for emendation or supplementation.

Although it has been treated by both its adoring fans and its adjuring detractors as something more, *The Passion of the Christ* is, after all, just a movie. As a movie, however, *The Passion* managed to generate an ecstatically supportive fan community. Like other cult communities, *The Passion*'s devoted audience engaged in repeated, communal viewings obsessing over the details of their beloved text, its meaning and its significance. Like other cult artifacts, this text created a world that seemed real and complete to its fans, that was separable into memorable scenes and images and that left some room for imaginative engagement. Like other cult audiences, but with greater strictures, *The Passion*'s fan-interpreters appealed to canonical resources to resolve interpretive ambiguities in their cult text. In a manner similar to other cult audiences, fans of *The Passion* used the film as a cultural artifact around which they could identify, demarcate, celebrate, solidify and encourage a community of like-minded individuals based on their appreciation of the cult object.

As noted at the beginning of this essay, however, some fans reacted to the films in ways that far exceeded traditional cult adoration. The Branches, for example, were willing to attribute miraculous efficacy to the film or, at least, to the experience of watching the film. The consistent claim of audience members that *The Passion* served as a window onto the central events of Christianity and revealed the truth at the heart of the Christian gospel were reacting in a fashion similar to the Branches. Certain audience members were able to see themselves reflected in this product of mainstream entertainment in a way that felt quite different from their general sense of exclusion from mass culture. Like almost no other cult artifact, *The Passion* was positioned – again, by both its detractors and supporters – as a lynchpin in a larger cultural war about religion, values, politics, citizenship and entertainment. As such, those who liked the film and saw themselves in it were almost compelled to adopt a Manichaean stance toward this text: the film and its supporters were wholly on the side of God and the good and any criticism was an attack on Christianity and the sacred. In this drawing of communal borders in relation to liking or disliking a movie, *The Passion* and its audience both mirrored and surpassed typical cult audiences. Unwittingly echoing the behaviors and sentiments of cult audiences before them, conservative Christian fans of *The Passion* used the film as both a rallying cry and litmus test in their struggle over the character of American society and their place in it. This might, in fact, be the ultimate irony of *The Passion* phenomenon. As much as its fans characterize the film as something radically different from the offerings of mass culture and as much as they understand themselves as doing something radically unique in response to the film, they responded as movie audiences have often reacted in the past. Like the Book says, "what has been is what will be, and what has been done is what will be done; there is nothing new under the sun" (Ecclesiastes 1:9).

Notes

[1] The observations in this essay concerning positive fan reactions to *The Passion* are based primarily on a careful review of two fan-generated websites. My-LifeAfter.com, which bills itself as "the definitive portal for media news and personal stories about the film and its effects", includes opportunities for real-time chatting, collections of news stories, discussion fora and an area to post prayer requests. The general discussion board contains more than 1,100 threads with more than 11,000 individual posts and had active participation as of July 2006, although regular participants noticed that postings and real-time chatting had diminished since the months following the film's release. (The lack of active monitoring of the discussion board was evidenced by the presence of "spam" e-mail among the

more recent threads.) The latest news posting on the site concerned the release of *The Passion Re-Cut* from March 2005.

SeethePassion.com was created by Women Influencing the Nation to "circulate" a petition to support the release of the version of *The Passion* that expressed the film-maker's vision and not one that had been "censored or deformed" to conform to the opinions of "enemies of the movie". This site had over 23,000 entries. The sponsors of the site claimed that they gathered 17,000 signatures; from my review, this would be a low estimate, even accounting for duplicate postings. Roughly 4,000 of the postings dated from after the release of the film. Postings prior to the film's release were mainly names or short statements of support for and excitement about the film. The list of news stories on this site provides a comprehensive account of the pre-release controversies, from the perspective of those news outlets that supported the film, but also ends with stories from March 2005. Neither website contained information about Gibson's 2006 release, *Apocalypto*. Two harshly worded postings concerning Gibson's July 2006 drunk-driving arrest and subsequent anti-Semitic remarks appeared on MyLifeAfter.com for a few days immediately following the incident, but were removed by the site's webmaster.

Other supportive websites include PassionforFairness.com, a petition addressed to the Motion Picture Academy urging that the film receive its share of accolades; SupportMelGibson.com, which has a picture of Gibson from *Braveheart* on its masthead and includes an area recording "hateful comments from the Jewish community regarding this website"; ThankYouMel.com, a collection of 369 thankyou letters that the site's host promised to send to Gibson by December 2004, and Passion-movie.com, the official international fan website. Because none of these sites contained fora for fan comments or discussion, I reviewed their contents less intensively. It is interesting to note, however, that the majority of the home page of Passion-movie.com is currently dedicated to the film adaptation of C.S. Lewis' *Chronicles of Narnia*, a film that was marketed to Christian churches with selective pre-screenings in the same manner and by the same company that managed the marketing of *The Passion*. The official website for the film, PassionoftheChrist.com, contained no site for fan interactions or contribution.

Finally, at least two websites were dedicated to ancillary products from the film. PassionOutreach.com, sponsored by the company that helped Gibson market the film, featured posters, door hangers, bulletin inserts, tracts, New Testaments with Jim Caviezel's picture on the cover and sermon manuscripts designed to help churches use the film as an evangelistic tool. SharethePassionoftheChrist.com, "the website for official licensed products", included t-shirts, calendars, art, collections of photographs, jewelry and coffee mugs.

Because they were not generated exclusively by fans of the film, I did not carefully review responses at the Internet Movie Database (imdb.com) or from RottenTomatoes.com. The discussion forum on Imdb contains almost 2,500 comments. The level of activity on RottenTomatoes.com demonstrates the interest generated by the film. The site contains 468 reviews of *The Passion*, compared to 385 for *The Matrix* (the next-highest revenue-generating R-rated film); *The Passion's* discussion board has 761 threads; *The Matrix's* contains a mere 48.

[2] A sizable group of conservative Protestant commentators have focused on Gibson's depiction of Mary as indicative of the film's Catholic (read "non-biblical,

borderline Christian") perspective. Although this "internal" disagreement about *The Passion* between Christians who share a set of assumptions about the significance of Jesus" death and the proper interpretive approach to the Scriptures is a fascinating topic in relation to film, I have chosen not to pursue it here for the sake of space and simplicity. Positive reactions to the film provide sufficiently rich material for examination and these materials have not yet been investigated in discussions of the film.

For those interested in pursuing the criticism of the film as "too Catholic", the premiere example can be found at LetGodBeTrue.com/TodaysWorld/Passion.htm. Other sites written by conservative Christians worried about the film's Catholic and extra-biblical content, as well as the moral tone of Mel Gibson's and Monica Belluci's prior work, include SeekGod.ca/gibson.htm, pawcreek.org/articles/end-times/PassionoftheChristCatholicTrap.htm, Creationists.org/passionmovie.html, Harpazo.net/EternalProductions/Passion.html and Av1611.org/Passion.

The arguments and observations about the overwhelmingly Catholic perspective of Gibson's film can also be found in T.A. McMahon's *Showtime for the Sheep?* (2004) McMahon's central argument, however, is about cinematic depictions of Jesus per se. Because any movie about Jesus or scriptural matters requires some kind of addition to, deviation from or interpretation of the biblical text, McMahon rejects the form regardless of its theological perspective or alleged adherence to Scripture. A similar critique has been made of *The Passion* (Brown, 2004).

References

Aitken, Tom, et al., "Table Talk: Reflections on *The Passion of the Christ*," in eds. Eric S. Christianson et al., *Cinéma Divinité: Religion, Theology and the Bible in Film* (London: SCM Press, 2005), pp. 311-30.

Bailey, John and Stephen Pizzello, "A Savior's Pain," *American Cinematographer* 85 (2004), pp. 48-61.

Bartunek, John, *Inside the Passion: an Insider's Guide to "The Passion of the Christ"* (West Chester: Ascension Press, 2005).

Baugh, Lloyd, "*Imago Christi*: Aesthetic and Theological Issues in Jesus Films by Pasolini, Scorsese, and Gibson," in Landres and Berenbaum (2004), pp. 159-71.

Beal, Timothy K., "They Know Not What They Watch," in Beal and Linafelt, pp. 199-204.

_____ and Tod Linafelt, eds., *Mel Gibson's Bible: Religion, Popular Culture, and "The Passion of the Christ"* (Chicago: University of Chicago Press, 2006).

Boyer, Peter, "The Jesus War: Mel Gibson's Obsession," *The New Yorker* 15 September (2003), pp. 58-71.

Brintnall, Kent L., "Mel Gibson's *The Passion of the Christ* and the Politics of Resurrection," *English Language Notes* 44 (2006), pp. 235-40.

Brown, Ian, *What You Need to Know about "The Passion of the Christ"* (Greenville: Ambassador Publications, 2004).

Caldwell, Deborah, "Selling *Passion*," in Fredriksen (2006), pp. 211-24.

Cardullo, Bert, "The Violence of the Christ," *The Hudson Review* 57 (2005), pp. 620-28.

Corley, Kathleen E. and Robert L. Webb, eds., *Jesus and Mel Gibson's "The Passion of the Christ": The Film, the Gospels and the Claims of History* (New York: Continuum, 2004).

Crossan, John Dominic, "Hymn to a Savage God," in Corley and Webb (2004), pp. 8-27.

Duncan, Jody, "Passion Play," *Cinefex* 97 (2004), pp. 27-37.

Eco, Umberto, "*Casablanca*: Cult Movies and Intertextual Collage," in *Travels in Hyper-Reality*, trans. William Weaver (New York: Harcourt, Brace and Jovanovich, 1986), pp. 197-211.

Eldred, Jody, *Changed Lives: Miracles of "The Passion"* (Eugene: Harvest House Publishers, 2004).

Fiske, John, "The Cultural Economy of Fandom," in ed. Lisa Lewis, *The Adoring Audience: Fan Culture and Popular Media* (New York: Routledge, 1992), pp. 30-49.

Fredriksen, Paula, "No Pain, No Gain?," in Beal and Linafelt (2006), pp. 91-98.

_____, ed. *On "The Passion of the Christ": Exploring the Issues Raised by the Controversial Movie* (Berkeley: University of California Press, 2006).

_____, "Preface," in Fredriksen (2006), pp. xi-xxiii.

Fuller, Christopher C., "Gibson's *Passion* in the Light of Pasolini's *Gospel*," *SBL Forum* (2006), www.sbl-sit.org/Article.aspx?ArticleID=508, accessed 4 March 2006.

Gilmour, Peter, "Text and Context: *the Passion of the Christ* and Other Jesus Films," *Religious Education* 100 (2005), pp. 311-25.

Goa, David J., "*The Passion*, Classical Art and Re-presentation," in Corley and Webb (2004), pp. 151-59.

Grace, Pamela, 'Sacred Savagery: *The Passion of the Christ*," *Cineaste* 29 (2004), pp. 13-17.

Ingersoll, Julie, "Is It Finished? *The Passion of the Christ* and the Fault Lines in American Christianity," in Landres and Berenbaum (2004), pp. 75-87.

James, Nick, "Hell in Jerusalem," *Sight and Sound* 14, April (2004), pp. 14-18.

Jancovich, Mark et al., "Introduction," in *Defining Cult Movies: The Cultural Politics of Oppositional Taste* (Manchester: Manchester University Press, 2003), pp. 1-13.

Jordan, Mark D. and Kent L. Brintnall, "Mel Gibson, Bride of Christ," in Beal and Linafelt (2005), pp. 81-87.

Juergensmeyer, Mark, "Afterword: the Passion of War," in Landres and Berenbaum (2005), pp. 279-87.

Kawin, Bruce, "After Midnight," in ed. J.P. Telotte, *The Cult Film Experience: Beyond All Reason* (Austin: University of Texas Press, 1991), pp. 18-25.

Kermode, Mark, "*The Passion of the Christ*," *Sight and Sound* 14 April (2004), pp. 62-63.

King, Neal, "Truth at Last: Evangelical Communities Embrace *The Passion of the Christ*," in Plate (2004), pp. 151-62.

Landres, J. Shawn and Michael Berenbaum, eds., *After "The Passion" is Gone: American Religious Consequences* (New York: AltaMira Press, 2004).

Lawler, Michael G., "Sectarian Catholicism and Mel Gibson," *Journal of Religion and Film* 8 (2004), www.unomaha.edu/jrf/2004Symposium/Lawler.htm, accessed 11 March 2005.

Le Guern, Philippe, "Toward a Constructivist Approach to Media Cults," trans. Richard Crangle, in eds. Sara Gwenllian-Jones and Roberta E. Pearson, *Cult Television*, (Minneapolis: University of Minnesota Press, 2004), pp. 3-25.

Leone, Massimo, "A Semiotic Comparison between Mel Gibson's *The Passion of the Christ* and Pier Paolo Pasolini's *The Gospel According to Saint Matthew*," *Pastoral Psychology* 53 (2005), pp. 351-60.

Levine, Amy-Jill, "Mel Gibson, the Scribes, and the Pharisees," in Plate (2004), pp. 137-49.

Linafelt, Tod, "Tragically Heroic Men and the Women Who Love Them," in Beal and Linafelt (2006), pp. 29-37.

Lyden, John C., *Film as Religion: Myths, Morals, and Rituals* (New York: New York University Press, 2003).

McMahon, T. A., *Showtime for the Sheep? The Church and "The Passion of the Christ"* (Bend: The Berean Call, 2004).

Maresco, Peter A., "Mel Gibson's *The Passion of the Christ*: Market Segmentation, Mass Marketing and Promotion, and the Internet," *Journal of Religion and Popular Culture* 7 (2004), www.usask.ca/relst/jrpc/art8-melgibsonmarketing.html, accessed December 2, 2005.

Márquez, José, "Lights! Camera! Action!," in Beal and Linafelt (2006), pp. 177-86.

Marsh, Clive, *Cinema and Sentiment: Film's Challenge to Theology* (Waynesboro: Paternoster Press, 2004).

Meachum, Jon, "Who Really Killed Jesus?" in Fredriksen (2006), pp. 1-15.

Middleton, Darren J. N., "Celluloid Synoptics: Viewing the Gospels of Marty and Mel Together," in Plate (2004), pp. 71-81.

Miles, Jack, "The Art of *The Passion*," in Beal and Linafelt (2006), pp. 11-20.

Miller, Monica Migliorino, *The Theology of "The Passion of the Christ"* (Staten Island: Alba House, 2005).

Morgan, David, "Catholic Visual Piety and *The Passion of the Christ*," in Plate (2004), pp. 85-96.

Neff, David, "The Passion of Mel Gibson," *Christianity Today* 48 (2004), pp. 30-34.

North, Gary, *The War on Mel Gibson: The Media v. "The Passion"* (Powder Springs: American Vision, 2004).

Noxon, Christopher, "Is the Pope Catholic… Enough?" *The New York Times Magazine* 9 March (2003), pp. 50-53.

O'Brien, Geoffrey, "Throne of Blood," *Film Comment* 40, May June (2004), pp. 26-29.

Ortiz, Gaye, "*Passion*-ate Women: the Female Presence in *The Passion of the Christ*," in Plate (2004), pp. 109-20.

Plate, S. Brent, *Re-Viewing "The Passion": Mel Gibson's Film and Its Critics* (New York: Palgrave, 2004).

Powell, Mark Allan, 'Satan and the Demons," in Corley and Webb (2004), pp. 71-78.

Prince, Stephen, "Beholding Blood Sacrifice in *The Passion of the Christ*: How Real is Movie Violence?" *Film Quarterly* 59 (2006), pp. 11-22.

Prothero, Stephen, "Jesus Nation, Catholic Christ," in Fredriksen (2006), pp. 267-81.

Reinhartz, Adele, "Jesus of Hollywood," in Fredriksen (2006), pp. 165-79.

Schaberg, Jane, "Gibson's Mary Magdalene," in Beal and Linafelt (2006), pp. 69-79.

Silk, Mark, "Almost a Culture War: the Making of *The Passion* Controversy," in Landres and Berenbaum (2004), pp. 23-34.

Smith, Leslie E., "Living *in* the World, But Not *of* the World," in Landres and Berenbaum (2004), pp. 47-58.

Tatum, W. Barnes, "*The Passion* in the History of Jesus Films," in Corley and Webb (2004), pp. 140-50.

Telotte, J.P., "Beyond All Reason: The Nature of the Cult," in *The Cult Film Experience: Beyond All Reason* (Austin: University of Texas Press, 1991), pp. 5-17.

Thislethwaite, Susan, "Mel Makes a War Movie," in Fredriksen (2006), pp. 127-45.

Veen, Robbert, "*The Passion* as Redemptive Non-Violence," *Mennonite Life* 59 (2004), www.bethelks.edu/mennonitelife/2004June/veen.php, accessed 2 December 2005.

Wallis, Jim, "*The Passion* and the Message," in Fredriksen (2006), pp. 111-25.

Whalen, Thomas, "*The Passion* of Mel Gibson," *Literature Film Quarterly* 32 (2004), pp. 240-43.

Wieseltier, Leon, "The Worship of Blood," in Fredriksen (2006), pp. 255-65.

Williams, Linda, "Film Bodies: Gender, Genre and Excess," in ed. Barry Keith Grant, *Film Genre Reader III* (Austin: University of Texas Press, 2003), pp. 141-59.

Woods, Robert H., Michael C. Jindra and Jason D. Baker, "The Audience Responds to *The Passion of the Christ*," in Plate (2004), pp. 163-80.

Websites

www.Av1611.org/Passion
www.Creationist.org/passionmovie.html
www.Harpazo.net/EternalProductions/Passion.html
www.LetGodBeTrue.com/TodaysWorld/Passion.htm
www.MyLifeAfter.com
www.PassionforFairness.com
www.Passion-movie.com
www.PassionoftheChrist.com
www.PassionOutreach.com
www.Pawcreek.org/articles/endtimes/PassionoftheChristCatholicTrap.htm
www.SeethePassion.com
www.SeekGod.ca/gibson.htm
www.SharethePassionoftheChrist.com
www.SupportMelGibson.com
www.ThankYouMel.com

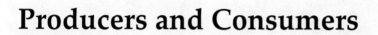

Producers and Consumers

Recasting the Revival Experience for the Youngest:
Celebrities, Rock Music and Action Sports

Silvia Giagnoni

According to the findings of the *2005 Newsweek* report on spirituality in the United States, a study conducted together with the multi-faith website Beliefnet.com, there is an indisputable "flowering of spirituality" in the United States that manifests itself not in an augmented church attendance (the phenomenon of mega-churches notwithstanding) but rather in the expression of religious-oriented practices outside the traditional institutions. As for the young, if organized religion (specifically denominational churches) is less and less the fitting answer to their needs, spirituality expressed through music and sport may be. This partly explains the success of Christian rock bands and the impressive, significant and academically intriguing crossover into the secular market of so many of them.

In the late 1990s, Luis Palau, an internationally acclaimed evangelist, friend and follower of Billy Graham, envisioned a new formula to spread the Good News. In 2006, these festivals, organized with the help of Luis Palau's two sons, Andrew and Kevin, have proved to be a win-win formula. Indeed, Palau's "Great music! Good News!" events have drawn record crowds all around the world: past Festivals have been held in Washington, Madrid (85,000 people), Lima (670,000), Manchester, Fort Lauderdale, Florida (300,000), Seattle, and Buenos Aires (1,000,000). Their aim is "to bring the message in a positive, culturally relevant style," as Andrew, son of Luis Palau, says in the video *Livin' It: the Unusual Suspects*. He further clarifies his point by saying that this is not about politics or "against this group or that group," as "people who don't go to church might think of Christians: so, one of the things that dad has always used as a catch-phrase for his festivals is "this is about what we are for, rather than what we are against."

In the present essay I will try to illustrate how evangelicals are trying to gain followers among the youngest generations through cutting-edge music, celebrity testimonies and the so-called action sports (or "expressive sports"). Thus, by making use of historical and descriptive analysis, I will primarily take into consideration the Palau festivals and their related promotional videos (specifically the *Livin It* series of films). The traveling sports ministry of the same name as the films is currently touring the United States as part of Palau events program. *Livin It: the Unusual Suspects* was apparently named after Stephen Baldwin's most famous movie, *The Usual Suspects*, although it plays on the idea that you would not expect to see the people who feature in the video today as committed evangelical Christians. I have also examined other similar DVDs (*Uncensored*) and TV shows (*OneCubed*, *Steel Roots*: on the Inspirational Networks, *Steel Roots* is a half-hour TV program highlighting today's top Christian athletes in surfing, skateboarding and snowboarding. Another similar show is the teenager-oriented "One Cubed USA" hosted by Jake Clemons and aired by a variety of stations among which ABC family. Moreover, I will make use of my own first-hand experience at another analogous events, namely the South Florida Festival in May 2006, along with articles on the phenomenon here under examination. I see these free events (among the ones I above mentioned only SFF charges) as a further tool deployed by evangelical Christians to spread the Gospel.

As for the theoretical background of this work, my thesis draws from Lawrence Grossberg's work on the relationships between popular culture (and specifically rock culture) and new Conservatism that he widely exposed in *We Gotta Get Out of This Place* (1992) and updated and expanded in his most recent *Caught in the Crossfire* (2005). In particular, I would like to develop the point Grossberg makes on the ability of the Christian Right to deploy popular culture products to achieve its religious, cultural and political goals. I am here arguing that the "action sports + Christian teen-oriented music + celebrity testimonies" formula is likely to be incorporated into the larger cultural strategy of New Conservatism that has been re-articulating what Grossberg calls the "rock formation" and thus re-adjusting hegemonic discourses according to the Right-wing political agenda.

Grossberg conceives the "rock formation" as an articulation of a "sensibility" specific to post-war contexts. From the outset, the articulation of private but common desires, feelings and experiences into a shared language has been imbued with an ideology of "authenticity." However, according to Grossberg, rock has always played with the idea of what he calls "authentic inauthenticity" (or "chronic nihilism") defined by the scholar as the proper sensibility of postmodernity. He views the rock formation as a power discourse which not only through music, but also via film, television, advertising, comics - and I would add today via internet, video-games, sports and video clips - has progressively come to take over significant spaces of our daily life thus shaping new ways in which people make sense of themselves and of the world.

Specifically, Grossberg's *We Gotta Get out of This Place* (1992) is based on the assumption that new Conservatism is being put into place through *cultural* rather than strictly political strategies and I will here provide some examples in relation to the cultural promotion of stereotypical gender roles. Finally, the phenomenon under investigation needs to be considered within the framework of the old-time American tradition of the marketing of religion: indeed, as Margaret Bendroth shows in her *Fundamentalism and Gender* (1993) and, more specifically, Lawrence Moore in *Selling God* (1994), American evangelism and business have been exchanging techniques since their respective beginnings.

Evangelical Christians are today recasting the revival experience by appropriating practices, styles, and narratives to which teenagers can easily relate. Historically, as social anthropologist Anthony F. C. Wallace noticed in his study on the topic, religious revivalist movements occur when there are conditions of high stress for individual members of the society combined with a disillusionment with a distorted cultural *Gestalt*; religious institutions fail to respond to the needs of important segments of society and thus must re-adjust to the new material, cultural and social conditions in order to maintain their power position in the society.

Like many Americans, Hollywood actor Stephen Baldwin went through a deep personal crisis after 9/11; for him this was "the day the impossible became possible," as he puts it in the *Unusual Suspects* video. He became a born-again Christian in solidarity with his Brazilian wife and since then has encouraged and reminded people to live "a life with a purpose" and, specifically, to spread the Gospel among teenagers using the testimonies of Christian action sport athletes. Stephen Baldwin declares on Beliefnet.com:

> we are not trying to reinvent the wheel, we are just trying to bring God and the Bible to the kids in a hard core way that they can relate to. There is almost nothing out there in the Christian Marketplace that the kids can connect with! This same idea holds true in the Mainstream Marketplace where the kids will start to see that the faith-based culture can be MORE hard core.

Although some organizations, such as Act One, are working at the grassroots level in order to change Hollywood from within, Baldwin does not consider it his "mission field" as he declared to Beliefnet.com:

> I have no interest in changing Hollywood. Right now, the best way to change Hollywood is *to convert the youth of this country to faith* so that they can go out and do whatever the Lord calls them to do. There is this *extreme movement* of the Holy Spirit that's coming to this country, and I think that's going to hit Hollywood as well [my emphases].

A case in point is Mel Gibson and his *Passion of the Christ*. He managed to create considerable excitement prior to the release of the movie with the help of successful marketing strategies. As Kent L. Brintnall shows in this collection, *The Passion* is considered by evangelical Christians to be a crucial moment in the history of evangelism. Many church groups promoted the film, both within their organizations and to the general public, in some cases giving away free tickets. Younger audiences appeared to like the film even better than older ones. As Woods, Jindra and Baker report:

> in most cases younger Christians tended to show higher levels of worship, personal growth, and appreciation of the film

than their older counterparts. Furthermore, women tended toward higher attitude levels in such attitudinal responses than men, but there did not appear to be interaction effects between gender and religious leaning. Evidently, then, the most favorably responsive group of Christians overall were women under age of thirty five. Perhaps the multimedia culture of the younger generations makes them more open to a visual and even theatrical presentation of faith than their older counterparts (2004: 174).

Other celebrities, such as Stephen Baldwin, are at the forefront of a remarkable movement that specifically target the "youth of the nation," to paraphrase the title of a famous P.O.D. hit. As far as popular music is concerned, P.O.D., a nu-metal band from San Diego, California, is probably the most significant Christian rock act that successfully managed to cross over into the secular arena in the last fifteen years; reportedly, the name P.O.D., which stands for Payable on Death. Although this is actually a banking term which means that when someone passes away, their belongings go to their heir, to the band, "Payable on Death" means that our sins were paid for on Jesus' death and He gave eternal life as an inheritance.

There are several evangelical organizations (the Fellowship of Christian Athletes, Pro Athletes Outreach, Athletes in Action) which aim at combining sport, physical fitness and religion and they mainly draw from the Anglo-American tradition of Muscular Christianity. In particular, Christian in Sports (CIS) in England and the Fellowship of Christian Athletes (FCA) send "sport ministries" to Latin America, South-east Asia and Africa, to spread the Gospel. Stephen Baldwin, indeed, has his own extreme sports ministry called *Livin It* (a skateboarding, BMX, motor cross outreach to the youth) along with a record company that he formed with ex-Korn founder Brian "Head" Welch after he became a "born again" Christian.

A non-confrontational stance and stress on positivity is a common (and winning) feature of new Conservative cultural strategies. It is partly the result of a lesson learnt by evangelicals in the last 10-15 years: in multicultural and pluralist societies to be "culturally relevant" means to be inclusivist in the preaching of salvation.

Moreover, the celebrity endorsement is meant to attract the widest audiences. For evangelicals it is important to share life experiences of spiritual struggle and of personal discovery of God's spirit as this is deemed to encourage fellows in the process of building their own personal relationship with Jesus Christ.

There are numerous festivals dedicated to Contemporary Christian Music (CCM) all around the country. Many of them blossomed between the late Seventies and the early Eighties, such as Cornerstone (Bushnell, Illinois; Orlando, Florida), Sonshine (Willmar, Minnesota), Agape Music (Greenville, Illinois), and Itchus (Wilmore, Kentucky) and Spirit West Coast (Monterey and Del Mar, California), just to mention some of them. Contemporary Christian Music, and more specifically, Christian rock was indeed born out of the counterculture as "the music of the Jesus movement." It has been a separate market for two decades and only recently has started to make significant incursions into the secular music sphere. Indeed, concomitantly with the prominent role that religion has come to play in public. Evangelical Christians have been able to finally impact the culture through a variety of media thanks to augmented financial means. As the current President of the Gospel Music Association and founder of CCM magazine John Styll noticed in the interview I had with him:

> the potential is there because, unlike thirty years ago when this all began, *the system is now wired for success* because the majors are involved so you can produce a record and if that starts to hit, they have the infrastructure to take it all the way and become really really big, whereas in the early days that wasn't even possible [my emphases].

About a quarter of the $3,500,000 cost of the Palau Festival in Washington was paid by corporations as David Kerley reported during the TV show *Good Morning America*. And this is not the exception: sports ministries have corporate sponsors that financially back up their activities. Moreover, it is worth remembering that contributions to religious organizations are tax deductible. Luis Palau justified the involvement of big business in the organization of his festivals as a way "to draw more people, a chance to convert them to Christianity" (ABC, 2005). Among the bands that perform at the Palau Festivals, the teen-pop group Jump 5 is involved with big corporations such as Nesquik (the "Snow Much Fun" promotion) and features in a commercial for J. C. Penney, and also with Radio Disney on various promotions. Chevrolet launched its promotional campaign and sponsorship of Third Day's Live Wire Tour with To-byMac. Today, these bands are able to take advantage of their status of "Crossover Christian artists," thus coming to occupy a position that allows them to endorse a variety of products; on the other hand, big corporations deploy these Christian personalities, true heroes in the evangelical subculture because they have succeeded in "getting out there" in the secular world, in order to brand their products and thus tap into the growing market of evangelical Christians. Artists such as Third Day and TobyMac of dcTalk belong to the so-called Third Wave of Christian rock, a movement of musicians started in the early 1990s within Contemporary Christian music who were emerging out of the "ghetto" of the Christian market to perform, produce and sell their records in the secular arena as well. In 2004, album sales in the Christian Rock genre grew 125%, according to the Gospel Music Association, and Contemporary Christian Music (CCM) is currently the sixth most popular in the U.S., behind rock, hip-hop, R&B/urban, country and pop music. I have to point out that this type of generic musical classification, although widely deployed, does not ring true when we speak of Christian bands, as in this case *the content* comes to define the genre, and not the style. Contemporary Christian Music (or CCM) is the most-used term to refer to Christian popular music in the press today. Specifically, the name draws from the well-known *CCM* magazine that was started in 1978 by John Styll. As Styll, now President of the Gospel Music Association, remembers in his column "History Makers with John Styll," "we name the new publication "Contemporary Christian MUSIC": and in so doing, he inadvertently helped the term to "stick" as the primary identifier of what was then a fresh new musical movement" (Styll, 2006: 70).

CCM is indeed known for transforming any musical form of popular music into a Christianized version of it, thus also posing serious questions in terms of rock ideology versus style which are beyond the scope of this essay. These bands have taken advantage of the different role that religion has acquired in public discourses, thus rendering the process of crossover smoother. Finally, independent Christian labels such as Re:think and Seattle-based Tooth and Nail are today distributed in the mainstream market by the majors and, thus, get higher exposure for their records. For instance, Charlie Peacock's Re: think was sold to the EMI Christian Music Group in 1997 and the group is now responsible for the artistic development, sales and marketing activities of the label.

However, these bands are often said "to water down the message" or to "to cross over without taking the cross over." Yet, their participation in Christian festivals, like the Palau events or the South Florida Festival is proof of their "loyalty" to the Christian community; it is an "authenticity marker," as Joli Jensen names it in talking about country music and the Nashville Sound (Jensen, 1998: 6-7). She explores the relationship between authenticity and crossover in her analysis of country music in the late 1950s and early 1960s when the so called Nashville Sound developed. Then, country music seemed to be losing its generic identity by turning into pop. Jensen analyses country music's authenticity in relation to charges of its commercialization. She also shows how the musical forms once regarded as non authentic can become authentic over time. A case in point is the "Nashville Sound". This ongoing presence on the Christian circuits signifies that the latter still "accepts" them and approves of their way of spreading the Gospel in terms of lyrical content, public behavior and "outspokenness about Jesus."

As far as I have been able to see during my research, evangelical Christians do not like to talk about politics – even though most of them seem to support conservative politics and specifically the Republican Party and prefer to leave two-party logics outside of their events. According to the Barna Research Group website, in 2006, 67% of evangelicals describe themselves as "mostly conservative" when it comes to political and social issues (compared to 30% of adults nationwide), 26% describe themselves as somewhere in between (compared to 50% of adults nationwide), and none call themselves liberal (compared to 11% of adults nationwide). Political affiliation is currently highly debated among evangelical Christians in the US. The majority of them is Republican and has supported the Bush administration; however, in Christian rock subculture we can find a variety of positions and, as I have pointed out, an overt reluctance to talk about two-party politics. It is worth-noticing, however, that explicit political activities would prevent churches and religious organizations from taking advantage of the exemption from income tax and other favorable treatment under tax law.

Neither did they like to be associated with traditional Fundamentalist Christians. In this sense, I regard the presence of former President Bill Clinton, "hired" as one of the "unusual suspects" in the homonymous video to endorse Luis Palau's ministry and the related cultural initiatives, as a rhetorical move geared to further prove that the Palaus are not supporting the Republican Party and that, consequently, the evangelical movement is indeed universal in its mission. On the other hand, Bill Clinton's participation in the video signifies his attempt to win credibility among evangelicals. This is in line with Senator Hillary Rodham Clinton's attempt to speak to religious America in her political activity after the 2004 Presidential election. However, it is worth noticing that Stephen Baldwin did side for George W. Bush. As he admits in the *Unusual Suspects* video, "when my faith-based motivation led me to wanna support the re-election of Bush at the Republican National Convention, let's say... that the boys were... concerned." "The boys" are Stephen's brothers, William and Ale, who, on the other hand, have always supported his spiritual drive but strongly disapprove of his political leanings. As Carol Baldwin, the mother, recalls in *The Unusual Suspects*, "they have differences of opinion. Stephen was at the Republican Convention and Billy was outside picketing the Republican Convention?!"

Actor Alec Baldwin does not like the re-affiliation of Christians with the Republican Party. According to Stephen, "what they [many Republicans] don't understand was... and what I think is the difference between myself and them now is... they're not having this experience;" in so doing, he retreats to an elusive comment as the then-Governor of Texas, George W. Bush, did once when asked to expound on his conversion:

> Well, if they don't know [what I am talking about] it's gonna
> be hard to explain it, when you turn over to Christ, when
> you accept Christ as a Savior, He changes your heart, he

changes your life. And this is basically what happened to me (*The Jesus Factor*).

This further proves how religion has been thrown right into the center of the political arena along with, paradoxically, the lessening of political and moral accountability.

Furthermore, the fact that the Palau events, sponsored by area churches (900 in Washington D.C.), are free, along with the voluntary activities in which the organizations get involved with the hosting communities (i.e. in Washington D.C., 800 volunteers cleaned up 10 schools in the two weeks before the event and donates more than $1,000,000), the way the festivals are advertised ("it's not a religious thing, it's a spiritual thing", as Luis Palau says in *Unusual Suspects* video), are all further attempts to evangelize but, most significantly, to "cross over." Indeed, the events, although mostly attended by white Christians, claim to bring together people of different racial, ethnic (and even religious) background. To be sure, festivals have always been essential venues for many Christians since the Jesus movement gatherings of the Seventies. Furthermore, the sense of communality that rock music concerts enable is here combined with a specific religious message. Besides, concerts resemble sacred rites: first of all, they are, to some extent, dictated by the equivalent need to share an experience with others and members of the audience raise their hands and close their eyes as if they were participating in a ceremony, although this is not going to happen with Christian hardcore sets where *mosh pits* are common. As a matter of fact, for these believers, a concert can be a worship experience, even if it is not clearly a proper "worship set" which is a part of the concert in which the band onstage openly invites the audience to pray and worship the Lord. The rock bands I interviewed in my research have often been asked by youth leaders to perform a worship set when they play at churches.

As far as the music itself is concerned, genre diversity reigns at the events organized by the Palaus although the common trait of all these bands it is not the genre that I have here widely defined as rock but their central appeal to teenagers: Third Day, the grunge/alternative rock band that won the Best Rock Gospel album in 2003; TobyMac, founder of the rap group dcTalk (well-known for the smash Christian hit "Jesus Freak"), pop singer Yuri, known as "the Mexican Madonna," and the mixed teenager pop band Jump 5 ("the Christian Backstreet Boys") are among the groups that have performed at the Palau festivals. As Luis Palau declared to the TV program *Good Morning America!*: "I feel music, sports, actors, Americans go for that." Palau's winning formula needs to be further analyzed. Undeniably, Luis Palau is not only "the Billy Graham of Latin America" but also, like the movie star Mel Gibson, a marketing genius.

In the second part of this essay, I would like to draw attention to skateboarding and thus shed light on the action sports component of these festivals. Skateboarding was born in the late 1950's but became a subculture on its own only in the 1970's in West Los Angeles (Dogtown). As a sport, it was derivative of surfing while, as a subculture, it was characterized by its primarily working-class character, an aggressive localism and the outcast behaviors of its practitioners as "urban guerrillas."

Skate parks are today one of the main attractions of the Palau's events. These festivals are not exploiting a completely novel trend. The Splinter Skate Park is located next to the Crossover Community Church in Tampa, Florida, and this church is just one example of a widely diffused practice. Reportedly, Rick Warren, author of inspirational best-seller *The Purpose Driven Life* (1993), is currently building a major skate park on his property in Lake Forest, Orange County, California. The 10,000-square-foot skateboard park built for the BeachFest held in Fort Lauderdale in March 2003 was then carted off to the local Calvary Chapel. It was right after the success of Beachfest that Palau planned to make sports a staple of future festivals. Likewise, Third Coast Sports, a Nashville company specializing in Church-marketing and event-planning for sports teams, has organized Faith Nights, which combine baseball and football games with Christian music and entertainment (including giveaways of the Bible and bobbleheads of the characters of the popular Christian cartoon *Veggie Tales*).

The "sports zone" is in fact very appealing to the youngest. At the South Florida Festival, the skate ramps ("Extreme Demo") were positioned right next to the "Xtreme Stage" where rock groups were playing: skaters and bands alternate in the afternoon schedule. To incorporate skate parks in the evangelical festivals (or to build them next to churches) means to appropriate a space of a subaltern "other" (here, outcast working-class kids playing a street sport) into an institutional (dominant) space, thus partly nullifying the potential counter-hegemonic power of this practice. More specifically, I believe this is a further attempt to blur the boundaries between resistant practices and commercialised teeanager activities. The skateboard subculture has been thus been co-opted, marketed and *mainstreamed* through a process of commercial and ideological incorporation.

Christian "Holmes" Hosoi grew in Venice Beach's Dogtown scene in the Eighties. Born in the Hawaii, he moved to California where, by the time he was 12, he was top amateur of the nation, "turning Pro" at the age of 14. Known as "the Michael Jordan of skateboarding," Hosoi's nickname, ironically enough, became "Christ" and in the late 1980s he even invented "the Christ air," a move intended to mirror Jesus on the cross. Christian Hosoi is today another prominent member of the Palau team. Hosoi used to party with Stephen Baldwin in Hollywood back in their "pre-born again" days. What happened was that in January 2000 Hosoi was arrested at Honolulu airport for carrying 1.5 pounds of crystal methamphetamine. He pleaded guilty to possession with the intent to distribute, saying he was a courier for money and drugs. Hosoi spent then four years at the San Bernardino prison, where he studied the Bible with his inmates, and once he came out in July 2004, he easily found his new place in the outside world: as he repeatedly says in the *Livin It* video, "when I went to prison, I found freedom." He started using his celebrity status in the world of skateboarding to spread the Good News of Jesus Christ. So, Hosoi was launched as a skateboard celebrity who went through a process of "extreme makeover:" he has become a born-again Christian. During the two-day event BeachFest, held in the midst of Fort Lauderdale spring break (March 22-23, 2003), where alcohol and dissoluteness generally fill the air, Stephen Baldwin learned that there were people who were communicating with kids, through skateboarding and propagating the Gospel of Jesus Christ. It was there that he then created, along with Christian Hosoi, the King of the Kings Skateboard Ministry.

As I mentioned earlier, since the late Nineties, these types of initiatives have flourished around the country. As of 2006, there were over 300 skateboard ministries in the United States: they gain followers by putting on an apparently strong anti-establishment attitude and offering hope, community and healthy entertainment. *Livin It* was filmed at the Skatechurch in Portland, Oregon, co-founded by skater Paul Anderson in 1997. Here, skateboarding has been co-opted and transformed from fun, resistant street practice into an indoor, highly-regulated activity. On the Skatechurch website we read: "Skatechurch is more than a place to skate. We exist to tell skaters about God. If you come to skate you must attend the Bible talk. If you are not willing to hear about God then Skatechurch is not for you." Similarly, the majority of Christian festivals require the bands to be somehow affiliated with a church or Christian organizations in order to perform. These restrictions have contributed to the creation of a separate market but also, through the years, have also given these bands the opportunity to play in front of substantial audiences at the beginning of their careers. Everybody is welcome as long as he (or she) is committed to Jesus Christ, which means to accept a certain definition of Christianity and thus follow its behavioral tenets - in other words, to abide by the strict control that the evangelical community exercises on its members.

Among the rules of the skate park, it should not surprise that there are also safety ones:

> Skating is permitted in the main room and warehouse only. No halls, walls, stairs, chairs or anything else that would need repairs. The upper parking lot, stairs, handrails, sidewalks and benches are off limits - no skating or hanging out up there. The lower lot is O.K. to skate but please don't do wall rides.

The strict disciplining of these physical spaces, which kids had previously appropriated precisely in order to resist the institutions of control (school, family, church), further shows how evangelical youth culture is thus re-inscribing its conservative practices into the rock and roll apparatus, thus nullifying any residual resistive stance.

On the other hand, watching the *Livin It* videos, skaters do not wear helmets, or knee and elbow pads or other types of guards; they do wear, instead, fancy clothes with their clearly visible brand names (i.e. "Apostle"). It is worth mentioning that there are many Christian apparel companies in the States such as A Different Direction Christian Apparel, Be the Message Christian Apparel, and Spiritual Wear. *Livin It* itself is both a clothing line for skaters and a book series. In fact, among named 'friends' promoted in the bonus material section of the *Livin It* DVD there are Untitled Skateboarders, Borders for Christ, Manna Skateboards, Dare2Share and Reliance Skateboards, all of which offer religious merchandise. In the "Our Sponsors" section of the *Unusual Suspects* DVD, a wider range of promoters are to be found, secular and Christian-oriented: the movie *The Chronicles of Narnia*, Interstate Batteries, Tyson Chicken, Meguiar's Car Products and, most interestingly, the new digital music site Songtouch.com which is advertised as "a community of inspiration and passion," where "music fans of Christian rock, hip hop to the bets pop can feel right at home." Song Touch "will move your body, mind and soul." *Narnia* has been "appropriated" by evangelical Christians as one of their movies. Although Narnia has not been promoted by its producers as a Christian movie, its soundtrack features exclusively Christian artists, such as Rebecca St. James, Jars of Clay, Jeremy Camp and tobyMac. All this is justified "in the name of Jesus", as Luis Palau seems to suggest in talking about the financial endorsement of corporations. Ethical consistency never questioned. Evangelicals need to be "out there in the world," which means gaining corporate money to spend on spreading the Word.

Moreover, in the videos athletes do skate in the abovementioned prohibited areas, thus conveying a sense of freedom and defiance that is not actually permitted for the kids who go there to skate (and, most importantly, to pray...). A disclaimer at the very beginning of the video warns viewers not to attempt to recreate the same stunts at home. We read: "*Livin It* features athletes performing stunts that are potentially extremely dangerous. Please do not attempt to duplicate any of the stunts seen in this video. The Luis Palau Evangelistic Association will not be responsible for the injuries suffered by individuals attempting to recreate the stunts seen in this video." Is this enough? It seems as if the *cool* "content" (read, ready-to-consume products, be they action sports or rock music performances), devoid of religious and political overtones, is deployed in order to appeal to teenagers, while the "context" (be it the Palau festivals, the skate parks next the churches, the promotional DVD, or the TV shows) remains Christian and, as I will show below, conservative in substance.

As Robert Rinehart has pointed out, alternative sports (also called action or extreme sports) such as skateboarding and surfing may have been an opportunity to create "a fundamental change in the way postindustrial society perceives sports" (Rinehart, 2005: 233). These are sports whose most important elements are considered "feminine" traits, such as timing, agility, balance, even grace ("That *looks* good, man!" is a comment that skaters would make to each others' performances), whereas in the mainstream American sports (football, baseball, hockey and soccer) other (masculine) qualities, such as strength, speed, power, are ideologically emphasized. As sport teaches its participants values, skills and lifelong lessons, it becomes clear the crucial importance that an alternative ideology, namely, a Christian one, could play in such a scenario. In this sense, other areas are worthy of further investigation, such as the long-term effects of the revival of the ideology of muscular Christianity in action sports.

After having taken into consideration these festivals, videos and TV shows geared to teenage audiences who love extreme sports and popular music, I would argue that these products work in order to construct a "cool" image of these athletes (stylish clothes, outlaw look, etc). Yet, although charged by a distinct religious ideology that can be traced back to the above-mentioned Muscular Christianity tradition these sports are constructed as more life-process-oriented than mainstream national ones. In the end, sports-practice represents just one step in a life devoted to the Lord. Among these athletes' life goals are priorities that go beyond a career in a specific field of sports, thus proving the virtues of the muscular Christian ethos. Vic Murphy, for instance, a BMX biker who is featured in *Livin*

It, dreams of becoming a pastor or of building a traveling sports ministry. Likewise, Christian rock artists often claim that music is a gift from God or just a tool to evangelize and spread the good news of Jesus Christ: having a family or becoming a minister is often in their future projects.

However, no other truly alternative elements seem to emerge from this Christian incorporation of extreme sports. In the United States, mainstream sports are to socialize and educate male youth, thus reinforcing both hegemonic masculinity and stereotyped femininity; for example, in football, we find the strength-centered performances of male players and the decorative, supportive ones of female cheerleaders. For example, the Christian organization Promise Keepers was born out of a movement begun by Bill McCartney, the University of Colorado football coach who left the team to focus on the organization whose purpose is to rearticulate gender roles according to conservative evangelical standards.

Finally, the videos I have analyzed portray a male world in which girls are only mentioned as obstacles (either as party girls or under the guise of "sport groupies") in the athlete's path of faith. In the narratives of these guys (collected through interviews), girls stand only for sex and purposeless fun. Therefore, they are to be erased from the whole picture, as they might interfere with the camaraderie-like climate that is being constructed. In the pre-punk era, girls were invisible in any youth subculture; they were in a position of "structured secondariness," thus mirroring their position in the larger society (McRobbie and Garber, 1975). To be sure, it should not come as a surprise that Christian values are being made to reinforce hegemonic (and thus currently conservative) representations of femininity. However, this total invisibility is worth emphasizing. Indeed, it is as if women were not to be part of the repeatedly mentioned Christian revolution that these guys are advancing through sport.

How are we to understand this invisibility? It might be argued that action sports, skateboarding, for instance, are street sports, and girls are not supposed to hang out in the streets like guys, bearing in mind that Skateboard Culture has been constructed as very chauvinistic in advertising as Robert Rinehart (2005) has pointed out. However, this does not mean that they are not there. The recent performances at the Winter Olympics in expressive sports such as snowboarding and free-style skiing prove the contrary: significantly enough, the documentary *AKA Girls Surfer* (2004) shows talented female (secular) athletes and provides a counter-intuitive insight into the subculture of surfers.

It is here worth noticing that Muscular Christianity was born in England precisely in order to fight against the supposedly "feminization" of the Anglican Church. It might be argued that the "feminine" features that expressive sports present are likely to endanger the building of the manly character of these guys, necessary it has been be argued, in these times of the "war against terror". Further research is required in this direction. To be sure, the absence of girls from representations of a Christianized sport world works to reinforce stereotypical gender roles; moreover, the growing circulation of these types of media products further proves that, as many intellectuals have pointed out, conservative culture is dominant in the United States today.

To conclude, the combination of action sports, celebrity testimonies and teen-oriented music seems to be the latest among the evangelicals' endeavors to gain acolytes among American youth. It is hard to tell to what extent these videos or festivals are achieving their goal of converting young people to Christian values. However, as Lauren Sandler reports, *Livin It* sold 150,000 copies in fifteen months (2006: 101). The money is rolling in. It is clear that the evangelicals' attempt to convert non-believers is massive and has been operated through such a variety of media and venues (videos, movies, TV shows, songs, festivals and other events) that it might deeply affect not only the "rock formation" but also, in the long term, the future of the United States.

References

ABC, "Rocking the Pulpit Christian Festival in Washington D.C.," *Good Morning America*, ABC News (Transcript) 8 October (2005), http://abcnews.go.com/gma, accessed 1 July 2006, resource has since been removed.

Adler, Jerry, "Special Report: Spirituality 2005: in Search of the Spiritual," *Newsweek* 29 August - 5 September (2005), pp. 46-65.

Banks, Robin, *The Hardcore/Punk Guide to Christianity* (San Francisco: AK Press, 1999).

Banks Adelle M., and Judith Cebula, "Palau Redefines Mass Evangelism with Party-Like Approach ", *Religious News Service,* 28 September (2005), http://www. beliefnet.com/story/176/story_17602_1.html, accessed 1 July 2006.

Bendroth, Margaret Lamberts, *Fundamentalism and Gender, 1875 to the Present* (New Haven: Yale University Press, 1993).

Cebula, Judith, "Party Hearthy Luis Palau Festival Create New Evangelism Model", http://www.beliefnet.com/story/168/story_16859.html, accessed 7 October, 2005.

Davis, James D., "The New Evangelism: Jumbotrons, Skateboards at Beachfest", *Sun Sentinel* 20 April (2002), p. 7D.

_____, "Palau-Palooza! Edgy Mix of Contemporary Christian Music Expected to Draw 100,000 to BeachFest this Weekend," *Sun Sentinel* 21 March (2003), p.30.

_____, "Palau Organization Tidies up After Beachfest," *Sun Sentinel* 29 March (2003), p. 12D.

Doolittle, Amy, "Festival Draws 40,000 to Mall: Christian Event Overcomes Rain," *The Washington Times* 10 October (2005), p. B01.

Grossberg, Lawrence, "Is there Rock and Roll after Punk," *Critical Studies in Mass Communication* 3 (1986) pp. 50-74.

_____, *We Gotta Get Out Of This Place: Popular Conservatism and Postmodern Culture* (New York: Routledge, 1992)

_____, *Caught in the Crossfire. Kids, Politics, and America's Future* (Boulder: Paradigm Publishers, 2005).

Hebdige. Dick, *Subculture: the Meaning of Style* (London: Metheun, 1979).

Jensen. Joli, *The Nashville Sound: Authenticity, Commercialization and Country Music* (Nashville: Vanderbilt University Press.1998).

McRobbie, Angela, and Jenny Garber, "Girls and Subcultures," in eds. S. Hall and T. Jefferson, *Resistance through Rituals: Youth Subcultures in Post-war Britain* (London: Hutchinson, 1975) pp. 209-222.

Moore, Lawrence R., *Selling God: American Religion in the Marketplace of Culture* (Oxford : Oxford University Press, 1994).

Negus, Keith, *Music Genres and Corporate Cultures* (London: Routledge, 1999).

PR Newswire, "SIRIUS Satellite Radio Expands its Christian Music Programming with Launch of New 'Revolution' Music Channel," Lexdon Business Library, 20 September (2005), http://www.lexdon.com/article/SIRIUS_Satellite_Radio_Expands_its/9420.html, accessed 1 July 2006.

Putney, Clifford, *Muscular Christianity: Manhood and Sports in Protestant America 1880-1920* (Cambridge, Mass.: Harvard University Press, 2001).

Rinehart, Robert, "'Babes' and Boards: Opportunities in New Millennium Sport?" *Journal of Sport and Social Issues* 29.3 (2005) pp. 235-255.

Sandler, Lauren, *Righteous: Dispatches from the Evangelical Youth Movement* (New York: Viking, 2006).

Sheahen, Laura, "Hardcore Faith: Interview with Stephen Baldwin," *Beliefnet. com,* http://www.beliefnet.com/story/172/story_17222.html, accessed 1 July 2006.

Styll, John, "Looking Forward to the Past," *CCM: Contemporary Christian Music* January (2006), p. 70.

Thompson, John J., *Raised By Wolves. The Story of Christian Rock and Roll* (Toronto: ECW Press, 2000).

Thornton, Sarah, *Club Cultures: Music, Media and Subcultural Capital* (Middletown: Wesleyan University Press, 1996).

Wallace, Anthony F. C., *Religion: an Anthropological View* (New York: Random House, 1966).

_____, "Revitalizations and Mazeways," ed. R. S. Grumet, *Essays on Culture Change* (Lincoln: University of Nebraska Press, 2003).

Warren, Rick, *The Purpose Driven Life* (Philadelphia: Miniature Editions, 2003).

Watson, J. Nick, Stuart Weir and Stephen Friend, "The Development of Muscular Christianity in Victorian Britain and Beyond," *Journal of Religion and Society* 7 (2005), http://moses.creighton.edu/JRS/2005/2005-2.html, accessed 1 January 2007.

Wise, Brian, "Bringing Christian Rock to a New Stage," *Connecticut Weekly Desk*, 23 October (2005), p. 6.

Woods, Robert H., Michael C. Jindra and Jason D. Baker, "The Audience Responds to 'The Passion of the Christ'," in ed. S. Brent Plate, *Re-Viewing The Passion: Mel Gibson's Film and Its Critics* (New York: Palgrave, 2004), pp.163-80.

Zoll, Rachel, "Billy Graham-style crusades may be on their way out," *The Associated Press*, Domestic News, 8 September (2005), http://www.fuller.edu/news/html/1quarter_mediasummary05.asp, accessed 1 July 2006.

Websites

1cubedusa.com/index2.asp
www.barna.org
www.beliefnet.com
www.cbn.com/700club
www.gospelmusic.org
www.palau.org
www.pao.org
www.songtouch.com
www.thirdday.com

Videography

AKA Girls Surfer, dir. Todd Saunders, Produced by Joe Guglielmino (2004).

Dogtown and Z-Boys, dir. Stacy Peralta, Distributed by Cinemien (2001).

Livin' It, dir. Stephen Baldwin, PalauFest Productions (2004).

Livin It, Unusual Suspects, PalauFest Productions (2005).

OneCubedUsa, Promotional Video (2005)

The Jesus Factor, Boston: WGBH Educational Foundation, distributed by PBS Home Video, (2004).

The Hollywood Crisis, Promotional Video, Hollywood Prayer Network (2005).

Uncensored, Redline Studio LLC (2005).

The Santafication of Hanukkah:
Escaping the "December Dilemma" on Chrismukkah.com

Elizabeth Bernstein

In *Adventures in Yiddishland: Postvernacular Language and Culture*, Jeffrey Shandler includes an examination of the way kitsch (funny, sentimental, popular and mass-produced material objects often fusing sacred and profane) has represented the dilemmas of Jewish American life since the post-World War II era. At that time, Yiddish, disappearing as a living language, was simultaneously "fetishized and mocked" on "comic, lowbrow items (T-shirts, coffee mugs, novelty items, etc.)" (Shandler, 2006: 29). This same Yiddish kitsch is still for sale by Hamakor Judaica, Inc. Their summer 2007 catalogue features a "No Kvetching" coffee mug, "Bubbie" and "Zeyda" caps and T-shirts and *From Schmear to Eternity: the Only Book of Yiddish You'll Ever Need*. The same page offers a traditional memorial candle holder, the book *Jewish Fathers: a Legacy of Love* and a prayer shawl and yarmulke set (Hamakor Judaica, 2007: 48). Hamakor Judaica's *The Source for Everything Jewish* catalogue exemplifies what Clement Greenberg explained in 1939 in *Partisan Review*: "the pre-condition for kitsch, a condition without which kitsch would be impossible, is the availability close at hand of a fully matured cultural tradition, whose discoveries, acquisitions and perfected self-consciousness kitsch can take advantage of for its own ends" (Greenberg, 1939: 40). In the U.S., genuine ritual objects (prayer shawls and candle holders) share visual space in the Hamakor catalogue with kitsch (coffee mugs and casual wear), just as genuine Jewish religious observance shares emotional space with Jewish silliness. Jewish kitsch exists alongside serious judaica because Jewish American life has adapted itself to a multifaceted reality which simultaneously laughs and prays, and laughs at what it prays about. According to Stephen J. Whitfield, Jewish humor "has become one of the enduring features of communal life, an adhesive that has exhibited about as much staying power as religious belief and that has helped to bind Jews to one another" (Whitfield, 2005:34).

In the late 1990s, "[a] marriage of hip and Jewish... emerged [and] redefined religious identity for irony-loving Jews in their twenties and thirties from New York to Los Angeles and beyond" (Zoll, 2005). These young Jews celebrated their identity, and the questioning of it, by going to "all-night multimedia celebrations of Jewish holidays... nightclubs where Jewish storytellers are the headliners; and [these events see the start[ing of] magazines, journals and web sites" (Zoll, 2005). Older traditionalists saw this trend as "a superficial fad as welcome as a Hanukkah bush"; however, "the young thinkers spearheading new cultural ventures say their elders should look beneath the kitsch. There, they say, Jewish leaders will find the modern-day answer to the question that has vexed every generation: how to keep the religion alive" (Zoll, 2005). At

Fig. 30. Festive Chrismukkah balls, www.Chrismukkah.com, photograph Ron and Michelle Gompertz.

the turn of the twenty first century, web sites offer virtual shops full of kitsch. ChosenCouture.com sells Yiddish phrase travel bags and "Let My People Go" toilet seat covers. Jewcy.com offers a Moses action figure and Star of David kosher soap. At the same time that Jewcy.com is selling kitsch, however, the web site also presents articles; some funny, like "Purifying My Colon—And My Soul" by Jay Michaelson (27 April 2007), and some not, like "Guns, God and Virginia Tech" by David Klinghoffer (17 April 2007).

This mixture of serious thought and satirical stuff is also available to consumers on Chrismukkah.com, which sells holiday kitsch for a blended celebration known as Chrismukkah, which "begins on the 1st night of Hanukkah, or Christmas Eve, whichever comes first and lasts until Christmas day, or the last night of Chanukah [sic], whichever comes later," according to the web site. Chrismukkah entered wider American popular culture in December 2003, when Fox aired an episode of its night-time drama *The O. C.* called "The Best Chrismukkah Ever." Chrismukkah.com was launched a month later by Ron and Michelle Gompertz. Ron Gompertz published *Chrismukkah: Everything You Need to Know to Celebrate the Hybrid Holiday* in 2006. The book and web site are very funny; the kitsch sold on the web site is grotesque and irreverent and the whole enterprise might appear insensitive, another "superficial fad." The homepage of Chrismukkah.com features tree ornaments sporting Stars of David (fig. 30) and a DIY Matzoh House; material combinations of Christmas and Hanukkah symbols that humorously represent the reality of Chrismukkah.com's target audience: interfaith families. However, even though the funny hybrid "menoraments" featured on Chrismukkah.com do evoke laughter, there lies, underneath that laughter, the very real anxieties of Jewish parents raising children in multi-faith homes. Chrismukkah.com comically presents a secular consumer hybrid celebration whose history and continuing controversy reveal serious issues of Jewish identity underlying the grotesque mixture of Hanukkah and Christmas.

Ron Gompertz is Jewish, but his wife Michelle is not. The birth of their "hybrid daughter" Minna prompted them to launch Chrismukkah.com. Although the web site sells holiday merchandise, Chrismukkah is not a holiday. As Ron Gompertz writes, "we think of Chrismukkah as a 'state of mind' for the season." For some interfaith families, the state of mind during the winter holidays is one of ambivalence known as the "December Dilemma," created when these families face choosing between Hanukkah and Christmas observances. These conflicts are serious because Christmas and Hanukkah cannot be combined meaningfully in a religious way. Christmas celebrates the birth of Jesus whilst Hanukkah commemorates the Jewish victory over the Greco-Syrians in 170 BC. These holidays have nothing in common except their proximity in the secular calendar. Nevertheless, some Jews have long adopted/adapted various Christmas rituals as an expression of national solidarity with their non-Jewish majority neighbors. According to Rabbi Joshua Eli Plaut (2006), earlier in the twentieth century, many elite German and other Western European Jews observed Christmas rituals, without becoming Christianized, so as to achieve and demonstrate their "secular inclusion in society". One such was no less than Theodor Herzl, the father of modern Zionism. Germans called this mixed secular celebration *Weihnukkah*, a word that combines *Weihnachten* (Christmas) and "Hanukkah."

In America at this time, Christmas was becoming increasingly secularized and commercialized (Belk, 1987) and some American Jewish families combined both Christmas and Hanukkah symbols in their home décor: "those Jews sharing in the tenor of Christmas without partaking in its religious elements would engage in selective borrowing of Yuletide accoutrements, lending a festive spirit to Hanukkah by appropriating decorations such as garlands, wreaths, and evergreen boughs" (Plaut, 2006). When German Jews immigrated to the U.S., many brought their *Weihnukkah* memories and traditions with them. Ron Gompertz's mother, a German Jew who survived the Holocaust, was one of these. Gompertz explains on the "Ghosts of Chrismukkah Past" page of his web site: "my mother's mother was Jewish, but her father was Lutheran. The Nazis categorized my [m]other as a "Mischling", German for mixed breed or mutt... Mom grew up celebrating the Christmas rituals at the insistence of her strict and protective father. Years later, as an adult, she missed those Christmas traditions ... and enjoyed decorating a tree." The Gompertz family in New York decorated a silk kumquat tree "with little mesh Santa Claus stockings filled with chocolate

Hanukkah gelt." By decorating a tree in her Reform Jewish home in America, Mrs. Gompertz reinterpreted for her sons the German Jews' non-religious mixture of Christmas and Hanukkah customs. Gompertz explains, "this bush symbolize[s] the roots of Chrismukkah for me" (www.chrimukkah.com).

Although Gompertz grew up in a home with two Jewish parents, the 2000-01 National Jewish Population Survey reported that "Jews who have married since 1996 have an intermarriage rate of 47%," and 33% of those intermarried Jews were raising their children as Jews (UJC, 2001). Interfaith couples who raise children attend to their children's religious upbringing in various ways, but most "who decide to raise their children in one religion realize that they cannot do so without honoring and respecting the ethnic and religious traditions of both parents," according to Edmund Case, the president and publisher of InterfaithFamily.com. Case's organization conducts an annual December Dilemma Survey. In 2006, "80% of the respondents were raising their children as Jews, 80% participated in both Hanukkah and Christmas celebrations, and 53% had a Christmas tree in their home. These couples resolve potential conflicts by treating Hanukkah, but not Christmas, as a religious holiday" (Case, 2006). Furthermore, many parents in the survey asserted that "their children's Jewish identity was not weakened by their participation in Christmas celebrations, but in fact was strengthened" (Case, 2006). As evidenced by the German Jewish *Weihnukkah* tradition, participation in Christmas *as a secular national celebration* does not threaten Jewish identity. Case admits that Chrismukkah is meant to be light-hearted in concept, but has nonetheless written an article called "'Chrismukkah' is a Bad Idea" because, he says, "as the antithesis of maintaining special traditions, [Chrismukkah] could only confuse children being raised with one religious identity in an interfaith family" (Case, 2006). Case's argument misinterprets Chrismukkah as serious *religious* syncretism, yet Chrismukkah has nothing to do with Jesus, divinely inspired Maccabean victories or miraculous cruses of oil. Chrismukkah provides American Jews with the opportunity to participate in the larger cultural Christmas consumer celebration in the USA in the way that *Weihnukkah* allowed German Jews the chance to participate in their larger national holiday by leaving religion out of the

Fig. 31. Child in dreidel costume, www.Chrismukkah. com, photograph Ron and Michelle Gompertz.

Fig. 32. Hanukiyah and swastika, www.Chris-mukkah.com, photo-graph Ron and Michelle Gompertz.

blend; cultural holiday symbols, not religious beliefs, get mixed into kitsch during Chrismukkah.

A further essay on InterfaithFamily.com illustrates one way interfaith families adopt and adapt holiday symbols. Jim Keen, a Protestant raising Jewish daughters, writes: "we decided to tell Gabby [the Keens' older daughter], 'Santa brings you Hanukkah presents on Christmas, because he knows you're Jewish'" (Keen, 2000). This is Hanukkah seen through the mainstream lens; this is Jewish Christmas, and it is nothing new. As far back as 1931, *What Every Jewish Woman Should Know* advised, "Jewish children should be showered with gifts, Hanukkah gifts, as a perhaps primitive but most effective means of making them immune against envy of the Christian children and their Christmas" (quoted in Plaut, 2006). Santa Claus, bringing stuff, becomes the intermediary for the Jewish and non-Jewish parents in some interfaith families, and their blended holiday celebration is a *cultural* fusion, not a religious one. However, Santa Claus, described by Belk as "a secular god" who has presented "an alternative to the celebration of the birth of Christ" for Jewish Americans, is still problematic as a mediator between Jewishness and Americanness because "the religious celebration of Christmas preceded the Santa Claus myth and the two are inseparably linked" (Belk, 1987: 95). In fact, Santa has recently been reclaimed as a *Christian* symbol of the holiday in the form of the Kneeling Santa: Christian kitsch situating a praying Santa before the manger (http://www.houseoffontanini.com/product.sc?cat egoryId=13&productId=429).

Chrismukkah.com visitors meet Santa Claus in "the Chrismuk-kah Timeline," where he appears last in a line of four photos which seem to constitute an alarming "which one doesn't fit" game. Sand-wiched between photos of a children's Hanukkah play (fig. 31) and the cover of a German children's book is a picture taken through the window of a Jewish home during Hanukkah (fig. 32). The viewer is positioned inside the home, looking at a window sill on which sits a menorah fitted with unlit candles for the last night of Hanukkah. Beyond the menorah, outside the window, hung on a building fac-ing the Jewish home, is a Nazi flag. This juxtaposition of symbols is hair-raising and, regardless of its place between photos of a child costumed as a dreidel and the big bellies of Santa and a comical rebbe, the picture of the menorah and the swastika can never be just one more silly combination of symbols for the holiday season. That picture underscores the Jew's historically precarious position in non-Jewish society and emphasizes the real, if unacknowledged, anxiety that produces, and is produced by, the final juxtaposition on the "Timeline" page: Santa Claus lighting a menorah. Perhaps "what most appalls often most amuses" (Bloom, 2003: 141), but the laughter evoked by Santa lighting Hanukkah candles is a nervous laughter which reflects the challenges and ambiguities of American Jews in interfaith families negotiating identity during the holiday season.

Religious Jews will not be amused by the hybridization of Hanukkah and Christmas on Chrismukkah.com. Ron Gompertz acknowledges this when he writes, "Chrismukkah is not intended for those who are deeply observant." He assures visitors to the site that he and his wife "are not recommending combining the religious observance of Christmas and Hanukkah into one." While Chrismukkah.com's target market is the interfaith family, religious faith is not the focus of this celebration. Santa's presence suggests that what interfaith families can celebrate together is not religious faith but materialism: "most of all, children (and grown-ups too) like Chrismukkah because there are more presents!" As the American Santa lights the menorah, he validates Hanukkah as an American-style gift exchange under the nostalgic rubric of a Jewish Christmas. Elaine M. Kauvar asserts, "[t]he third generation of American Jews... maintains its tie to tradition only tenuously... and for many of them the religious tradition continues as Jewish activism, nostalgia, and even mere kitsch and sentimentality" (Kauvar, 1993: 339). Kitsch and sentimentality are Chrismukkah's driving forces, as Ron Gompertz is the first to admit: "shhhh. Don't tell my daughter, but Chrismukkah isn't a 'real' holiday. No more real than Frosty the Snowman, Rudolph the Rednosed Reindeer, Santa Claus or Hannukah [sic] Harry." Chrismukkah.com's kitsch allows interfaith families to make fun of their potentially destructive mutually exclusive beliefs. The mixture of Christmas and Hanukkah greetings in cards that read "Merry Mazeltov" and "Oy Joy" are linguistically senseless but amusing reflections of the patois of interfaith family life.

On Chrismukkah.com, interfaith shoppers can take a break from serious *religious* considerations and enjoy cultural fusions. Visitors to the web site's homepage face the following questionnaire: "so, what's it going to be? Candy canes or chocolate gelt? Figgy pudding or gefilte fish? Latkes or fruitcake? Spin the dreidel or get kissed under the mistletoe?" Nothing on this list exemplifies religious belief or practice, but the foods and activities are recognizable as culturally distinct, symbolic of *either* Christmas *or* Hanukkah. Although this playful quiz does imply the serious choices faced by the interfaith family, purchase on Chrismukkah.com offers a safe haven through the culturally inclusive rite of consumption. Interfaith customers are reassured:

> Well, you've found the one place where you don't have to choose! Here you can have it all. Here we celebrate Chrismukkah - the merry mish-mash, one-size-fits-all, unisex, alternative, non-denominational, non-judgmental, non-polluting, all-inclusive, sustainable, holistic, X-treme hybrid holiday celebrating diversity, religious tolerance, ideological, theological and political freedom, peace on earth and the interconnectedness between all animals, plants and minerals.

Using the hyperbolic style of a carnival barker or snake oil peddler, Chrismukkah.com promotes not only irreverent hybrid stuff, but serious Judeo-Christian values and American Dream ideals. Matei Calinescu sees kitsch as a valuable steppingstone to the "fully matured cultural tradition" Greenberg wrote about in 1939. In Calinescu's opinion, "kitsch suggests (sometimes with more accuracy than we would like to believe) the way toward the originals. After all, in today's world no one is safe from kitsch, which appears as a necessary step on the path toward an ever elusive goal of fully authentic aesthetic experience" (Calinescu, 1987: 262). Ron Gompertz sees Chrismukkah's imaginative secular playfulness as a way to communicate important values to his daughter. He writes that while he and his wife "are not religious, [they] are both proud of [their] cultural heritage. At the same time, we are curious to learn about, and happy to help each other celebrate our respective traditions and customs." The Gompertzes are "determined to respect and honor our traditions, while acknowledging our new combination family. Most importantly, we want Minna to grow up informed, tolerant and balanced" (Gompertz, 2006: 16). At least since the nineteenth century, American Jews have seen the Christmas season as a time to assert their Jewish identity by performing "*mitzvot*—charitable deeds that one's Christian neighbors were also expected to do in 'the spirit of Christmas'" (Plaut, 2006). Plaut concludes his discussion by looking at "[p]erhaps the most ironic manifestation of the Christmas mitzvot phenomenon," which is "the Jewish volunteer in a Santa suit," whose volunteerism represents "an established means of combining the Jewish value of *tikkun olam*, repairing the world, with the Christmas message of bringing joy to the world" (Plaut, 2006).

Chrismukkah.com and other web sites humorously exploring American Jewish identity through kitsch are, ironically, part of what Samuel G. Freedman calls "The Jewish Reformation" in his epilogue to *Jew vs. Jew: The Struggle for the Soul of American Jewry* (2000). Because cultural assimilation has been so successful, Freedman argues, religion is the only thing left that makes American Jews feel Jewish. This "central premise of Orthodoxy, that religion defines Jewish identity," represents a rebellion by "that fraction of American Jews who worship on a regular basis against the vast majority who show up only for the High Holy Days or a Passover seder or send out one of those popular new on-line holiday cards featuring Santa Claus and a menorah" (Freedman, 2000: 338-9). Clearly, kitsch is one defining feature of American Jewish religious identity, even for those who do not find it funny. There are, as I have shown, good reasons for regarding such interfaith kitsch as a serious business.

References

Belk, Russell W., "A Child"s Christmas in America: Santa Claus as Deity, Consumption as Religion", *Journal of American Culture* (1987), pp. 87-100.

Bloom, James D., *Gravity Fails: the Comic Jewish Shaping of Modern America* (Westport: Praeger, 2003).

Case, Edmund, "'Chrismukkah' is a Bad Idea", Interfaith Family, www.interfaithfamily.com/site/apps/nl/content2.asp?c=ekLSK5MLIrG&b=297377&c, accessed 1 December 2004.

Freedman, Samuel G., *Jew vs. Jew: the Struggle for the Soul of American Jewry* (New York: Simon and Schuster, 2000).

Gompertz, Ron, *Chrismukkah: Everything You Need to Know to Celebrate the Hybrid Holiday* (New York: Stewart, Tabori and Chang, 2006).

Greenberg, Clement, "Avant-Garde and Kitsch", *Partisan Review* 6.5 (1939), pp. 34-49.

Hamakor Judaica, Inc., *The Source for Everything Jewish* (Niles: Hamakor Judaica, 2007).

Kauvar, Elaine, "Introduction: Some Reflections on Contemporary American Jewish Culture", in ed. Thomas Schaub, *Contemporary Literature* 34.3 (Madison: University of Wisconsin Press, 1993), pp. 337-357.

Keen, Jim, "Will Santa Bring Me Presents, Even If I'm Jewish?" InterfaithFamily, www.interfaithfamily.com/site/apps/s/content.asp?ct=515407&c=ekLSK5MLIrG&b=297377&ct=515407, accessed 1 December 2000.

Plaut, Joshua Eli, "What Attitudes Toward Christmas tell us about Modern Jewish Identity", My Jewish Learning, www.myjewishlearning.com/holidays/Hanukkah/TO_Hanukkah_Themes/Wolfson_December 864/JewsChristmas.htm, accessed 10 October 2006.

Shandler, Jeffrey, *Adventures in Yiddishland: Postvernacular Language and Culture* (Berkeley: University of California Press, 2006)

UJC, *National Jewish Population Survey 2000-01: Strength, Challenge and Diversity in the American Jewish Population*, United Jewish Communities (2001), www.ujc.org/page.html?ArticleID=33650, accessed 27 April 2007.

Whitfield, Stephen J., "Towards an Appreciation of American Jewish Humor," *Journal of Modern Jewish Studies* 4.1 (2005), pp. 33-48.

Zoll, Rachel, "It's Jewish Identity with Twist of Irony: Young People Exploring Tradition in New Ways," The Washington Post, November 12 (2005), http://orthodoxanarchist.com/press/washpost.html, accessed 30 March 2007.

Websites

www.chosencouture.com
www.chrismukkah.com
www.houseoffontanini.com
www.jewcy.com

Contributors

Kathaleen Amende is Assistant Professor of American Literature at Alabama State University in Montgomery, Alabama. Her primary interests are in American literature of the South and, particularly, Southern women's writing. She has most recently published an article on Anne Moody in the forthcoming book *Emmett Till in Literary Memory and Imagination* (LSU Press). Having completed her doctorate from Tulane University in the spring of 2003, she is currently at work on her first book, an expansion of her dissertation work on religion and eroticism in the works of southern female authors. Dr. Amende has also completed work for conferences and guest lectures concerning critical race issues and the Civil Rights Movement. After spending a year teaching at China Incarnate Word in a small town outside of Guangzhou, China, she has returned to the United States and settled at Alabama State University where she teaches most of the American Literature courses.

Elizabeth Bernstein has been an instructor in the First Year Composition Program and a tutor in the English Department Writing Center at the University of Georgia since 2001. She also tutors in the Athletic Department Writing Center. In both departments, she works with many multilingual students, and her composition courses are made up entirely of international students. She directs the Carol L. Bush Education Center at Congregation Children of Israel, Athens, Georgia and she homeschools her daughter. As a scholar she is interested in culture studies and life writing.

Kent L. Brintnall is a doctoral candidate in the Graduate Division of Religion at Emory University. His research focuses on contemporary visual culture and Christian theological discourses with a particular emphasis on depictions of the suffering male body and theologies of the cross.

Harry Coverston is an instructor of humanities, religious studies and philosophy of law at the University of Central Florida, Orlando. He is an ordained Episcopalian priest and a former practicing attorney. His Ph.D. in Religion, Law and Society was awarded by Florida State University where he also served as the assistant chaplain at the Episcopal student ministry, the Chapel of the Resurrection. He also earned a Masters of Divinity from the Episcopal seminary of the Graduate Theological Union in Berkeley, CA, and his Juris Doctor from the University of Florida in Gainesville. He is a fifth-generation Floridian and also a fifth-generation educator.

Jennifer Fleeger is a doctoral candidate in the Department of Cinema and Comparative Literature at the University of Iowa where she teaches courses in film theory, cinema sound, and literary adaptation. Her research interests include sound theory and the intersection of mass media and evangelical Christian culture.

Silvia Giagnoni currently teaches in the Department of Communication and Multimedia Studies at Florida Atlantic University where she is finishing her PhD in the Comparative Studies Program. Her dissertation is on the crossover of Christian rock bands in the United States. Her academic interests are mainly focused on the cultural studies of popular music.

Darren E. Grem is a Ph.D. candidate in U.S. history at the University of Georgia. His forthcoming dissertation examines Christian entrepreneurs and their impact on post-World War II American politics and culture.

Dominic Janes is a lecturer in the history of art and religion at Birkbeck College, University of London. His core research interests focus on Christian discourses of materialism, incarnation and sexuality. His PhD dissertation was published as *God and Gold in Late Antiquity* by Cambridge University Press in 1998. He has just completed his third book, *Victorian Reformation: The Fight over Idolatry in the Church of England.*

Jennifer Lee is a graduate of the State University of New York at New Paltz where she is now an adjunct instructor in the English department. Her poetry has been featured in numerous independent publications, and she has presented papers at the Conference on College Composition and Communication (CCCC), the SUNY Counsel on Writing, and the New York College English Association. Her MA thesis, "The Corporatization of the American Dream: Satiric Portrayals of Consumerism in Douglas Coupland's *All Families are Psychotic,* Chuck Palahniuk's *Survivor,* and Harry Crews' The *Mulching of America,*" was the inspiration for the following paper. She is currently in the process of applying to PhD programs in the United States.

Monica Pombo is an Assistant Professor at Appalachian State University, Department of Communication, where she teaches media criticism and production courses. Dr. Pombo received her Ph.D. from Ohio University in 2003. Her research interests cover visual communication and media education. She worked at the Office of Communication, United Church of Christ from 1992 to 1997 as a radio/video producer and media advocate.

Diane Carver Sekeres is a member of the literacy faculty in the elementary education program at the College of Education at the University of Alabama. After she and her husband raised four children, she earned a doctorate from the University of Georgia. She has studied Christian children's fiction published in the United State for 8-12 year olds as framed by theories of the political economy of publishing, multiculturalism in children's literature and liberation theology. Her areas of interest include children's literature, how it is used in elementary education, writing instruction, teacher education, and literacy instruction in home schooling.

Printed in the United States
114829LV00001B/403-408/P